Family Dynamics in Individual Psychotherapy

FAMILY DYNAMICS IN INDIVIDUAL PSYCHOTHERAPY

A Guide to Clinical Strategies

ELLEN F. WACHTEL
PAUL L. WACHTEL

THE GUILFORD PRESS
New York   London

LIBRARY OF CONGRESS CATALOGING IN PUBLICATION DATA

Wachtel, Ellen F.
    Family dynamics in individual psychotherapy

    Bibliography: p.
    Includes index.
    1. Psychotherapy. 2. Psychotherapy patients—
Family relationships. 3. Family — Psychological aspects.
I. Wachtel, Paul L., 1940-   . II. Title.
[DNLM: 1. Family. 2. Psychotherapy—methods.
WM 420 W114f]
RC489.F33W33   1986   616.89'14   85-27242
ISBN 0-89862-663-3

FOR KAREN AND KENNY

Preface

THE LINES OF DIVISION that for so many years have kept the field of psychotherapy unproductively divided into competing "schools" seem to be dissolving. New challenges are appearing daily to the conservative assumptions that have led many therapists to define their practice more by what they don't do than by what they do. Practitioners from all the major therapeutic orientations are increasingly questioning the presuppositions that have circumscribed their work. More therapists now describe themselves as eclectic than as adhering to the tenets of any particular school. A new organization, the Society for the Exploration of Psychotherapy Integration (SEPI), has recently been formed with membership worldwide.

In the context of this growing trend, this book attempts to build a bridge across one of the most significant chasms that still divide our field—that between individual and family perspectives on therapeutic work. It is our firm belief that the discoveries and innovations that have emerged from work with troubled families in the last few decades are among the most important that the therapeutic field has produced. But we remain convinced as well that those discoveries complement, and in some ways modify, but do not replace the earlier foundations on which individually oriented efforts have been based. We hope in the pages that follow to show how work with troubled individuals can be enhanced by an appreciation of developments in family therapy, and how each of these major perspectives on human behavior can be enhanced by an understanding of the other.

This book evolved out of the initial explorations of one of us (EFW), who has been trained in both individual psychodynamic therapy and family therapy. The order of authorship accurately reflects the relative contributions of the two of us. Most of the specific therapeutic innovations derive from the first author's close familiarity with both traditions. In her own practice (with individuals as well as with couples and families), and in her teaching of family therapy to graduate students, psychology interns, and psychiatric residents, she found that there were ample opportunities for the creative application of ideas from one domain to the enrichment of the other.

The second author (PLW) was intrigued by her descriptions of these therapeutic experiments and was eager to try them out in his own practice. He was struck as well by how the concepts devolving from family systems work converged with his own efforts to spell out a version of psychodynamic thought more attentive to the crucial role of context in the evolution and daily expression of psychodynamic structures. It had already become clear at the completion of an earlier book (P. L. Wachtel, 1977a) that his evolving theoretical perspective had interesting points of similarity with the theories that guided family therapy, particularly in its emphasis on circular processes in providing the link between past and present.

Thus a collaborative effort seemed like a natural step to take. The clinical explorations of one of us dovetailed beautifully with the theoretical inquiries of the other. By now, to be sure, each of us has contributed to both aspects of the book, and we have each gone over many drafts of each chapter both individually and together. But it remains clear to each of us that the heart of the book lies in the contribution of the one of us (EFW) who actually has spent thousands of hours with couples and families as well as with individuals, and it was she who wrote the largest portion of the initial draft on which the book is based.

A central feature of this book is abundant case material designed to make clear and concrete to the reader just what we are describing. In order to insure confidentiality for our patients, these case illustrations are of course disguised. In some instances we have presented composite portraits based on several cases that shared similar properties. The clinical material is not presented as "proof" of the correctness or effectiveness of our approach; that will require controlled research (cf. Grünbaum, 1984). Rather, our aim is simply to illustrate as vividly as possible the phenomena and interventions we are referring to. It is our hope that this will enable other clinicians to get a clear enough picture that they can experiment with these methods themselves, and that what we have presented will have heuristic value in stimulating the kind of controlled research that can determine more definitively the value of the approach described here.

A husband and wife cannot work closely on a professional project without having to deal with and work through the welter of sex-role stereotypes that afflict our society. On a personal level we feel we have done this rather successfully, but in one respect we must acknowledge we have failed: In our efforts to make our prose as clear and readable as we could, we have been unable to eliminate the occasional use of pronouns such as "he" to refer to a person in general rather than only to a male. The history of the English language reflects the social forces and assumptions that have shaped the people who spoke it, and this history is woven into its very structure. Some authors' prose lends itself readily to phrases such as "his or her" where "his" would once have been used. In our own writing, we too have used this more modern form where feasible. But many of our sentences sound intolerably awkward in such locutions and so have remained in traditional English phrasings. We hope that the fact that it is the woman who is the first author of this volume will prove sufficient reminder to the reader that the old stereotypes are no longer valid.

A powerful sustaining force in the long, hard work that any book requires has been the pleasure we have derived from our children, Karen and Kenny. It is to them that we lovingly dedicate this book.

Ellen F. Wachtel
Paul L. Wachtel

Contents

Family Dynamics in Individual Psychotherapy

1. *The Contextual Unconscious*

DEVELOPMENTS in family therapy ought to be useful to the individual therapist. Most psychotherapists, after all, are concerned with the "family dramas" that have influenced their patients' lives, and almost all address themselves to the patient's significant personal relationships.[1] Yet up to now, individual therapy and family therapy have been rather separate clinical approaches. Frequently, practitioners of family therapy have belonged to different professional communities and reference groups from those of individual therapists; even when the same individual has practiced both individual and family therapy, there has been a tendency to compartmentalize—to do "family therapy" when one sees families and "individual therapy" when one sees individuals.

We believe that this separation and compartmentalization are unfortunate. In our experience, there is a great deal of interest among individual therapists in the burgeoning developments in family therapy. Many individual therapists sense that their work could profit from a better understanding of the family systems in which their patients are enmeshed. Others are intrigued by a variety of new intervention methods and perspectives on clinical work that family therapy offers. Still others sense that it would be useful to know more about—and perhaps to have firsthand contact with—the people who are important in the patient's life. But to many therapists it is unclear just how to use these new developments. How can the therapist who has spent years de-

---

1. Some readers may find the term "patient" too evocative of a medical model. We ourselves see problems with the term and most decidedly do not operate from a medical model. But "client" seems to us also unsatisfactory, because it places in the foreground what is true but should be in the background—that it is a business relationship. "Analysand" cannot solve our dilemma, because we are not speaking strictly of "analysis." Therefore we elected simply to proceed with the term we grew up with—"patient." The reader is asked to put aside whatever connotations the term has for him or her and to focus on the way of working we are advocating.

veloping empathic or interpretative skills, or who, on the basis of
clinical experience, has come to hold strong convictions about human
development and the therapeutic process, make use of what family
therapy has to offer without giving up these core features of his or
her professional identity?

In this book, we intend to show how this can be accomplished
and to indicate why we believe it will enrich the clinical work of most
therapists. The book's primary focus is on the work of the individual
therapist, illustrating in concrete clinical detail just how the methods
and perspectives of family therapists can be incorporated into a more
traditional insight-oriented approach. But in shedding light on the
relation between individual and systems perspectives, the book should
be of interest to the family therapist as well. Its most central message
is that neither the dynamics of individuals nor the context in which
they operate can be ignored, and that the two codetermine each other
in ways it is essential to understand.

Psychotherapists are a very diverse lot. Compilations of the variety
of different schools or "brands" have been estimated at figures between
130 and 250 (e.g., Goldfried, 1982). Obviously, we cannot address
fully the concerns of practitioners of all these competing schools. But
despite the distinctions, there is in fact considerable overlap among
many of the central assumptions of the major points of view. Though
some of the most important approaches were originally developed at
least in part as a challenge to then-prevailing Freudian ideas, most of
them nonetheless share Freud's central assumption that psychological
difficulties are largely the result of the person's disavowal of aspects
of his or her own experience and that greater self-knowledge or self-
awareness will contribute to desirable change.

There are, to be sure, differences among approaches in the language
used to express this basic idea. These reflect important differences in
values, in epistemology, and in the image of man. There are significant
differences as well in precisely what aspects of experience or psychological life are assumed to be warded off; in how this is seen as being
accomplished; and in the role of interpretations, empathic communications, advice, confrontation, therapist self-disclosure, and a host
of other dimensions of therapeutic technique and orientation.

Nonetheless, we believe that, despite all the differences, there is
enough of a common core among the various psychodynamic schools,
the Rogerian or client-centered approach, Gestalt therapy, the existential
approach, and other related orientations that the following discussion

will have relevance for a wide range of therapists. There are indications, in any event, that the largest and fastest-growing group of therapists consists of those who do not identify exclusively with one or another school, but seek instead to combine the best of several—or, to put it differently, whose allegiance is precisely to this common core that unites most therapists.

Our own orientation in working with individuals is a version of psychodynamic thought that, as we explicate in what follows, has particular affinities to the ideas of family systems theorists. We describe our theoretical position in some detail, in order to provide an orienting framework for the clinical discussions and examples that constitute the largest portion of this book, and to show how we believe the apparent contradictions between traditional insight-oriented therapies and the approaches dominant in family therapy can be resolved. But we wish to make it clear to the reader that our intent is not necessarily to convert others to our theoretical approach. We believe that many of the points we make here, with regard both to theory and to technique, will be useful as well to the reader whose professional identity is as a Freudian, a Rogerian, a Gestaltist, a humanistic therapist, or an eclectic. What we wish to show is that some of the key ideas of most traditional therapeutic schools can be viewed from a slightly different vantage point, and thereby can lend themselves to an incorporation of developments in family therapy.

To borrow a family therapy term, our aim in this chapter is to provide a kind of "reframing" of traditional clinical ideas, a reframing that will facilitate the individual therapist's use of ideas and methods from family therapy. The theoretical position spelled out here—one we call "cyclical psychodynamics"—was originally developed as part of an effort to integrate psychodynamic and behavioral points of view. It is spelled out in more detail elsewhere (e.g., P. L. Wachtel, 1977a, 1985). Here we wish to highlight the particular affinities that this approach has for family systems considerations.

A Reexamination of Some Key Assumptions

We wish to consider here a number of key assumptions that are widely held by individual therapists and to see how they may be recast in ways that open up new possibilities for therapeutic assistance. Our intent is to present a reformulation that is true to the observations that have shaped clinicians' views over the decades, yet at the same time provides a window through which can pass the fresh and exciting ideas that have evolved in the past quarter century of intensive study of family dynamics and the family roots of psychological distress. We seek a theoretical view that stays close to clinical observation, but also provides a perspective on how clinical observation itself is constrained and unwittingly channeled by the assumptions and methods that have been dominant in the field. It is our hope that most readers will find that the facts and experiences in which their work is rooted are evident in the pages that follow, but that they take on new configurations that present new prospects for change.

Circular and Linear Causality

Writers on family therapy have increasingly argued that the development of family therapy represents an entirely new epistemology—one in which the central concepts stress a picture of causality that is circular, rather than the linear view of causality that is evident in psychodynamic and other traditional approaches to therapeutic work with individuals. According to L. Hoffman (1981), for example,

> Mental illness has traditionally been thought of in linear terms, with historical, causal explanations for the distress. . . . But if one [sees the troubled individual] with his or her family, in the context of current relationships, one [begins] to see something quite different. One [sees] communications and behaviors from everybody present, composing many circular loops that played back and forth, with the behavior of the afflicted person only part of a larger, recursive dance. (pp. 6–7)

This distinction between the perspectives of family therapists and individual therapists does seem to capture something typical of much of the literature in the two fields. The distinction is not an essential one, however. It is possible to embody all the key observations and almost all the key concepts that characterize a psychodynamic view in a framework that is fully circular in the same sense that family therapy theories are. Indeed, that is the aim of the cyclical psychodynamic theory we present here. The theory builds in particular on the contributions of Erik Erikson, Karen Horney, and Harry Stack Sullivan, though as it has evolved it has gone in directions those theorists and their followers would not always be comfortable with. A key feature of the cyclical psychodynamic view—and one that particularly aids its articulation with family systems perspectives—is its approach to the role of the patient's history in his present difficulties.

Almost all psychological theories regard a person's childhood as a crucial time in the shaping of his personality. But there are considerable differences among theories in precisely *how* childhood influences are supposed to shape adult experience, as well as in just how much an adult difficulty or characteristic is seen as reflecting the influence of childhood and how much as reflecting circumstances in the present.

Most (though not all) family approaches stress the crucial role of present interpersonal presses and communication patterns in shaping the experience of any individual in the family. The development of the particular pattern of interaction in which the family is caught occurs over time, of course; it has a past and a history. But any individual's behavior is seen not as the linear, causal product of past events or experiences, but as part of a system of transactions between people that codetermine each other in the present. The history of this system of interactions is a process of "coevolution" (Bateson, 1972). Behavior patterns mutually evolve: A does not cause B's behavior, nor does B cause A's; rather, they each shape each other's behavior (and therefore their own).[2]

Once the pattern has evolved, it seems to be relatively self-sustaining. A continuity may be discerned from past to present to future, but earlier events are not viewed as the sole or direct cause of later events. Instead, a recursive chain of events is identified in which even the ideas of "before" or "after" seem in some ways arbitrary, the result of how the sequence is "punctuated" (L. Hoffman, 1981).

Parents are familiar with the fruitlessness of the question "Who started it?" Each child says with utter conviction, "He [she] started it," and both are both right and wrong; it depends on with which act of the repeated circle one starts.

The cultural cliché of the alcoholic husband and the nagging wife—he drinks because she nags; she nags because he drinks—provides another image of the arbitrariness of punctuation.

The individual therapist seeing either the husband or the wife of such a pair alone might arrive at a very different picture of why his or her behavior is what it is. Not every man, after all, drinks in response to his wife's nagging. Nor, for that matter, would every man marry

---

2. As we discuss later, this mutual shaping and participation is not limited to pairs of people. Patterns among larger numbers of people are of concern to family therapists, too. Triangles (and sets of triangles) are a particular focus of concern.

such a woman, or experience her behavior as nagging, or evoke that particular behavior from her. It is certainly possible to find events and experiences in the man's past that seem to be factors, even *sine qua nons*, in his having become enmeshed in such a pattern. Had he had a different mother or father, had he had certain needs met or other feelings accepted, he might not have ended up where and how he did.

Such a perspective has yielded important advances. Guided by such a view, therapists have learned to listen to their patients or clients with a freshness and sensitivity not normally encountered in daily life. Not merely the manifest message or experience being communicated, but subtle, tentative, partly hidden meanings have become able to be addressed as well. Psychoanalytically oriented investigators have discovered important regularities in what kinds of psychological contents people tend to ward off. More phenomenologically oriented therapists, concerned about the dangers of overgeneralizing and fitting clients' experiences into a procrustean theoretical bed, have focused on the process of listening and communicating, stressing the therapeutic qualities of empathic sensitivity. Increasingly, among therapists of most persuasions, when the voice of the child is heard, it is not just the childishly antisocial impulses that are noticed, but the voice of the frightened child as well, the self that hides behind an outward adaptation, the true self that is in danger of being crushed by the imperatives of a self-image erected as an emergency structure under perceived parental pressure.

It is unfortunate, however, that frequently these insights have been embodied in formulations that draw an unnecessarily sharp distinction between an "internal world"—whether conceived of in negative terms as more primitive, or in positive terms as more genuine—and the more "external" world of overt behavior and adaptation to environmental events. In our cyclical model, the relation between unconscious psychological processes and structures and the person's everyday social world is understood differently. Rather than regarding unconscious wishes, ideas, fantasies, and images of self and others as persisting in spite of the person's present life conditions, they are understood as persisting precisely *because of* those conditions. On close scrutiny, one finds that these seemingly unrealistic or "internal" psychological processes have a good deal to do with the person's present life. Life circumstances, it turns out, maintain these inner structures, which in turn contribute to maintaining the same basic life circumstances. The cycle is repeated over and over again.

A CASE ILLUSTRATION: RICHARD R

To illustrate some of what has been presented thus far, consider the case of Richard R. Richard felt thwarted in many ways. The only child of successful parents, he was stuck in a low-level accounting job about which he felt ashamed. In his social and sexual life, he seemed to be constantly struggling against inclinations to be exploitative, hurtful, or manipulative with women. These inclinations were only very occasionally experienced with any degree of awareness, and were considerably at odds with his conscious aims and qualities. In the center of his consciousness were concerns very much the opposite—an overly responsible attitude that didn't permit him to have much fun. He felt trapped in relationships he wished he could break off but felt he couldn't because the woman needed him and to leave would be to treat her shabbily.

In some ways, the guilt that beclouded the life of this overly responsible man seemed out of keeping with the actual conduct of his affairs. He was in many respects considerably more scrupulous than average. Moreover, it would not be difficult to relate his present conflicts to his experiences in growing up, which both stirred resentment at his mother and required him to bury that resentment under a crushing burden of responsibility. Nonetheless, closer scrutiny permitted a formulation of his difficulties that maintained a dynamic formulation of conflict and defense and incorporated the important shaping role of his early experiences, yet at the same time presented a fully circular picture of the relevant causal sequences.

Whatever the origins of the pattern, at the time he came to therapy Richard was caught in a vicious circle that refueled itself continually. His excessively responsible attitude led to experiences that stirred feelings of resentment and frustration. Moreover, it left him feeling inadequate and inhibited, and secretly longing to be a bold, marauding male. He was thus tempted to be considerably more aggressive and even exploitative than his conscious value system permitted, and also to become involved with needy and vulnerable women.

This last-mentioned piece of the pattern reflected still another part of the circular chain of consequences: Because he was in fact inhibited, he did have trouble attracting women who could be more independent or choosy. But when he responded to the desperate reachings out of a needy woman, he was gratified and flattered by the attention, but also ashamed of his readiness to "use" a woman who was weak and vulnerable. So he "tried" very hard to really care about her, with consequences that were all too predictable: She would sense the lack of real interest, feel hurt, yet also hope against hope that his overt message was true. Consequently, she would be drawn in still more deeply.

Richard, in turn, in response to both the woman's deepening involvement and her increasing hurt, disappointment, and anger, would feel more and more trapped and angry himself. Moreover, as a secondary response to his own inhibitions, he was susceptible to stirrings of sadism evoked by her desperation and helplessness. His attempted solution to this (far from fully conscious) dilemma? Still more earnestness, more being good and responsible in order to turn back the unacceptable feelings. And the consequence of such a strategy? As we have just seen, it strengthened the very feelings he wished to make disappear.

What is the starting point of such a pattern? Is the defense a response to the impulse? Or is the impulse itself an ironic consequence of the very defense against it? We have here not a linear, causal sequence, but a case of the chicken and the egg (and, if we may say so, a matter difficult to unscramble).

A CASE OF "NARCISSISM": ALLEN M

Even the "narcissistic" disorders that have been of such concern in recent years—and whose origins tend to be traced to the earliest years of life—can be understood in this cyclical, nonlinear fashion. Whatever the origins of the person's fluctuating self-esteem and grandiose fantasies or difficulties in maintaining a coherent sense of self, it is possible to see how the pattern is maintained in the present. Allen M, for example, alternated frequently between extreme grandiosity and feelings of worthlessness. A wheeler–dealer in real estate, he lived his life in "the fast lane." At the many parties he attended, he managed always to let people know of his accomplishments, of his wealth, of the famous people he knew.

Allen was good at doing this. He trumpeted his message in a low-key, subtle way rather than in a gross or obvious manner; indeed, his delivery was so smooth he was able not to notice it himself, either. (He was, of course, highly motivated not to notice.) Nonetheless, the message came through very clearly, and it had significant consequences for him.

When Allen entered a new social group, he had a strong (though not always conscious) need to enter as a leader, to be admired and fawned over. His talents were such that he was often able to accomplish this. But his success was usually a mixed blessing. The result was, in large measure, to lock him onto an exhausting treadmill that made Sisyphus look like a loafer.

Almost everyone who interacted with Allen for any time came to expect great things from him. He was known as relatively insensitive to others' needs, as moody and unreliable; however, this was tolerated because he was so unusual, so accomplished, so much a live wire when he came forth at all. He thus occupied a role in most relationships that absolutely *required* him to be special. Others might be accepted in terms of more mortal standards, but not Allen. Allen, after all, was not someone to look up for simple human support, for the sharing of weaknesses that reassures others and fosters intimacy, for the various everyday qualities that make each of us seem *simpatico* with at least some other people. Allen, rather, was to be sought after and accepted for his specialness, his unusual accomplishments and talents. It was these qualities that enabled him to be admired and pursued in spite of his other failings.

What was harder to recognize was that it was his very pursuit of specialness that created his failings on a simpler human level. Allen felt under too much pressure to succeed and stand out for him to feel able to take time to pay attention to others' needs. But, in circular fashion, it was in large measure that inability to attend seriously and sincerely to others' needs that fueled his frantic efforts to achieve. He sensed that he must compensate for his lack of ordinary human response, but didn't recognize how that lack was a product of his very efforts to cover it and compensate for it. Increasingly locked into but one dimension of human existence, he squeezed out of himself those softer aspects he could not afford; and having done so, he needed even more to develop, out of all proportion to a balanced and potentially stable existence, the one source of security upon which he could at least somewhat rely.

Needless to say, this pattern made it difficult for Allen to attain satisfying intimacy. He was caught in a similar circle here. His style of living was both a way of dealing with his loneliness and isolation and a major reason why that isolation persisted.

Of course, this way of living was not something that Allen just accidentally fell into and then got caught in its maw. Its origins lay in experiences of childhood and in his compensatory efforts to deal with those experiences. But, as with Richard R, the pattern developed its own momentum once it was begun. No longer was Allen dealing with the experiences of the past in any direct way; the legacy of the past was many years of skewed interactions with other people, which seemed to prove that what he must do (today) was precisely what he had been doing for so many yesterdays.

In one sense, Allen's way of life was "unrealistic" and a continuation of his experience as a young child. He lived as if ordinary humanity could never be the basis for warm, accepting responses from others; as if the ways that most of us find comfort, reassurance, and human contact could not work; and, significantly, as if the parental expectations of perfection and the bewildering and terrifying tendency of his parents to withdraw unpredictably were a characteristic of his world today. In this sense, Allen lived psychologically in the world of the past.

But if one appreciates the interpersonal consequences of having lived one's life this way for so many years, Allen does not seem quite as out of tune with his present reality. As we have seen, in Allen's particular idiosyncratic version of the "real world," people *did* expect prodigious achievements of him all the time. None of us in fact live in an "average expectable environment" (Hartmann, 1939). For no two of us is the world really the same place. On close inspection, each of us lives in a world skewed by our particular personality. Part of this skewing—an extremely important part—can be thought of as "subjective," as our idiosyncratic way of *perceiving* situations, making of them something different from what another would. This is the focus of most psychotherapeutic efforts, the basis for such concepts as transference and parataxic distortion. But this subjective dimension has a more objective counterpart as well. By our selectivity in whom we interact with, and by our particular way of evoking responses from others, each of us actually does encounter different events and different responses from those of anyone else.

Allen encountered a far higher proportion than most of us do of people either highly competitive or dependent on and (frequently ambivalently) admiring of the successful and powerful. Moreover, with whomever he met, he was more likely than most of us to intimidate, to provoke competition, and/or to establish a relationship in which he was expected to outshine others. Many of the people who were important in his life, whose admiration provided some of the glue that felt as though it held him together, were people whose own vulnerabilities were salved by identification with a powerful other. Though meek and fawning in one sense, these people were at the same time harsh taskmasters. Their own needs required that the Allens in their lives be more than human, and their admiration had an element of demand and threat: If he failed to maintain the image that (in turn) provided *them* with the glue that held them together, they would need to go elsewhere. Nothing needed to be said, and little of this was in the awareness of either party, but the admirers that people like Allen attract tend to be as fickle as they are fervent. Allen sensed on some level that however much he was top dog, if he ceased to do his tricks he would find himself alone. This was not just a matter of seeing the world through a lens distorted by his early experience. It was also a reasonably accurate perception of the idiosyncratic world he had created for himself in the long journey that was launched by that experience.

Allen's prodigious demands on himself were further fueled by another circular process. For a different subset of the major cast of characters in his life, his bragging (however subtle and often unconscious) evoked a quite different response—an anxious need to compete, to measure up, to pick up the challenge that Allen had thrown down. These people, whose character structures were more like Allen's own, would respond in kind. They would say, in effect, "Oh, you know the Queen. How nice. Say hello to Lizzy for me next time you see her."

The effect of such responses was often devastating for Allen (as no doubt his were for them; such people unfortunately tend to attract— and torture—each other quite regularly). He would feel in over his head, small, foolish, humiliated. He would also be confirmed in his inner sense that he must strive even harder to succeed and to present himself as powerful, sophisticated, and "in" with the right people. Thus would he again proceed in a way that provoked similar challenging responses from others, responses that called forth still more of the same. In psychology at least, the perpetual motion machine is all to easy to find.

The Importance of Irony

Central to the foregoing accounts of how maladaptive patterns develop and are maintained is *irony*. The consequences of people's behaviors are not assumed to be always those that are intended. Often they are close to the opposite. In this respect our account is similar to a number of others, both in the psychodynamic and family systems traditions, but it differs in important respects from other equally prominent approaches, which seem to posit a much more direct link between intention and outcome.

It is closer, for example, to Horney's picture of how past experiences affect present behavior than to Freud's. Horney (e.g., 1939) usually stressed the vicious circles in which people become enmeshed, and her accounts of how efforts to defend against anxiety tend to undermine rather than bolster security reflect an acutely ironic vision (P. L. Wachtel, 1979b).

One can certainly discern an ironic vision in Freud's work too, but it is tempered more by other competing perspectives (Messer & Winokur, 1980; Schafer, 1976). There are ironies and vicious circles in Freudian accounts of neurosis, but irony is not as central; Freud's favored lens was a tragic one (P. L. Wachtel, 1984).

Freud's greatest contribution was in enabling us to recognize the powerful and pervasive role of hidden intentions in the lives of all of us. He showed that behaviors that might seem incomprehensible or lacking any real meaning could in fact be understood as reflecting a multiplicity of intentions of which the person is not aware. He showed as well that even in the realm of "ordinary" behavior, where it was conventional to think of actions as intentional, there could be construed a far more complex and portentous network of intentions than convention conceived of. Freud's entire career, in fact, can be understood as a monumental effort to expand our understanding of intention. His arguments on behalf of "psychic determinism" were not really about physicalistic cause-and-effect relationships, but rather about the determining influence of *desire*. In effect, he sought to demonstrate that whatever we do we in fact want to do, even though "want" had to be reconceived both to go beyond the conscious understanding of our aims and to take into account the acutely conflicting nature of those wants; most outcomes are compromises among several competing desires.

This ability of Freud's to discern intentionality to an unprecedented degree, as well as his implicit recognition that it was in this realm that lay his claim to enduring fame, placed limits on the role that could be attributed to *un*intended consequences. In Freudian accounts, we seem always in some way or other to be striving (however conflictedly) for just what turns out to occur. This tendency in Freud's thought finds its most extreme expression in the idea of the death instinct; even here, Freud says, we are ultimately dealing with the striving after a goal (though of course also the striving to avoid it).[3] But it is clearly evident as well in a first cousin of the death instinct, an idea introduced in the same set of arguments (Freud, 1920/1955)—the repetition compulsion.

Unlike the death instinct, the repetition compulsion is an idea that is widely influential among clinicians. Here, in similar fashion, the fact that people do seem to repeat the same pattern over and over is taken to show that people *strive* to repeat—indeed, that the urge to repeat is one of those primal longings that admit of no further analysis. Here, we are told, is bedrock.

In our view, the concept of the repetition compulsion is a hindrance rather than an aid to clinical understanding and therapeutic effectiveness. For us, the fact of repetition is a question, not an answer. To attribute the repetition to an urge to repeat is to give an explanatory-sounding *name* to the phenomenon, rather than a genuine explanation. It seems to us very much like Moliere's satirical explanation of sleep as the result of the "dormitive principle."

Somewhat more useful is the idea, implicit in the more psychological aspects of the concept of the repetition compulsion—as opposed to the biological and metaphysical aspects, which we view so negatively— that we strive to repeat in order to "work through" old traumas. Certainly it is true that some such tendency is widely evident. How often, for example, do we go over again and again what we "should" have said, what we wished we had said, in some encounter that left us uncomfortable. Here, though repeating the experience in our minds brings us pain, it seems reasonable to assume that we have nonetheless "chosen" to do so in order to come to terms with it somehow (and in order to prepare ourselves for the next time).

But the idea of the repetition compulsion seems to us to have been overextended by many clinicians, leading to an overestimate of intention and an insufficient appreciation of ironic, unintended consequences. This seems to us the case, for example, when a repeated pattern of choosing a certain kind of (inappropriate) sexual partner or of confronting an authority in a self-destructive way is understood

3. The critical tone of this comment is not meant to imply that it is never appropriate to postulate self-destructiveness in behaviors other than outright suicide; that the decay of our bodies is not in part a result of psychological factors; or that death is not sometimes welcomed. Rather, it is the almost inexorable tendency in Freud's thought to find a motive behind every outcome that is our concern here.

as an intentional (though of course unconscious) repetition in order to try one more time to, in effect, make one's mother or father different.

We are not saying that such fantasies cannot play a role in patterns like this, but rather that we are more impressed with a different set of influences — those leading people to try solutions to their problems that end up making things worse. From this perspective, the main intention (conscious *or* unconscious) is *not* to encounter the same old situation again, but precisely to avoid that situation. But motives are not omnipotent, and often we do not get what we intended. Indeed, in the ironic realm of psychological maladaptation, we often get quite the opposite.[4]

In the field of family therapy, too, there are widely differing views of how intentional the patterns that bring people to therapy are. In an interesting discussion of therapy with depressed married persons, Coyne (1984) succinctly differentiates the position of the Palo Alto school from those that take a less ironic perspective:

> Although our assumptions implicate spouses and family members in the persistence of depressive interactions, it does not necessarily follow that they have a compelling investment in the status quo or that depressive behavior serves a "function" in the larger system. Indeed glib functional accounts of depressive interactions pose the risk that therapists will minimize or ignore the profound distress and deprivation that depressed people and those around them inflict on each other. (p. 55)

Therapists of the Palo Alto school view the client's presenting problems as largely the result of the very efforts the person makes to solve the problem. Such a view has clear and interesting parallels with Horney's more intrapsychically oriented description of how defensive efforts end up stirring the very feelings and the very anxieties they were designed to ward off (cf. Horney, 1939; P. L. Wachtel, 1982).

---

4. Strictly speaking, in the "working-through" version of the repetition-compulsion idea, the person *also* does not want the same old situation. In effect, he wants the same start so that that start can have a different finish. In contrast, however, we are suggesting that in many instances even the start is largely unintended—that finding a cold woman in order to make her warmer than one's mother was, or confronting an irate authority in order to convert him to a figure more sympathetic than one's harsh father, is not the person's primary goal. Rather, as elaborated below, it is in how one tries *not* to encounter such a figure, in all one does to avoid it, that one ends up there. (We hasten to add that it is not a matter of all or none—that, from a psychodynamic perspective, wanting to avoid a situation does not necessarily preclude also wanting to approach it. Nonetheless, we clearly differ at least in emphasis from those who make considerable use of the repetition-compulsion idea.)

Family therapists who stress instead the ways in which the system "needs" its members to act as they do have more of a structural parallel with Freudian accounts. In each, there is a sense that what one observes is something striven for (however ambivalently), rather than an ironic and unintended consequence. There are important ways in which our own approach differs from that of the Palo Alto school, but in this important respect, that family systems perspective and our psychodynamic view have a significant commonality.

A Cumulative View of Development

As befits our psychodynamic training, we do take a developmental perspective in understanding the people we work with. We are interested in how the people who consult us came to be mired in their self-defeating patterns, and we believe that early experiences play a crucial role in personality development. But we find that it is entirely possible to reconcile this concern and perspective with a strong emphasis on the forces operating in the present and manifested in the system of transactions in which the person repeatedly participates.

The resolution of the apparent contradiction between a concern with developmental experiences and a stress on the present lies in a picture of development somewhat different from that usually offered in the psychoanalytic literature. It has frequently seemed to us that Freud's theory is actually less a developmentally oriented one than a theory of how development is *prevented*. Accounts that stress fixations and developmental arrests seem to imply that although development may have proceeded in other aspects of mental life, the most crucial influences on the personality are those parts of the psyche that did *not* evolve, that have remained essentially as they were at an early stage.

In an earlier publication (P. L. Wachtel, 1977a), this idea has been addressed in terms of the metaphor of the "woolly mammoth": Much as Arctic explorers have found the remains of these ancient creatures, preserved hair, flesh, skin, and all by the layers of ice that served as a Paleolithic deep freeze, so too have archaic psychological structures been thought to be preserved in their original form by being kept out of the organized ego, where modification by perceptual input is possible. As a consequence, it is possible in the traditional psychoanalytic framework to characterize a patient's problems—indeed, his basic character—

as, say, "pre-Oedipal." Key features of his personality are assumed to remain just as they were when he was aged 1 or 2; in important realms he is thought to have not gone through crucial developmental experiences, experiences that perhaps only analysis can enable him to undergo.

Such accounts have the difficulty of excluding or relegating to secondary status later experiences, and they pose a problem in utilizing insights picked up about the present family system in which a person is immersed. They can illuminate how perception of present interactions is distorted by earlier experiences, but they leave little room for seeing how internal structures can be modified (or maintained) by later experiences in the various interaction systems in which the person participates.

Our preferred model of development is a cumulative one. Early experiences are seen as crucial not because they are somehow stamped into the psyche in an almost indelible way, but because they *influence the kinds of later experiences the person will have*. "Pre-Oedipal" experiences are crucial for adult personality not in any direct way, but because they skew the kinds of "Oedipal" experiences the person will have— or, to put it more precisely, because they in turn produce an almost infinite series of skewed and skewing experiences. Among psychoanalytic writers, Erikson (e.g., 1964) comes closest to presenting such an account. For Erikson, development never stops, is never really "arrested," even for those with severe early traumas. Later behavior and experience show the effects of such traumas indirectly, in the particular way the person encounters, interprets, and (partially) masters a lifelong series of developmental tasks.

In our own work, we have been struck by the ways in which apparently anachronistic ways of thinking and perceiving turn out, on close inspection, to be tied to continuing patterns in the person's life. We too see evidence of unconscious wishes, ideas, fantasies, and self-images that seem in some way "infantile" or "primitive." But rather than regarding them as persisting in spite of the person's present life conditions, as we might if we held to a model of fixation and arrest, we find that they can be understood as persisting precisely *because of* present conditions.

This is by no means to suggest that the relationship is one of simple stimulus–response connections. There is indeed a complex structure to psychological experience: The meaning and impact of events is not simply "given" in the events themselves; they take on meaning in terms of our expectations, desires, and previous experiences. Rather, what we are arguing is that "inner" structures do not just persist regardless of what is going on in one's life, but rather reflect—often symbolically or indirectly—the ongoing structure of one's daily encounters.

For example, in our experience, dreams or fantasies suggestive of castration concerns are not merely a stored memory of a fear or misperception of childhood, but occur only when in some way the person is *presently* being cut down to size, undermined, belittled, or otherwise emasculated. The unconscious fantasy may not be a literal representation of what is going on, but it does point to a significant feature of the person's present life experience.

The relationship we see between unconscious wishes and fantasies on the one hand and manifest interactions on the other is a two-way street. Existing psychological structures certainly do influence (very considerably) how we perceive events and how we act in relation to others. At the same time, however, the actual transactions that result—including, very centrally, the way others react in relation to us—feed back to maintain or to modify the internal structure.

As one of us has put it (P. L. Wachtel, 1977a), every neurosis requires accomplices. Without the feedback from others that intentionally or unintentionally confirms or strengthens existing structures of fantasy and desire, change in neurotically based perceptions of self and others could occur. It is precisely because of this that attention to the interpersonal context and to the interaction systems in which the person participates is so crucial.

Transactional and Nontransactional Visions of Psychodynamics

The cumulative vision of development just outlined seems to us to hold the key to integrating individual and family therapy perspectives. It is what most of all distinguishes our approach from that of a number of other writers whose work has been nourished by both traditions (e.g., Boszormenyi-Nagy & Spark, 1973; Framo, 1981; Skynner, 1976). We have learned a great deal from these writers, but believe that they have not fully resolved a contradiction between a view of the personality as the container of a history that the person carries around with him as an influential foreign body in the psyche, and an appreciation of how the person continually *makes* (and remakes) his history through his interactions with others in the evolving present.

Friedman (1980), for example, in a generally interesting attempt to address the interface between individual and family therapy, refers to the two perspectives as akin to the wave and particle theories of light—two complementary ways of viewing things, each valid and essential, neither reducible to the other. Such a view seems to us to surrender too soon the possibility of a full and genuine integration. The seeming irreconcilability, we believe, is due largely to the equation of a psychodynamic point of view with a linear, intrapsychic version thereof. The cyclical psychodynamic theory we have pointed to above seems to us very much a psychodynamic account of the individual. It emphasizes the important role of unconscious wishes and thoughts, of conflict and defense, and of the monitoring and distorting of subjective experience in the service of maintaining a particular conscious image of the self. But its account of the influence of current interpersonal patterns and communications is not an additional, complementary perspective, separate but necessary; rather, these interpersonal patterns are viewed as part of the warp and woof of just how the intrapsychic state is maintained—indeed, of what the intrapsychic state *is*. One's hidden "inner world" is, in this view, not a realm unto itself, but at once a product, a symbolization, and a cause of the interaction patterns in which the person engages.

Sander (1979), whose *Individual and Family Therapy* is an effort to integrate the two schools of thought, contributes usefully to breaking down stereotypes and false barriers; he fails, however, to come close to a true integration, because the psychodynamic aspect of his thinking remains primarily linear and intrapsychic. Consequently, the main conclusion of his foray into the interface seems to be that there are certain cases for which family therapy is appropriate and others for which psychoanalysis or psychoanalytic therapy is the treatment of choice. He usefully challenges the claims of more strident adherents of both points of view who see one or the other as universally applicable and preferable, and points out as well places where an additional perspective is useful. But such a strategy of separate domains does not really take us very far toward an integration, as his subtitle suggests is his aim.

The point is not that Sander's conclusion is wrong per se; we too believe there are cases that, given the methodologies presently available, would benefit more from family therapy and others for which an individual approach is more useful. Rather, it is that his equating psychodynamic thought with Freudian and other individualistic variations (cf. P. L. Wachtel, 1983) diminishes the possibility of *theoretical* integration, which is a prologue to new and as yet unimagined variations in clinical technique.

Closer to our own account are the contributions of such writers as Beutler (1983), Feldman (1979, 1982), Feldman and Pinsof (1982), Gurman (1978, 1981), Kramer (1980), Pinsof (1983), Segraves (1982), and Wile (1981). We have learned much from these theorists and clinicians, and we recommend these works to the reader as further examples of how the interpersonal and the intrapsychic can be usefully brought to bear in a comprehensive and unified approach.

Multiple Processes of Change

In our view, psychological change is a highly complex matter that is not readily captured by one or two overarching concepts. Emphasis in therapy and in theories about therapy must include a variety of methods and ideas. We wish here to indicate some of the main considerations we regard as significant and to provide a perspective on them that may help to facilitate fruitful cross-pollination.

The reader will note that here, as later in describing the range of active intervention methods we employ, we do not limit ourselves solely to systems-oriented concepts and methods. Although the main task of this book is to demonstrate how systemic considerations can facilitate the work of the individual therapist, it would be strongly counter to the spirit of our work to make of the question "Is it systemic?" a new fetish that excludes potentially valuable methods on *a priori* ideological grounds.

Thus, for example, in the ensuing description of therapeutic processes, and in our later description of intervention methods, some behavioral ideas and techniques are included along with the psychodynamic and family systems notions that are at the heart of the present effort. The reason for such an inclusion is simple: We believe that therapeutic work is thereby enhanced. Moreover, the additional methods and perspectives we discuss can be shown to be compatible with the rest of what we are here describing and advocating (cf. P. L. Wachtel, 1977a).

The Value and Limits of Insight

The belief that the path to personal liberation lies through insight and self-understanding has a lineage that can be traced back to antiquity ("The truth shall make you free"). But the convictions of modern psychotherapists about the curative power of insight have a more specific source. They derive rather directly from the observations of Breuer and then of Freud about a century ago.[5]

Breuer and Freud's reports (Breuer & Freud, 1895/1955) were dramatic (indeed, far more dramatic than later psychoanalytic claims regarding therapeutic success). When patients remembered with full affect the powerful experiences they had intentionally (though unconsciously) cast out of awareness, their debilitating symptoms disappeared. Excruciating bouts of blindness, paralysis, wracking pains, twitches, writhings, and other tortures—of mysterious origin, and unyielding to the most powerful medical methods of the day—gave way before the ministrations of a new kind of doctor, whose tools were simply listening and talking, together with a persisting concern with eliciting the memories of long-forgotten events. The truth, it seemed, could indeed make one free.

As time went on, however, the durability of these cures became less certain. Moreover, some of the basic premises began to seem questionable as well. The actual occurrence of sexual traumas turned out to be an erroneous assumption. In most instances the patients had *not* encountered the events they remembered.[6]

Freud, of course, found a brilliant way to reinterpret his findings and insure his place in history. By turning from specific traumas, which only some individuals experienced, to wishful fantasies, which were viewed as an inevitable part of growing up, he achieved a theory that had claims to universal applicability. Much of what is most central in

---

5. It will shortly become clear why we think this an accurate statement even with regard to Rogerians, Sullivanians, and others who do not think of themselves as followers of Freud; it will also become clear why it is appropriate for modern Freudians, many of whose ideas (e.g., regarding the ubiquitous importance of infantile fantasies) derive from the reformulations Freud made when he *rejected* some key ideas put forth in the "Studies on Hysteria."

6. That Freud's original conclusions were in fact erroneous has recently become a matter of some controversy (cf. Malcolm, 1984; Masson, 1984). As should be clear from our overall argument, we regard both as overly dichotomizing the issue. It is not really a matter of either–or, but of how the actual events (e.g., whether, gross sexual advances or subtle, symbolic seductions) are construed and given meaning.

modern psychoanalytic thought really *begins* with the rejection of the theory of actual infantile trauma and the emergence of an emphasis on fantasy instead.

But the earlier theory had a fateful impact on psychoanalysis nonetheless, and on many of the therapeutic approaches that subsequently followed. The powerful impact of seeing people change dramatically upon remembering what they had tried to forget gave an enduring cast to Freud's work. *What* was thought to be cast out of consciousness changed, and, later, *how* the person might come not to know significant things about himself came to be an increasing matter of concern; however, the basic emphasis on self-deception as the disease and honest confrontation with the frightening truth as the cure remained intact in the new theory.[7]

For most of the 20th century, not only Freudians but other psychotherapists as well have maintained a central concern with promoting insight on the part of the patient. Even as dissidents appeared within the psychoanalytic movement, and others, like Rogers, developed alternative therapies outside of the psychoanalytic context altogether, the emphasis on insight or self-awareness remained dominant.

In the cold light of controlled research, and as the experiences of thousands of therapists and patients accumulated, it began to seem that the various psychotherapies were not as dramatically successful as had once been hoped. But plenty of successes nonetheless accrued, and they were understood as primarily the result of insight. Indeed, when behavior therapy appeared on the scene in the late 1950s and early 1960s, its proponents tended to couch their comparisons with all other approaches in terms of behavioral versus "insight-oriented" therapies. Insight was the common thread that united approaches as diverse as those of Freud, Sullivan, Horney, Rogers, and Perls.

---

7. Also relevant to the arguments presented here, the early observations from which psychoanalysis arose gave another significant direction to the theory as well: The emphasis was not just on knowing the truth about oneself, but on knowing the truth about something in the *past*. Hysterics suffer from reminiscences, it seemed to Breuer and Freud; even when the memories recaptured were recognized as *false* memories, the concern with past rather than present experiences remained. "Earlier" remained synonymous with "deeper" and "more significant," and a memorial rather than a transactional emphasis remained as a powerful residue of the early observations even after the falsity of these observations was acknowledged (P. L. Wachtel, 1977a, Chap. 2). The memorial and the transactional were to some degree united in the concept of transference, but the union was far from complete (cf. Gill, 1982; Schafer, 1977; P. L. Wachtel, 1981a).

If one looks at the actual practices of various therapists, however, rather than just their theories, one readily sees that they do many things beside impart insight. A great many theories might have developed regarding what were the actual curative factors in "insight-oriented" therapy. Over the years, some theories did develop that placed insight in a less central place in the understanding of therapeutic change.[8]

Among the most significant and controversial of these theories was Alexander's (Alexander, 1956; Alexander, French, *et al.*, 1946). Alexander suggested that frequently insight is not the primary cause of therapeutic change, but rather a later by-product *following from* change. At the center, he argued, is a "corrective emotional experience," whereby the patient's experience with the therapist provides a contrast with a significant earlier and shaping experience he had with his parents. Alexander's approach was highly controversial in analytic circles, not only because he challenged the supremacy of insight, but because he implicitly challenged the supremacy of the classical analytic technique as well. Perhaps in response to the strongly rejecting attitude of the analytic community, Alexander later muted some of his bolder arguments: He suggested that his emphasis on corrective experiences was not intended to question the crucial role of insight, and that he was not directly contradicting the orthodox position that the classical analytic technique was without question capable of producing more extensive change than any other technique. Nonetheless, Alexander continued to discuss the process of psychotherapy with a noteworthy clarity and openness to new ideas, and his ideas and observations about the relative contribution of insight to the therapeutic process remain a significant challenge to the orthodox position.

In our own thinking about psychotherapy, insight remains a significant concern. It is difficult to get what one wants if one doesn't know what that is. Self-deception resulting from conflict prevents people from being clear about their aims or about the connection between their good and bad feelings and the events to which they are related.

Dollard and Miller (1950) are particularly illuminating in this regard. Their discussions of the ways in which conflict interferes with

8. Jerome Frank (1973), for example, noted the comparable success rates among various competing therapies with presumably different theories and practices, and suggested that a common thread (not only in formal psychotherapies, but in traditional religious and folk remedies as well) is the imparting of a sense of hope that overcomes demoralization.

cognitive functioning and problem solving, and disrupts labeling of experiences and desires, are seminal. So too is their detailed analysis of the central importance of anxiety in the generation and maintenance of neurosis. As becomes readily apparent in the next section, we too regard anxiety as a critical consideration in understanding the difficulties that bring people to therapists.

The Centrality of Anxiety

On a number of occasions Freud described repression as the "cornerstone" of psychoanalysis. Not only was it the key theoretical concept in understanding psychopathology; its undoing was the key to Freud's approach to therapy as well. If not knowing something about oneself was the problem, then knowing was the solution. Hence the emphasis on insight.

Late in his career, Freud made a crucial change in his theory that implicitly shifted the cornerstone. In "Inhibitions, Symptoms, and Anxiety," Freud (1926/1959) clarified a matter that had been a source of confusion from the very beginnings of psychoanalysis. Originally Freud had thought of anxiety as a discharge phenomenon, a way of releasing the pressure of dammed-up libido that resulted from repression. This formulation seemed consistent with Freud's observations: Anxiety was frequently found in the same individuals who showed signs of significant degrees of repression. Moreover, the phenomenology of anxiety suggested a discharge phenomenon; the sense of being all stirred up and on edge was evocative of something being dumped into the autonomic nervous system. Finally, in many of the anxious patients Freud saw, direct discharge of libidinal urges was minimal, suggesting an alternative mode of discharge instead. These considerations all lent weight to the image of repression as the basic, initial phenomenon and anxiety as a secondary consequence.

Freud, however, also had from the beginning a conception of repression as *motivated*, and motivated in particular by the wish to avoid distress. What he made clear in 1926 was that the distress being avoided was anxiety, and that when anxiety appeared in conscious experience it was due not to an *excess* of repression (leading to anxiety as a discharge or release), but to a *failure* of repression; repression was an action undertaken in order to avert anxiety,[9] and when it was

9. For further discussion of repression as an *action*, see Schafer (1976).

insufficient to do the job, conscious anxiety (or various manifest tension equivalents) was the result. Thus, anxiety could be seen as logically underlying repression, rather than vice versa.[10]

As, earlier, Freud had described a developmental sequence of impulses that were likely to become the objects of repression, now he spelled out a developmental sequence of threats and fears (Freud, 1926/1959). This new developmental sequence was not, to be sure, intended to replace the earlier picture of developmentally scheduled impulses; in the Freudian scheme, these impulses remained a primary category, biologically programmed and not reducible to anything else.[11] And, indeed, even the evolving ego's aversion to those impulses and tendency to shrink from them was to some degree regarded as innately programmed (e.g., see Anna Freud's [1936/1946] discussion of the ego's fear of being overwhelmed by the instincts). Nonetheless, the ground was being laid for a theory in which personality development and psychopathology could be understood most centrally in terms of a series of efforts to cope with or ward off the terrifying feeling of vulnerability we call anxiety.

If ultimately anxiety underlay repression, rather than vice versa, then anxiety rather than repression would seem to be the cornerstone. And, in a crucial corollary, becoming less afraid, rather than knowing more about oneself, would become the heart of the therapeutic process. As we shall see, this shift in perspective opens up for the therapist a variety of methods that have heretofore tended to be eschewed in the name of insight; it leads as well to a different understanding of insight itself.

Freud took a crucial step in refining his conception of the psychotherapeutic paradigm when he moved from an emphasis on "making the unconscious conscious" to the idea of "where id was, let ego be." Potentially, his new understanding of anxiety pointed to a still further refinement: "Where blind fear was, let realistic appraisal (and expanded opportunity) be."

10. Actually, matters are not as either–or as these one-directional formulations seem to require. It does seem to us that anxiety is in some ways more basic than repression, in the sense of being both temporally and logically prior. But it is clearly also the case that one of the consequences of repressing important aspects of one's psychic life, rather than coming to terms with them and integrating them into the developing personality, is a greater vulnerability to anxiety. As discussed throughout this book, most psychological phenomena require a circular conception of causality.

11. This was not the case, of course, for dissident psychoanalytic theorists such as Horney (e.g., 1939).

Freud himself, of course, did not put forth such an explicit formulation. By the time "Inhibitions, Symptoms, and Anxiety" appeared,
he was already 70 years old and ill. Moreover, he had (remarkably)
achieved a major overhauling of his theory just 3 years earlier. Under
the circumstances, still another major working through of all the revisions
that his new anxiety theory required was more than could be expected
even of a Freud.

One might, however, have hoped for such a reworking by younger
analysts. This did not turn out to be the case. By and large, repression
continued to be treated as the cornerstone and insight as the heart of
the process of therapeutic change. This was essentially true even in
the work of Horney and Sullivan, who did make anxiety very central
in their formulations. In important respects, the basic point of view
we are advocating takes as its starting point Freud's later anxiety theory
and the anxiety-centered theories of Horney and Sullivan. But it attempts
to carry through more fully on the new understanding of anxiety's
key role.

In our view, the patient's chief difficulty is not that there are things
about himself that he is not in touch with, but that he is not in touch
with them because he is afraid. It is not a matter of either–or, of
course. There can be profound consequences simply of not being in
touch with aspects of one's own experience. But there are important
clinical consequences of a shift in emphasis, in which the recovery of
lost experiences is to a large extent conceived of as a secondary consequence of therapy rather than a primary focus. At the heart of the
work is enabling the person to overcome the anxiety that has motivated
the defensive avoidance of experience.

In Chapter 6 we discuss in some detail a number of ways of
helping the patient overcome the anxiety. Here we wish simply to
indicate in a general way the processes and procedures we believe are
involved. Here as elsewhere, we conceive of therapeutic change as a
complex, multifaceted affair that is not reducible to one or two overarching notions, such as insight, transference, or deconditioning.

EXPOSURE

Exposure to what has been fearfully avoided is one of the most important
contributors to the process of anxiety reduction. Whether one is considering the psychoanalytically identified defenses or the more overt
avoidances evident in phobias, a key feature in the maintenance of

anxiety is avoidance of what is feared. If one is not confronted with the feared situation, one cannot find out whether it is still dangerous.

Almost all therapeutic procedures, in one way or another, serve to get the patient to confront what has been anxiously avoided. The behavioral procedures of flooding and systematic desensitization are the most obvious instances. But psychoanalytic interpretations of warded-off thoughts and feelings have a very similar effect (Dollard & Miller, 1950; P. L. Wachtel, 1977a). The interpretations stir, call to mind, bring to focal attention the cues associated with those thoughts and feelings; where once they were defensively avoided, now they are in the person's line of sight, as it were. Consequently, it becomes possible to begin to notice whether the expected danger may perhaps not appear.

Dollard and Miller's (1950) account of the therapeutic effects of exposure in terms of the process of extinction seems to us illuminating, and its implications for therapeutic practice are intriguing (e.g., see P. L. Wachtel, 1977a, 1978). But for the reader who is put off by the application of such terms from the learning laboratory to the travails of everyday clinical work, there is still a value in thinking of exposure (*sans* "extinction"). As Freud said, one cannot slay the enemy in effigy. Where the adversary of therapeutic progress is the anxiety stirred by forbidden thoughts and feelings, confrontation with those thoughts and feelings is essential if they are ever to seem less forbidden.

THE PRINCIPLE OF GRADUALISM

"Gradualism" is a principle we will see cropping up in a variety of contexts throughout this book. It is not absolutely essential to the overcoming of anxiety—sometimes being thrown right into what is most frightening is just what it takes (e.g., see Marks, 1978; Stampfl & Levis, 1967)—but it is frequently the most humane and effective way to help someone confront what he or she is afraid of. As we shall see, gradualism is even more crucial when the development of social skills is also a central concern. In those instances, encouraging the patient to plunge right in instead of employing (implicitly or explicitly) a more graduated regimen may almost insure failure.

In our cyclical view of interpersonal dynamics, gradualism is particularly important to take into account. If, as we believe, reciprocal interactions between people are crucial in maintaining—or changing—maladaptive patterns, then enabling the patient to confront challenges only severe enough to elicit relatively mild anxiety is essential. Too great anxiety is likely to produce interpersonal behavior that is ineffective or counterproductive; the likely result is that the other person will respond in an unhelpful way that—far from contributing to the reduction of anxiety—will only confirm the patient's sense that the particular feeling or behavior is dangerous.

Indeed, one of the most significant considerations in our adoption of an interpersonal, systems-oriented approach to psychodynamics has been precisely this sort of occurrence. Traditional intrapsychically oriented psychodynamic accounts do not take sufficient notice, it seems to us, of how crucial the responses of significant others are in the person's life. As a consequence, good psychotherapeutic work in the sessions is frequently undermined by what happens outside the sessions. It is our belief that a failure to pay sufficient attention to the reverberating interactions in the patient's life is a major reason why psychoanalytic therapy is so protracted and its results so ambiguous.

MASTERY

From another perspective, what we are talking about with respect to anxiety is mastery. The idea of mastery brings together the previously discussed perspectives of exposure and gradualism. Exposure is of value only if the exposure is one that contributes to persuading the individual that a danger no longer exists. If the patient confronts what he fears (be it an external situation or a feeling or thought of his own) and does encounter a distressing event, the exposure will obviously not be therapeutic. It is not just exposure per se that diminishes anxiety, but exposure combined with disconfirmation of the anxious expectation.

But it is important to be clear that what the patient learns is usually not that no danger exists at all. Rather, what he must recognize in order to change in a therapeutic direction is that the danger is not so great or so probable that it is not worth taking the risk of changing. This is generally true whether one is addressing a phobia regarding some external situation or an inhibiting (and very likely unconscious) fear of one's own wishes or feelings.

For example, if one is dealing with a dog phobia or an airplane phobia, it is not the therapist's task to persuade the patient that dogs never bite or planes never crash; this is clearly not the case. Rather, the aim is for the patient to cease to be so preoccupied with a possible but unlikely danger that he is limited in his pursuit of other values in his life. Similarly, it is certainly true that sometimes people do get into trouble for expressing anger or even for expressing love. It is not the purpose of therapy to convince the patient that this cannot happen. But one hopes that the patient will reassess the risks and probabilities so that he dares to try things he has previously fearfully avoided. After all, it is precisely because he senses, at least dimly, that he has not chosen an optimal point of balance between risk and opportunity— that his life is more limited than prudent concern for safety alone would require—that the patient has come to therapy in the first place.[12]

Overcoming anxiety, then, is not really based in most cases on discovering that one's fears are completely unfounded. Rather it is a matter of placing the possible risk in proper perspective and of feeling that one can handle the discomfort that comes with any uncertainty and possibility of danger. It is in this sense that mastery must be considered as a crucial concern. Exposure to what was previously feared without experiencing untoward consequences helps to facilitate a sense of mastery over what was previously too frightening to confront. Gradual approach similarly serves to enhance mastery in many instances, enabling the patient to feel up to the task of encountering what was previously avoided. And certainly the promotion of social skills that have failed to develop fully because of the patient's avoidances—a topic to be addressed shortly—plays a critical role in enabling the patient to gain a sense of mastery.

INSIGHT

Notwithstanding our earlier comments about the overemphasis on insight in many therapeutic approaches, we do believe that insight plays a significant role in therapeutic change. In our view, however, it is but one of a number of aspects of the change process, rather than its heart and soul.

The overcoming of anxiety is considerably facilitated when the processes noted above are complemented by the patient's progressively greater understanding of his own desires and assumptions, of his

12. In order to make a particular point here, we have used a rather rationalistic language of probabilities, prudent risks, and the like. This is clearly not the language one is likely to use most of the time in the actual therapy sessions. One should not sound like an investment advisor or a seller of mutual funds when talking to patients. Even for theory such language, while useful for highlighting certain issues, has serious limits when used too exclusively.

feelings and fears, of his strengths and deficits, and of the patterns of interaction in his life. Both understanding of himself and under-standing of significant others can aid the patient in mastering the anxieties and inhibitions that have cramped his life. Recognition of how his present circumstances differ from those of his childhood in which his fears were first learned can also help considerably in over-coming anxieties more appropriate to the situation of childhood help-lessness than to the realities of adult life. As Dollard and Miller (1950) put it, overcoming repression enables the patient to find words to express and label previously inchoate experiences. This permits the development of discriminations between past and present, safe and unsafe.

Greater understanding of oneself and one's life patterns also helps to consolidate changes brought about by other aspects of the therapeutic process. One learns to apply what one has learned in the therapy session to other facets of one's life, thereby extending and strengthening therapeutic gains. Developing the ability to put things in perspective helps to place limits on one's anxiety. As we will see, the concept of "reframing" in family therapy points to similar considerations. The therapist's efforts at reframing point troubled individuals toward a new understanding of their lives, and usually one that is pragmatically suited for mastery of their anxieties.

Overcoming Skill Deficits

As important as it is, reduction of anxiety is not the only important contributor to therapeutic change. A variety of interrelated processes and procedures need to be taken into account in understanding how people change. One very central contributor to patients' difficulties is a deficit or deficits in social skills, and, correspondingly, efforts to aid patients in developing skills are an important part of the change effort.

A deficit in skills, it is important to understand, does not necessarily imply obvious or complete social incompetence. Some of the "smoothest" people we know have odd lacunae in particular situations, and some of the most assertive people we know have areas in which they are more hesitant than the average person to make their views known forthrightly and effectively. As we stress repeatedly throughout this volume, theoretical power and therapeutic power are enhanced by accounts that appreciate how much people's behavior and experience vary as a function of context. Indeed, this is in many ways the heart of the integrative effort that informs this book.

It should be noted that a concern with the presence of odd lacunae even in apparently well-functioning people is quite consistent with our emphasis on the central role of anxiety. Like Horney, we assume that anxiety is an almost inevitable occurrence early in life; the very fact of our species' initial helplessness, and the many years it takes before we achieve adult understanding of the complex social world we inhabit, make for a frequent experience of confusion and apprehension even with the best of upbringings. That this distressing state is not widely apparent in all children is due to the anxiety-reducing efforts it strongly spurs—efforts that are frequently quite effective in yielding a short-run feeling of safety, but that can be a mixed blessing in the longer-run course of development. Many of the skill deficits evident in adults (or in adolescents or older children) are the result of earlier safety measures, which, as they prove successful in the short-run reduction of anxiety, and thereby persist, introduce biases into the course of development. Certain kinds of experiences are consistently avoided; particular kinds of people are chosen to interact with; particular kinds of relationships are established; a particular side of whomever one relates to is drawn out over and over; and all in all, despite the potentially enormous variety of meanings that events can have for one, their subjective interpretation tends again and again to point to particular sequences and outcomes that seem to—but by no means actually do— exhaust the range of possibilities.

"SPECIALISTS IN LIVING"

In all these ways, all of us in effect become "specialists" in particular kinds of human relationships—and inevitably become less expert in other ways of relating (which are easy for other people with different "specialties"). One person may be able to haggle with authorities but may also have difficulty expressing heterosexual affection; either he is too subtle, hedged, or hesitant to really get across that he cares, or he wears his heart so much on his sleeve that he scares people off or invites rejection. Another person may do fine on both scores, but may have difficulty handling the competitive aspects of same-sex friendships. And so on. The kinds of skills required for full functioning in a society such as ours seem almost infinite, and the most competent of us have situation-specific peaks and valleys.

Of particular importance in understanding the maladaptive patterns that bring people to therapy is the way in which anxiety and skill deficits interact. The deficits originate because of the tactics used to avoid anxiety, but their effect is to maintain the person's sense of vulnerability. By avoiding experiences that are threatening, the individual fails to learn to cope with them and consequently continues to feel threatened. He overweights his adaptive efforts in particular directions and does not feel solidly grounded and realistically accepted in his daily life.

For example, the individual who relies on what Horney called the "moving-toward" neurotic trend relies for security on being loved, taken care of, attached. To the extent that this is not normal or healthy love, but a neurotic pattern based on avoidance of anxiety, this behavior becomes rigid and gradually becomes associated with a skill deficit. Initially, the person does not engage in assertive actions or seek mastery or leadership in order not to threaten his basic adaptive strategy: He fears that if he is too independent or too threatening, he will cease to be regarded as someone to be taken care of. After a while, however, his options become more and more constricted. Years of avoiding the normal developmental experiences that yield a variety of kinds of competency leave him no longer able to handle effectively many tasks or situations his peers perform comfortably. Consequently, he feels even more desperately committed to being attached and protected; his earlier fantasies that not to be so would be disastrous are now bolstered by his sense that he has rendered himself genuinely less able to handle life's challenges than other people. And, in turn, he again deals with this sense of vulnerability by dependent attachment, which further inhibits the development of skills. As the Palo Alto group of family therapists put it, the solution has become the problem.

Interrupting such vicious circles can be approached in a variety of ways. Sometimes, simply focusing on the primary avoidance pattern spurs actions that begin to reverse the circular process in which the patient is caught; he may begin spontaneously to reappropriate potential abilities that have been forsaken or sidetracked. When this happens, it is usually due to the therapist's having at least implicitly understood some of the circular processes discussed here, and of his having in some way encouraged such new actions or indicated that understanding alone, without efforts to act differently, will not suffice.

On other occasions, more explicit attention to building skills is necessary. In such instances, the therapist may offer explicit advice or instruction and/or may discuss with the patient a series of graduated tasks to perform in his daily life. Both in the sessions and at home, practice may be stressed, aided in the sessions by modeling, role playing, and role reversal. A detailed discussion of these procedures and of how they can be reconciled with the basic orientation of psychodynamic therapies can be found elsewhere (P. L. Wachtel, 1977a).

What is most relevant in the present context is that whether the therapist's attention to these matters is explicit or implicit, understanding them fully requires an understanding of how other people serve (usually unwittingly, and sometimes unwillingly) to reinforce the pattern in which the patient is trapped. This means considerably more attention than has been typical to the cast of characters in the patient's life. One must ask these questions, for example: What kinds of people does the patient consistently choose to interact with? Who are the people who are presently most significantly involved in the patient's main interaction systems? Do these people have a considerable stake in keeping things as they are, or are they likely to be fairly flexible if the patient initiates new behaviors? Are there people around who will support change in the patient?

As we discuss in some detail later, it is often helpful actually to meet the important other people in the patient's life. We do this in a session together with the patient, rather than meeting alone with the other people. Our rationale for this and its effects on the therapeutic process are discussed below (see Chapters 7 and 8). Later in this chapter, we consider some of the objections traditional individual therapists might have to such a procedure. Here we wish simply to indicate that working to help the patient expand his abilities in interactions with other people requires an understanding of the feedback loops that maintain the patient's deficits and of the other people who contribute to those loops.

New Feedback: Altering the Actions of Accomplices

Closely related to the issues and processes addressed above is a change in the feedback the patient receives from other people. As we have already indicated, we view the enduring psychological structures that have been of central concern to psychoanalysts and other insight-oriented therapists as maintained by the responses that the patient tends to evoke from other people, rather than as a direct residue of early experiences. In principle, if this feedback could be altered, the psychological structures would alter as well. But as we have also discussed, the problem is that in fact the feedback is *not* very likely to change, because the evocative aspects of the patient's behavior tend to bring forth the same response again and again. It is this that centrally constitutes the vicious circle of neurosis: On the basis of past experiences, the person tends to act in particular ways that call forth further experiences confirmatory of the necessity of proceeding in the same way. Given the skewed set of experiences each of us selectively encounters, the world seems to us to require precisely more of the same—and more of the same, then, is what comes about, over and over again.

A central feature of the therapeutic process as we conceive of it is the disruption of this repeated pattern. This disruption requires an understanding of how not only the patient but those who interact with him keep it going. But, much of the time, understanding is not enough. It is also necessary to encourage the patient to engage in actions that are likely to bring about a different response. This can occur in a variety of ways, varying from teaching new skills (see above), to advice or mutual discussion and planning, to the use of paradoxical interventions designed to evoke from the patient a response different from what has been typical so far. The procedures relevant to accomplishing this aspect of the therapeutic process overlap a good deal with those relevant to helping the patient overcome deficits in social skills. The difference lies mainly in the perspective from which the task is approached. The "skills" perspective and the "feedback" perspective are complementary, two sides of the same coin.

Education

Most accounts of therapy give little, if any, attention to the educative aspects. This is largely a result of a more general reluctance to be directive in any way or to assume a stance that seems to imply that the therapist knows better than the patient how to live. As we have indicated, we are sympathetic to these concerns, but feel that the way they have usually been addressed has placed severe constraints on therapists' ability to be helpful to their patients. One need not be a superior specimen of the human species in order to see something that the patient does not. Often all it takes is not to be immersed in the patient's life in the same way he is, or not to have precisely the same blind spots as he does (which is quite different from not having any blind spots at all). We all know that therapists are as capable as anyone of being bewildered, self-defeating, or unable to see the obvious in their own lives. It is the therapist's stance vis-à-vis the patient, the combination of involvement and detachment (which is not the same as "neutrality"), that enables him to be educative without being arrogant or invidious.[13]

There is no reason to believe that all this can't be communicated as readily as the reasons for, say, not answering a direct question. (In either case the patient may experience what we are doing in a way other than it is intended, and in either case the transferential response is "grist for the mill.")

In particular, the therapist can usefully be educative with regard to the ways in which other people may experience the patient's behavior and their likely responses. An important product of a successful therapy is not only greater self-understanding, but better understanding of other people as well. Such improved understanding is also part of the *process* of therapy. If we can help our patients to gain a clearer grasp of what is going on with the important people in their lives, we can increase the chances that the vicious circles in their lives can be reversed. To put it differently, helping the patient to understand the behavior of other people is part of the process of helping him to understand the process or system he himself is caught in. As we indicate in Chapter 2, for example, understanding of triangulation can clarify how in fact the patient's own experiences may depend considerably on what is going on between two other people.

Divided Loyalties and "Psychic Reality"

One problem that arises for many therapists, once one begins to consider the viewpoint of significant others in the patient's life, is that of divided loyalties. A number of colleagues have expressed to us concerns bearing on this issue. One of the uniquely valuable features of the therapeutic

13. It is, of course, also a function of training: Well-trained therapists *do* know more about human relationships, about the likely consequences of particular lines of action, about the signs that someone is construing an action in an idiosyncratic way, and so forth. If we didn't, we would have little justification for accepting the fees we receive.

relationship, they point out, is the patient's having someone totally dedicated to understanding things from his point of view.

This concern has been particularly evident in initial reactions to the procedures that are introduced in Chapters 7 and 8, which involve occasionally bringing into sessions the patient's parents, siblings, partners, or other significant figures in his life. The therapists with whom we discussed this were intrigued by the idea that such meetings could enable the therapist to gain a clearer understanding of the key people in the patient's life and of how he interacts with them. They were skeptical, however, about including such meetings in their own work. A central hesitation involved the question of divided loyalties. They sensed that if others were in the room, they might feel some responsibility toward them as well as toward the patient, and they felt that this could interfere with their commitment to seeing things through the patient's eyes.

A related concern found expression in the position that it didn't matter what the parents, say, were "really" like; what mattered was psychic reality. To attempt to "correct" the patient's perception, based on what could be observed in such a meeting, would be implicitly judgmental or critical; it would also present the danger of setting up the therapist's perceptions as a standard against which the patient's were to be matched. Moreover, it was felt, such a "corrective" orientation would deny the validity of the patient's experience on its own terms, whereas it is precisely the affirmation of the person's private experiential world that is one of the central therapeutic elements in the therapy relationship.

We are sympathetic to these concerns, and to some extent we share them. However, we believe they represent but one pole of our ethical responsibilities as therapists and of the path to psychological healing. It is essentially the individualistic pole, the pole that recognizes our basic separateness and aloneness. In a profound sense we *are* ultimately alone, trying to make contact with others across an abyss. We are born and die separately, and we cannot directly feel another's pain or joy or even be sure whether he is having the same experience when he says an object is green or red. This is why whatever feeling we do have that another understands our experience is so precious. At the same time, it is why it is important for the therapist not to impose his own view on the patient (who needs to recognize the legitimacy of his unique experience, rather than submerging it in the effort to accommodate to the perceptions of others).

But as profoundly as we are alone, we are just as profoundly interdependent and interconnected. We cannot survive in isolation. We exist always in a context and in relation to the world around us. This "duality of human existence" (Bakan, 1966) is so basic that no therapist can avoid it. There is no individual therapist whose theory does not take into account to some degree the significance of context, and there is no family therapist who would deny that he studies not just a system but a system composed of individual human beings who think, want, and feel. But therapists do differ in the balance they choose between conceptions that emphasize our separateness and conceptions that stress our connectedness. They also differ, we believe, in how well they manage at least partially to integrate and reconcile these competing perspectives.

Our unique individuality need not be conceived of in terms of properties exclusively inside us; it can be understood in terms of the particular way each of us interprets and gives meaning to the events of our lives. The approach we advocate neither ignores input from the environment (social and otherwise) nor elevates it to a primacy that makes our subjectivity a mere epiphenomenon. Rather than conceiving of the influence of environmental input in ways that portray us as merely reactive, as slaves to stimuli, it stresses a vision of man as actively *responsive* to the world about him (P. L. Wachtel, 1977a, Chap. 12).

In our view, most of the conceptions that presently guide individual therapy do not integrate our separate and our context-related natures as well as they might. They tend to overemphasize both the desirability and the possibility of autonomy; as a consequence, they rule out many potentially valuable ways of providing assistance.

Support

In the view of most therapists, support is something antithetical to exploration in psychotherapy. "Supportive therapy" is thought of as superficial patchwork and often as implying that the therapist encourages the patient to ignore cogent realities (e.g., fostering an attitude of "it isn't important" about some potentially disturbing matter, or telling the patient everything is okay without encouraging him to examine the range of his reactions and feelings).

In our framework, support is viewed rather differently. For us, support is a crucial part *of* exploration. Only with a good deal of support from the therapist will the patient be able to face up to the anxieties associated with the conflicting strands of his feelings. To some degree, to be sure, what we are suggesting is of concern to most therapists. The emphasis in recent years on transcending the image of the therapist as a blank screen, or the coldness seemingly implied in Freud's analogy between the analyst and a surgeon,[14] attests to recognition on the part of many leading figures in the field that some warm or supportive element must be included in the process (e.g., Greenson, 1967; Schafer, 1983; Stone, 1961). But we believe that the full importance of a supportive stance, and the full compatibility between such a stance and the facilitation of exploration, have been constrained by the traditional terms of the discourse. A significant exception has been Daniel Wile (e.g., 1981, 1984), who has forcefully argued for an exploratory approach designed to allay the patient's anxieties and misgivings while pursuing all the strands of the patient's feelings. Our own approach has much in common with Wile's. The work of the Psychotherapy Research Group at Mount Zion Hospital in San Francisco, stressing a version of psychoanalytic thought they call "control–mastery theory," also stresses that good interpretations are likely to reduce rather than increase the patient's anxiety (e.g., Weiss, Sampson, & The Mount Zion Psychotherapy Research Group, in press). There are ways in which they too are contributing to overcoming the false dichotomy between exploration and support.

We do not believe that the growth and self-expansion at which psychotherapy aims is best achieved through a lonely struggle. Indeed, to us, that romantic image is one of the important impediments to patients' progress (cf. P. L. Wachtel, 1977a, Chap. 12; Wheelis, 1973). Fruitful self-exploration involves the overcoming of deep-seated anxieties. The courage to explore and discover is fostered by benevolent attachments and patient encouragement, not by a stance of dispassionate analyzing. Certainly there is a kind of support and encouragement that can be a substitute for rather than an aid to exploration. But for most therapists who aim for an exploratory approach, the danger lies

---

14. It is important to be clear that we are not implying that Freud himself was cold and surgeon-like. Rather, the point is that Freud uncharacteristically chose a poor metaphor. There are many indications that Freud himself was far from a caricature analyst in his own practice. Indeed, we suspect that his departure from a surgeon-like stance accounts for much of the therapeutic success he did achieve.

more in the opposite direction: Too severe an interpretation of neutrality or too great a suspicion of "support" is more likely to impede therapeutic progress.

Especially important in the context of the present book's mission is the importance of support from significant others in the patient's life. The success or failure of therapy ultimately depends far more on the response of the people with whom the patient shares the bulk of his interactions than on the therapist. The therapy, in our view, is more than anything else a catalyst. It is essential and significant, because often without it the more powerful forces operating in the patient's daily life might not be called into play in a positive fashion. But if the effort is made to cure through the therapy, rather than using the therapy to help cure come through the forces of everyday life, the results of the therapeutic enterprise are likely to be disappointing.

The Question of Neutrality

The stance that is often offered as an alternative to the supportive one described above is that of "neutrality." Neutrality, properly under-stood, does not imply a cold indifference. Neutrality, too, is conceived of as a way of being on the patient's side, but in a way that takes into account very centrally the ubiquity of conflict. To the proponent of neutrality, it is short-sighted to be too overtly supportive; since people almost always want contradictory things at the same time, explicit affirmation of anything the patient says, does, or thinks very likely also implies being on the *other* side of some other desire or inclination of his.

The proponent of neutrality wishes to affirm most of all the person's right to make *his own* judgments. For this reason, he regards the neutral stance as a more liberating one. Most often, he also takes as an important corollary a central concern with fostering autonomy.

Related concerns have led other therapists to advocate a stance of "unconditional positive regard." There are differences—in some respects, rather significant differences—between "neutrality" and "un-conditional positive regard," to be sure; however, in important ways, the latter is embedded in a set of assumptions and values very similar to that associated with the idea of neutrality. Here, too, the therapist's task is to achieve accurate empathic understanding, eschewing value judgments or approval or disapproval of particular things the person does. And here as well, one finds a strong emphasis on the person choosing for himself. Indeed, it would not be too far off the mark to think of the difference between the model of the mirror or the blank screen on the one hand, and that of unconditional positive regard on the other, as "cool neutrality" and "warm neutrality."[15]

Therapists operating from the orientation of either "warm neutrality" or "cool neutrality" are concerned with not intruding on the person's experience, with letting the patient discover what is inside himself unbiased by input from the therapist. This concern tends to be a moral concern as well as a technical one. The therapist does not want to impose his own values on the patient. He does not want to distract the patient from his own inner experience or to promote a surface adaptation to others. Rather, his aim is to foster the patient's looking deep within himself and in some profound way coming to see what he genuinely wants.

This set of ideas regarding the appropriate ways for the therapist to be truly on the patient's side can seem to place limits on the applicability of methods and viewpoints from family therapy. It is likely to discourage the therapist from using the various active intervention methods that family therapists have developed, since they imply a greater directiveness than the notion of "neutrality" suggests. It is likely as well to direct the therapist's attention rather exclusively to what appear to be spontaneous upwellings from within, rather than seeing the person's actions and subjective experience as a response to what is going on around him (cf. P. L. Wachtel, 1982). The "neutral" therapist believes that by keeping a low profile he can see, and help the patient to see, the patient's genuine feelings and desires, undistorted by the therapist's input.

Our own approach, guided more by Sullivan's concept of participant observation than by the classical idea of neutrality, permits a wider range of interventions. We do not believe that the therapist can ever avoid influencing the patient (certainly not if he is an *effective* therapist!); nor do we believe that avoidance of influence is to be desired. There is appropriate influence and inappropriate influence, to be sure; some

---

15. As the earlier discussion of support implies, the gap between "cool neutrality" and "warm neutrality" has narrowed in recent years. The modifications of psychoanalytic technique (or of the attitude behind the technique) offered by such analysts as Stone (1961), Greenson (1967), Kohut (1977), and Schafer (1983) have—in different ways— shifted psychoanalysis in a "warmer" direction while continuing to emphasize the idea of neutrality.

matters are more the therapist's business than others, and some methods are more coercive (see P. L. Wachtel, 1979a). But to confuse the effort to sort out salutary and baneful influences (even if such an effort is always only partially successful) with the possibility of ruling out influence altogether is a pursuit of folly.

Our emphasis on the importance of context leads us to be strongly skeptical about any claims that a particular stance reveals the "true" personality hidden behind superficial appearances. It also leads us to conclude that in those instances where the therapist's influence is somehow reduced, the result will not be some kind of purer, more spontaneous expression of what is within, but rather an increase in the influence of others in the patient's life. And this is not because we view people as mere puppets or passive reactors, but because we believe that people's activity and unique individuality consists in their particular way of integrating a host of interpersonal influences, rather than in somehow ignoring those influences or becoming independent of them. In Piagetian terms, one might say that the development of what is frequently discussed in terms of "autonomy" can better be understood in terms of "decentering": We become more independent of the influence of our parents (or of our therapist) by attending to a wider array of influences, integrating many sources of information about the world and about what produces satisfaction. In the process, we create a unique identity and personality.

A Transactional View of Transference

The clinical implications of the discussion above can perhaps be further clarified by considering how we conceive of and work with transference. For many therapists, transference is the single most crucial consideration in the entire therapeutic process. The possibility of diluting, distorting, or short-circuiting the transference is for many therapists the primary concern that would inhibit them from taking advantage of the developments in family therapy we are considering in this book. It is therefore essential for us to indicate, at least in brief, the transactional view of transference that guides our work.

Consistent with the contextual emphasis that we have put forth throughout, we regard transference manifestations as always best understood *in relation to* some action or quality of the therapist (cf. Gill, 1982; I. Hoffman, 1983). Our view of transference borrows from

Piaget's concept of "schema," a psychological structure characterized by both assimilation and accommodation (cf. P. L. Wachtel, 1981a). The assimilative aspect of transference is the one that has always been stressed in psychoanalytic discussions; transference is evoked as a concept when new persons or events are experienced in terms of old expectations and structures. But as Piaget (e.g., 1952, 1954) has put it, there can be no such thing as pure assimilation or pure accommodation; both are implied in all psychological processes.

In those reactions that are labeled as "transference," assimilation predominates, to be sure, but we do not adequately understand what is going on without also considering the accommodative aspects of the process—the ways in which the transference experience is also a reaction to what is actually going on. From such a perspective, it becomes clear that transference does not simply "emerge" or "unfold" spontaneously, nor is there a single underlying true transference (cf. P. L. Wachtel, 1982). Rather, there are a host of potential transference reactions to the almost infinite number of ways in which the patient–therapist relationship can evolve.

These various reactions are not a random hodge-podge or simple sum of reactions to stimuli. They have a coherence that reflects the person's history and defines his personality. They are the product of our active and continuing construction of our experiential world. But, like all of psychological life, their locus of causality lies neither in external stimulation nor in internal structures, but in the active joining of the two. The therapist's actions and characteristics do not lie outside this process, but are part and parcel of it.

Consequently, there is no privileged position from which the therapist can observe transference reactions without influencing them, and no one "true" transference reaction from which other observations represent a distortion. Whatever the therapist does, he will evoke a transference reaction, and whatever that reaction is, it can potentially help patient and therapist understand how the patient construes and constructs the events of his life. There are actions by the therapist that can "spoil" the therapy—not all therapies are equally successful, after all—but none that can "spoil" the transference. Neither the patient nor the therapist can "not behave," and their behavior with each other is the raw material from which transference interpretations are fashioned.

Within our framework, transference interpretations remain an important part of the therapeutic process. But they are interpretations that recognize the therapist's actions as a crucial element. They are thus contextually oriented interpretations, which are fully consistent with a general emphasis on understanding people in relation to others. As should be clear, they are also interpretations for which the illusion of neutrality is not necessary, and hence the therapist is permitted to entertain a wider range of therapeutic efforts without having to give up the special advantages of focusing on the transference. Just how we put this greater leeway for therapeutic intervention into practice will become evident as the book proceeds.

In the next chapter, we outline some of the major conceptual approaches to understanding family dynamics, attempting to sort them out in a way that will be useful to the therapist who is considering bringing some of these ideas and methods into his or her work. Then, in Chapter 3, we discuss various lines of clinical inquiry that can help the clinician to explore the relevant family dynamics that contribute to his or her individual patients' difficulties. The discussion of modes of clinical inquiry is extended in Chapter 4, which describes the use of the genogram, an emotional family tree used by family therapists to track significant patterns across generations. We suggest some new ways to use the genogram that make of it a kind of projective test for individual and family dynamics. Chapter 5 discusses the use of interpretations in a way that highlights the possibilities of systems-oriented interpretations, and that indicates how interpretations can be integrated into an approach that includes the possibility of active intervention in troubling life patterns. Chapter 6 addresses a variety of active intervention methods that can help the therapist to make use of the new insights gained from consideration of the patient's family and context. These methods derive mainly from the practices of family therapists, but some other methods that are compatible with the overall approach presented here are also examined. Finally, in Chapters 7 and 8, we describe how work with individual patients can be enhanced by including occasional sessions with parents, spouses, and other significant others. These sessions can provide extremely useful clinical material, as well as providing the patient with unique opportunities to modify old patterns and perceptions.

2. *The Family as a Unit*

ALTHOUGH THERE ARE by now many different schools of family therapy, some assumptions are held in common by almost all who call themselves family therapists. The primary principle upon which all agree is that the family must be regarded as a psychological unit. By this is meant that the family has certain properties existing over and above the characteristics of the individuals of which it is comprised.

The repetitive patterns and sequences one sees in families are described as the "family system." These patterns are not determined by any one person. Nor are they the simple sum of two individual psychodynamic histories coming together. Families have something that might be described as a life of their own. There are family feelings, family defenses, family realities, family myths. There is a way a family has of being in the world. There are family rules both conscious and unconscious, concerning things as varied as attitudes toward strangers; the permissibility of particular feelings; or the role of education, sex, or pets in one's life.

Since there are repetitive and predictable ways in which family members interact, a change in behavior on the part of any one family member automatically disrupts the system. A change on the part of one individual in a family invariably produces changes in the behavior and feelings of others in some way. We see continually actions, reactions, and actions in response to reactions—a state of affairs referred to in the family therapy literature as a "reverberating feedback loop" (L. Hoffman, 1981). As we have noted in Chapter 1, most family therapists conceptualize problems in terms of circular rather than linear causality. They are concerned with sequences, patterns, simultaneous events, and circular interactions.

It is assumed by all family therapists that the behavior of individuals will change if there is change in the system of interpersonal relationships of which they are a part. But despite a language or rhetoric that might lead the uninformed reader to assume otherwise, most family therapists are concerned as well with the inner experience of the individual. They assume, however, that not only his behavior, but his thoughts, feelings, or wishes as well will change with a change in the context in which the person lives.

Such a perspective influences from the onset one's exploration of the nature and origin of the individual's distress. In a first meeting with a patient, one would broaden the use of inquiry to include events in the life of intimates that may be having reverberating effects on the individual with whom one is consulting. For example, if a woman states that she is depressed, in addition to the usual questions regarding precipitating events that directly affect her one might inquire as to events in the life of her husband and children. Perhaps, for instance, the husband's father, with whom he has always argued, is critically ill. In the face of this illness, the husband may feel increased guilt toward his father. As a way of coping with his feelings of guilt, he may in turn alter his behavior toward his own children, showing them much more attention than ever before. The effect on the mother (the patient) may be to leave her feeling displaced in her role as nurturant parent, thereby contributing to her depression.

A systemic view would also lead the therapist to inquire into the reactions of family members to the patient's symptoms. Is there something, say, about the family's efforts to be "helpful" that actually ends up exacerbating the problem? For example, in the hypothetical illustration above, if the husband were to respond to his wife's depression by becoming solicitous and even more caring, he could inadvertently further her distress at being usurped in the role of "nurturant one."

It is useful to note here, amplifying the key theme we are developing throughout this book, that such an interactional and systemic view of the patient's difficulties is in no way antithetical to a psychodynamic, individually oriented perspective. Why, for example, this woman's sense of meaning in life depends so desperately on being the main provider of nuturance is a question that can—and should—be pursued on many levels.

Homeostasis and Evolution

Family therapists have adopted a number of concepts from other sciences. The concept of "homeostasis," which is the tendency of a biological system to maintain a relatively stable internal environment through the interaction of numerous quasi-independent but interlocking processes, was originally applied to family systems by Gregory Bateson and others at the Mental Research Institute in the 1950s (Jackson, 1957). In family systems theory, it means the propensity within a family to keep a certain established equilibrium. Family members will attempt to restore the stable environment when it is disrupted in any way.[1]

Families are thought to progress (or get stuck) at predictable developmental stages (Carter & McGoldrick, 1980). Many family therapists see symptoms as developing when the family system is not flexible enough to allow for changing patterns of interactions to meet the new developmental needs of its members. Thus families are evaluated by most family therapists in terms of how flexible or inflexible the family structure is (Minuchin, 1974). The "meta-rules" (rules about rules) of flexible families permit revisions of roles and functions. More rigid family systems are more apt to experience developmental changes as a threat to the cohesiveness of the family unit.

When family stability is threatened, a symptom may develop in one of the family members only. It is important to note, however, that for family therapists, a symptom in an individual is thought of not as his alone but as belonging to the whole family. Thinking in these terms, a family therapist asks himself questions such as these: What function does this individual's symptom serve for the family as a whole? How would the family be stressed if the individual were to change? Does the symptom serve to restabilize a system whose stability has been threatened? Is the symptom a result of a "solution" that has backfired and itself become the problem? Is the symptomatic individual acting out someone else's upset? These ways of thinking are elaborated

---

1. The notion of homeostasis has recently become a source of controversy among family therapists. Family *therapy*, after all, is based on the assumption that families can change their established patterns. Dell points out that if "homeostasis is understood as something that maintains the status quo—maintains the system *this* way—then when the system evolves to a different way, homeostasis is unable to account for it. On the other hand, system change can easily be explained if homeostasis is considered to be a tendency to seek a steady state, *any* steady state ... when a system is perturbed ... it tends to seek a steady state that is *always* slightly different from the preceding steady state" (Dell, 1982, p. 27). This notion, combined with increasing attention to the idea that living systems are always evolving and that small changes in a system can spontaneously lead to complex reorganizations, has led some family therapists to reduce their emphasis on families' resistance to change. For an excellent discussion of these questions, see Lynn Hoffman's *Foundations of Family Therapy* (1981).

upon later in this chapter. The reader may already have noted that some of these questions seem more compatible than others with individual therapists' orientation.

Important but Nonuniversal Concepts

Thus far we have been describing ways of thinking that are characteristic of almost all family systems approaches. The reader is probably aware, however, that there are a good many schools of family therapy with widely differing notions as to the cause and cure of family dysfunction. We next present a number of key ideas that, though not central in all family systems approaches, are in one way or another characteristic of several prominent positions in the field, and seem to us worthy of attention.

Stuck-Togetherness and Boundaries

Assessing how differentiated an individual is from his family is as important to family therapists as it is to individual therapists. The family therapist, however, emphasizes the entire family system that makes differentiation difficult. Rather than talking about a patient as borderline or poorly differentiated or symbiotically fixated, the family therapist describes the entire family system.

It is interesting to note that, despite the rather wide differences of opinion as to how best to conceptualize the causes and cures of family dysfunction, there is a fair amount of agreement on the descriptive level. Most observers of families have noted that some families seem almost to be stuck together, while others seem to lack cohesiveness. Minuchin (Minuchin, Montalvo, Guerney, Rosman, & Schumer, 1967) has described families in terms of "enmeshed" versus "disengaged" transactional styles. He points out that most families are not totally enmeshed or disengaged, but rather have enmeshed or disengaged subsystems. It is in extreme cases of enmeshed or disengaged families or subsystems that problems arise.

Enmeshed family members are described as being overly connected to one another in the sense that whatever affects one person has an unusually powerful reverberating effect on the others. In contrast, in systems that tend toward the extreme disengaged end of the continuum, "only a high level of individual stress can reverberate strongly enough to activate the family's supportive systems" (Minuchin *et al.*, 1967, p. 55). According to Minuchin, "Members of enmeshed subsystems of families may be handicapped in that the heightened sense of belonging requires a major yielding of autonomy. . . . Members of disengaged sub-systems or families may function autonomously but have a skewed sense of independence and lack feelings of loyalty and belonging and the capacity for interdependence and for requesting support when needed" (Minuchin *et al.*, 1967, p. 55).

Murray Bowen (1972) is referring to a similar phenomenon with his concept of the "undifferentiated ego mass." He too sees in many families togetherness paid for by a reduction in the members' sense of individuality. Like Minuchin, Bowen sees individuals in fused families as being highly reactive to one another emotionally. Bowen's account is not fully parallel with Minuchin's, however, since he does not place much emphasis on disengagement except as a defense against undifferentiation, which remains basic for him.

A similar emphasis can be found in the work of Stierlin (1977), who has studied the families of troubled adolescents in the United States and Germany. According to Stierlin, in families that are too tightly bound together, "members fail to articulate their needs, wishes and roles vis-à-vis one another" (p. 340). In his work, as in Bowen's, the central aim of family therapy is to promote each member's individuation, differentiation, and relative autonomy. Like Minuchin, he sees disturbed families as having insufficiently drawn boundaries between generations and genders.

Robyn Skynner, a British family therapist who also thinks of families in terms of how much separateness, individuality, and growth is acceptable, captures well the sticky quality of these families in observing that the greatest compliments in such undifferentiated families are "you haven't changed a bit" or "he's always the same" (1981, p. 43).

How can we understand this phenomenon of stuck-togetherness? It is at this point that there is a parting of the ways. Minuchin conceptualizes the enmeshed–disengaged continuum as basically a transactional style or interactional preference. He does not look for deep unconscious causes, but assumes instead that a given family structure affects inner psychic processes and not the other way around. By changing the patterns of interaction in the family, individuals can be helped to become more differentiated. Little attention is paid to just why a particular family has one pattern or another. When the family comes to treatment, that pattern is already an established fact, whatever its origin; changing it, not understanding its history, is viewed as the therapist's appropriate concern.

If one accepts the notion that altering the structure of the family can further the individual's sense of himself as a separate and differentiated person, then it is clearly useful for individual therapists to get a good sense of how the family is organized and operates. Minuchin (1974) describes families in terms of subsystems and boundaries. By "subsystems" he means the various groupings in the family. Subsystems, for example, might consist of "parents," "siblings," "females," "males," "older children," "younger children," "those who like sports," "those who do the parenting," and so on. As is probably evident, a particular individual can participate in several different subsystems in the family (e.g., as father, as husband, and as breadwinner).

Boundaries are necessary to protect the functioning of the various subsystems. By "boundaries," Minuchin means the rules as to who participates in certain activities and how. Boundaries help maintain the differentiation of the various subsystems. Thus, for example, in order for siblings to develop their own relationships, the sibling subsystem must have boundaries that protect it from parental intrusion. Similarly, for adults to function effectively as partners, there must be boundaries around their relationship.

In enmeshed families, the boundaries are not firm and clear. Stress reverberates rapidly, and everybody seems to be into everybody else's business. Disengaged families, on the other hand, have rigid boundaries so that access of one subsystem to another is difficult.[2] The therapist tries to help the family establish clear boundaries that are neither diffuse nor rigid.

This conception of family functioning can be useful in working with individuals as well. It is possible, with appropriate inquiry, to get a fairly good idea of the kinds of boundaries that exist in the patient's family. For example, if one is alert to these issues, one might ask a patient who says she is upset with her brother whether or not she has shared her upset with anyone else in the family.[3] It can be enlightening

2. Note that this includes difficulties for any *individual* in the family in gaining emotional contact with any other, since in this scheme an individual is also thought of as a subsytem.

3. Naturally, one would also be interested in the meaning her brother's behavior has to her, the conflicting feelings it stirs and so forth. We are not suggesting that family dynamics concepts be substituted for concepts of individual dynamics, but rather that the various concepts be integrated in a more inclusive fashion.

to determine whether siblings work out their differences by themselves or whether others get involved. Who confides in whom in the family? Does news travel fast? Do children get involved in parents' fights? Are there cross-generational alliances? What is the circuit along which information travels (e.g., does daughter report to mother what is happening with brother, and does mother in turn tell father)? Later in this book, we discuss a variety of interventions that the individual therapist might make on the basis of such an analysis. The first step is to get this kind of information in a systematic way.

Bowen's analysis is less concerned with structure; he sees the fused structure of some marriages as caused primarily by the individual difficulties of the marital pair. Emotional fusion in a family is seen as resulting from the marriage of two individuals who have never adequately differentiated themselves from their families of origin. Bowen (1972, 1978) describes the well-differentiated person as one who is able to choose to operate either on an intellectual or an emotional basis. People who function mainly on an emotional level (or use their intellect in the service of emotionality) are described as having a low degree of basic differentiation. According to Bowen, such individuals fuse with partners who have an equivalently low level of basic differentiation.

These individuals may appear to be the mirror opposite of each other, with one partner seeming extremely dependent while the other appears to be quite independent. Bowen claims, however, that each partner is overly reactive emotionally to the other and is therefore fused with the spouse. According to Bowen, the problems that arise from fusion in one's present family (to be elaborated below) can only be truly resolved by helping each partner differentiate from his or her family of origin. Thus, though both Bowen and Minuchin see some families as fused or enmeshed, Minuchin focuses on the transactional aspects of this state, whereas Bowen sees as primary properties residing in the individuals.

Stierlin's (1977) discussion of "homeostatically enmeshed" families presents still another explanation. The lack of differentiation between family members is seen as the indirect result of efforts by the marital couple to defend against disappointments with their own parents, as well as disappointments with themselves, by using what Laing (1965) has described as "mystification." By "mystification," he means the attributing of one's own negative feelings or traits to another and convincing this person that he or she *is* as perceived.

Skynner (1981) also sees the diffuseness of boundaries and unclear identity stance in disturbed families as derived from defensive efforts. In order to ward off emotions that have not been acceptable in a family over generations, projection is used, and others are manipulated into behaving in ways that confirm one's projections. In Skynner's view, it is projection that creates the confusion of identities and boundaries.

It is important to note that boundaries are of concern to family therapists not only within the family, but between the family and the rest of the world. Some families allow and encourage close relationships outside the immediate family. Others seem to have unspoken rules that prohibit or make difficult any real involvement with outsiders.

Lyman Wynne (Wynne, Ryckoff, Day, & Hirsch, 1958), one of the early researchers on families of schizophrenics, has noticed that these families have very little tolerance for individuation among family members. In order to preserve the illusion of family togetherness, or what Wynne calls "pseudomutuality," the family puts up a "rubber fence" between itself and the outside world. Like a rubber fence, these families' boundaries appear to have some give, while in fact remaining impervious to intrusion.

Interpersonal Defenses and the Transfer of Stress

Individual therapists have long known that the anxiety and emotional stress of one individual can be disowned or projected, often effectively transferring the anxiety to someone else (e.g., Searles, 1965; Sullivan, 1953). Although defenses of this sort involve more than one person— in contrast, for example, to the defense mechanisms of denial or intellectualization—individual therapists tend to focus on how the one individual who is their patient is protecting himself from emotional distress, rather than the impact this has on others. Family therapists, in contrast, look at defenses as interpersonal maneuvers. They have tried to explicate more precisely how, when, and to whom stress is transferred. They focus not on the transfer of stress that exists within any individual (intrapsychic), but on the transfer of stress that exists between two or more people (interpersonal).

Family therapists differ in their conceptions of where the stress that is being dealt with interpersonally comes from. Some family therapists, for example, view anxiety from a standpoint essentially derived from psychoanalytic object relations theory, whereas others are concerned strictly with current sources of tension. Both ends of the continuum, however, see defense operations as existing within an interpersonal system. All family therapists are in agreement that individuals use and help one another to defend against upsetting or unacceptable emotions. There is also a fair amount of agreement as to *how* this is done, despite the different conceptions of etiology.

Both Minuchin and Bowen, for example, who differ widely on the reasons for family and individual stress, see one possible "resolution" in the formation of three-person interactions, called "triangulation." According to Bowen (1978), one way a two-person system resolves stress is to bring in a third party. For Bowen, the stress between two people has to do primarily with balancing the individuals' needs for closeness with their need for individuation. The greater the underlying fusion in the partners (as a function of having failed to differentiate themselves sufficiently from their respective families of origin), the more difficult it will be for them to strike a stable and satisfying balance. Eventually one person in a fused relationship (typically the one who feels the most internal discomfort) will attempt to resolve the tension by establishing an intense (though not always overt) relationship with a third party. This third person can be a child, a parent, a lover, or even a therapist.

It is Bowen's view that these triangles are seldom stable. Alliances are seen as constantly shifting, though within limited pathways. The person who was part of the original twosome, for example, may become uncomfortable with being cast into the outsider role (though he may at first have been relieved); somehow conflict erupts between the other two members of the triangle, and alliances shift once again. Whatever course the shifting alliances may take, the important thing to remember is that each dyad in a triangle of this sort is in fact a function of the other two. Efforts to understand any of these dyadic relationships simply in terms of what is going on between the two people will be incomplete and misleading.

According to Bowen, the greater the anxiety in the system, the more activity and interaction there is between interlocking triangles. For example, mother, in order to deal with tensions between her and father, becomes very close to son; father as a consequence feels excluded and starts to fight with son; mother is then the outsider, and she fuses with daughter.[4] Note that in this illustration we are referring to four people, not just to three. Triangulation is a process that, particularly where there is a lot of tension and not very much resolution, tends to proliferate. Several interlocking triangles are usually the result, with each individual participating in more than one; the system is largely defined by the ways in which these various triangular arrangements intersect.

When tension in a family is moderate, a relatively stable triangle can develop, so that it may appear that the problem is between a particular twosome. The point is, however, that no relationship can be understood without considering it within the context of other relationships.

Whereas Bowen is impressed by the constant shifting within triangles, Minuchin (1974) gives more emphasis to relatively stable, albeit dysfunctional, patterns of triangular interactions. He calls these patterns "rigid triads." Minuchin uses the term "triangulation" to describe only one kind of rigid triad, that in which two parents who are in overt or covert conflict with each other attempt to enlist the child's support against the other. This pattern involves the child in shifting alliances with each of the parents. Another kind of rigid triad is one in which there is a stable parent–child coalition. In this pattern there is open conflict between the parents, and a child and one parent are joined in a close and constant alliance against the other parent.

A couple may also use their child to aid in the *denial* of conflict between themselves. Minuchin calls this triad "detouring." The "detouring–attacking" mode is one in which the parents unite in their assessment of their child as "bad" and in need of parental control. Similarly, parents can mask their differences by the "detouring–supportive" mode in which they jointly focus on a child who is considered "sick."

Individual therapists can readily incorporate the idea of triangulation into their work. To do this, one must think of relationships

----

4. Note that mother is the outsider even though father's interaction with son is a "negative" one. It is the *involvement* she is excluded from, the chance to play out something in relation to the other (cf. Sullivan's concept of "hostile integration"). Note also that the pattern has no real endpoint or beginning. It is only expository convenience that leads to a description starting with mother and moving toward son. Her "later" move toward daughter is likely to be met with by a response from father that again brings tension within the couple's relationship to the fore—and is dealt with by the mother's again moving toward the son.

in terms of their impact on other relationships. If a woman describes having terrible fights with her daughter, a systems perspective asks how this affects or reflects upon her relationship with her husband. Is the stress in the parent–child relationship deflecting attention from the conflict between husband and wife? Perhaps it is serving to join them in creating an alliance against the "difficult" daughter.

Again, we wish to reiterate that these systems interpretations do not invalidate an understanding based on individual psychodynamics. The woman, for example, may be having difficulty with her daughter because of her own conflicts centering around sexuality, power, and so on. At the same time, the individual psychodynamics may be interlocked with systems dynamics in a way that prevents change in either.

The systems perspective helps us to see how the problem is set in the context of other relationships. For instance, using Murray Bowen's notions, we might see a man's argument with his closest friend as part of a shifting triangle, in which he returns to a state of intense closeness with his wife until the time that he can no longer tolerate his loss of individuality. Or perhaps there is a stable triangle in which a comfortable balance between closeness and differentiation is reached by including in the marriage, as it were, a third party with whom one of the spouses is very close. If the relationship with this "third party" is interrupted through moving, death, marriage, or the like, the balance between closeness and distance that has worked for the couple will be disturbed, creating tension in the relationship that was not previously apparent.

Family members can use one another to defend against anxiety-arousing feelings in ways far more subtle than triangulation. Many family therapists from a variety of orientations have arrived at what Framo has described as the "discovery of the interlocking, multiperson motivational system whereby intimates collusively carry psychic functions for each other" (1980, p. viii). The idea here is more than that individuals project onto others feelings and thoughts that are unacceptable. Projection alone is a concept that leaves out the ways in which others are induced to confirm the projection, as well as the possibility of mutuality or *collusiveness* of projections. Some individual therapists, particularly of the object relations school, have been concerned with somewhat similar phenomena under the rubric of "projective identification," but their attention to the manifest details of the interactive process (as distinct from the subjective experience of the single individual) has tended to be considerably less than is the case for family therapists.

PROJECTIVE IDENTIFICATION ONTO CHILDREN

Many family therapists have observed that children often take on a role that embodies affects denied by one or both parents (e.g., Ackerman, 1966; Framo, 1965; Boszormenyi-Nagy & Spark, 1973). Again, though there is a good deal of disagreement as to the reason for or nature of the stress that is being displaced, there is agreement on an observational level that this phenomenon occurs. Children, because of their need for parental approval, can readily be induced to behave in the ways needed by their parents. The induction may start out through a parent's simply "seeing" something in a child that reminds him of conflictual aspects in himself. This parental characterization of the child may lead the child to see himself that way, and to conform his behavior to what has now become a *self*-characterization.

The parent may do more than merely "see" traits in a child. He may induce a child to play a particular role through the utilization of subtle cues, or by giving messages that say "don't" and "do" at one and the same time. For example, a parent who is conflictually defending against anger at authority figures may "disapprove" of a child's rebellious behavior in such a way that the child gets mixed messages. If the child acts rebelliously, the parent can reinforce his own defenses against anger by expressing disapproval, and at the same time can vicariously gratify the forbidden wish through identification with the child.

Laing (1965) has been particularly interested in the process by which a child is induced to play out roles needed for what he calls a "transpersonal defense." As noted earlier, he refers to this process as "mystification." Mystification occurs through the attribution of negative traits (weakness or badness) to a child, through the invalidation or disqualification of a child's self-determined and differentiated viewpoint, and through the induction of particular behaviors on the part of the child by actively but covertly molding his feelings and behavior. Laing points out that "the masking effect of mystification may not avoid conflict, although it will cloud over what the conflict is about" (1965, p. 345).

Such considerations might lead, for example, with a patient who describes herself as having been a fresh and rebellious child, to an exploration of the parents' attitudes toward the overt expression of their own hostility. In addition to trying to understand the origin of the patient's rage in terms, for example, of individual frustration or deprivation, one would also consider whether the patient was or is in essence speaking for another family member. Was she, and is she still, subtly encouraged to act irrationally in the service of a parent's conflicting needs?

PROJECTIVE IDENTIFICATION BETWEEN PARTNERS

Individual conflict can also be resolved through projective identification with a partner. As Framo (1981, p. 138) puts it, "a main source of marital disharmony is that spouses project disowned aspects of themselves onto the mate and then fight them in the mate." Other family therapists have also observed that partners often express for each other forbidden wishes and impulses. Bowen (1978), for example, sees fused couples as acting almost as one, with each partner playing out the mirror image of the other's behavior. A highly independent man may be married to an extremely dependent woman. Each individual is able to function in that manner because the partner is expressing aspects of the individual that he or she feels unable to actualize. Sager (1978) points out that in choosing each other as mates, these individuals may have unconsciously "contracted" to play out certain roles for each other. Much of his work involves teasing out these implicit contracts.

TRANSFERENCE AND INDUCEMENT TO PLAY OUT ROLES

Thus far we have been talking about the use of others to embody conflictual aspects of *oneself*. It is also possible to induce family members to play out roles of significant others in one's past with whom there is unfinished business. A spouse, for example, may be induced to act like an authoritarian father with whom one was never able to fight. This is more than mere transference distortion. Having unconsciously encouraged this aspect of the spouse's personality, one can now gratify (albeit by proxy) one's unfulfilled (and perhaps denied) aggressive urges toward the father.

Children too can be used in this way. A child, for example, may be used to gratify parental needs for nurturance—needs that are being displaced from either the marital relationship or the family of origin. It is not uncommon to see families in which one or both parents' needs for parenting are being met by the child. Many family therapists regard school phobia, for instance, as deriving from a parent's need to ward off feelings of emptiness and the child's need to comfort the distressed parent.

This defensive operation is an interpersonal one, since it can only work if the family member actually behaves in the manner needed. It is not simply that an individual "sees" or transfers onto a spouse or child certain aspects of other important figures, but that he gets people to *behave* in accordance with the transference expectations.

This view leads us to ask questions that help elucidate the ways in which a patient may be helping to create the very behavior he complains about. For instance, a woman who lives with a tyrannical man may have a need to exercise self-control in the face of irrational outbursts. This both reassures her of her "saneness" in comparison to her husband and enables her to stand up to him in a way she never did with her father. Thus the participation of others in the transference process—as well as an understanding of how the patient actually elicits that participation—becomes an important focus of the therapeutic work (cf. P. L. Wachtel, 1981a, 1982).

FAMILY DEFENSIVE OPERATIONS

Thus far we have been talking primarily in terms of the defensive needs of one individual rather than the family as a whole. It is important to remember that each interactional pattern exists as part of a larger system and serves to keep the entire family system stable. Thus, a child who nurtures a parent may also stabilize the marriage or the relationship with the extended family, in that these relationships will not be stressed by dependency needs. A child may in effect be delegated by the group to play out a role that is of benefit to the system as a whole, in that it provides stability in what otherwise might be emotionally strained relationships.

Families, moreover, like individuals, may assign members roles in order not only to fulfill certain family needs as described above, but also to serve the purpose of what might be thought of as group projective identification. Ackerman (1966), one of the earliest theorists in family dynamics, has observed that families need their "scapegoated" child in order to preserve the desired functioning of the family. The scapegoat "was not really the outsider, different and alien, as they had thought. Rather he was their spokesman in an important but neglected area of life" (p. 236).

Stierlin (1977) observes something similar. He describes families as selecting a delegate who is perceived by the family as the cause of the family's misery. The other family members observe in the delegate "their disowned badness or madness and . . . redeem themselves through him from their disowned guilt" (p. 203).

GROUP DEFENSES

Another way in which an individual can use the family defensively is to obtain group consensus for attitudes and world views that protect the individual's version of reality. Laing (1965) points out that "if the one person does not want to know something or to remember something, it is not enough to repress it (or otherwise 'successfully' defend himself against it 'in' himself); he must not be reminded of it by the other" (p. 349). This defense differs from projective identification, in that it involves bolstering one's denial through a shared group belief system, rather than by the displacement onto another of one's own wishes.

A group can be induced to bolster denial in a variety of ways. Family members can be persuaded to maintain defensively necessary beliefs through direct indoctrination or through indirect means like mystification. These belief systems are referred to by family therapists as "family myths" (Ferreira, 1963) or "realities" (Minuchin & Fishman, 1981). Family myths are of course strongest in families that are enmeshed or undifferentiated. It is necessary for the preservation of the myth that no individual express a contradictory viewpoint. When family members have trouble with the distortion of reality implicit in "myths," and cannot challenge them directly, they may develop symptoms.

It is important to note that family myths are seldom directly expressed or explicitly acknowledged in a family. It is the very fact that these assumptions are held without being verbalized that enables them to go unchallenged. Myths may be about the different family members (what they are like, who is close to whom, etc.), or they may be more generalized. Generalized myths express an attitude toward life and assumptions about the world outside the family circle.

A number of common family myths have been described by Glick and Kessler (1980). Among those they list are these: (1) "Marital partners should be totally honest with one another at all times"; (2) "marital and family life should be totally happy, and each individual therein should expect either all or most gratifications to come from the family system"; (3) a "happy marriage is one in which there are no disagreements, and when family members fight with one another it means that they hate each other"; (4) "marital partners should be as unselfish as possible and give up thinking about their own individual needs";

(5) "positive feedback is not as necessary in marital systems as is negative feedback" (pp. 77, 78).

The concept of family myths is widely shared among family therapists. Selvini Palazzoli, Cecchin, Prata, and Boscolo (1978) regard the uncovering of family myths as the foundation on which the rest of therapeutic work is built. In one interesting family, for example, they describe the myth of "one for all and all for one" as the source of much unacknowledged stress. "The iron rule never mentioned forbade them not only any comment but also any gesture that could be said to be motivated by jealousy, envy or competition" (p. 89).

Minuchin and Fishman (1981), too, in their book on family therapy techniques, devote a chapter to the importance of modifying the family's "realities" and expanding their world view so that a symptom is not necessary. A similar kind of concern is evident in the writings of numerous other leading figures in family therapy.

Myths tend to be associated with unspoken but nonetheless powerful prescriptive and proscriptive rules. Thus in families that regard the world outside the family as dangerous, there is an implicit rule that one must not make close alliances with "outsiders." If there is a myth of "togetherness," there is probably a corresponding rule that one should not talk openly of differences. If there is a myth that "men are emotional and women are not," there is a corresponding prohibition against behavior that would disconfirm the myth. As noted above, myths may concern family relationships or the attributes of individual family members, rather than a general philosophy about life. These sorts of myths tend to lock family members into rather rigid roles. One might call it a family myth, for example, that one daughter is viewed as being fundamentally "brains" while the other is related to as the "beauty." Statements such as "Johnny is just like his dad" or "Susie and her younger sister are inseparable" provide other examples.

Often families have "myths" about family members that are connected with family communication patterns. Such statements, either overt or covert, like "Dad is highly volatile, so don't tell him upsetting news" or "Mom is sensitive" or "Susie can't keep a secret" may lock the family into rigid communication patterns.

We encourage patients to become conscious of the myths their families have held and how these myths may have influenced the patients' behavior or limited their choices about themselves or relationships to others. One man, for instance, who was having a very difficult time making a commitment to a woman, recalled that his family always said, "You can only trust your family." Another man who consistently resisted conventional success recalled his parents' contempt for money-hungry professionals. More often than not, people are unaware of the "mythology" they carry around. Until these myths become conscious, the patient is hampered in evaluating his own opinions and options.

The Stresses That Underlie the Symptoms

Though there is a fair amount of agreement on the observational level that such phenomena as triangulation or family myths characterize family functioning, theories range widely as to the nature of the stress that is at the root of these family defense operations. It is possible, however, to group the various views into two very broad categories. The first category puts greater emphasis on the more immediate interpersonal sources of family tension; the second emphasizes the individual's inner conflicts and how they are manifested and affected by interaction with other family members. It should be remembered that the theories in both these theoretical categories look at *systems* rather than individuals, in that both are concerned with repetitive patterns and sequences, and both subscribe to the view that the whole is more than the sum of the parts.

The Structural View

We have already described Minuchin's classification of families along the enmeshed–disengaged continuum, and his concern with the boundaries between family subsystems. For Minuchin, it is the structure of the family that causes stress and symptoms in family members. According to Aponte and Van Deusen (1981), the most important dimensions of family structure are "boundaries," "alignment," and "power" (or "force"). The boundaries of a subsystem are the "rules defining who participates and how" (Minuchin, 1974, p. 53). "Alignment" refers to the joining or opposition between family members. For instance, "alignment statements would indicate whether the father agrees or disagrees with his wife's disciplinary action towards the children" (Aponte & Van Deusen, 1981, p. 313). Power or force is "the relative influence of each [family] member on the outcome of an activity" (Aponte, 1976, p. 434).

The family experiences stress when the family structure is such that it doesn't meet the needs of its individual members and/or the larger social environment of which it is a part. Family members develop symptoms when their needs are being thwarted because of rigid family structures. The true source of the stress, however, may be defended against through triangulation as described above.

Consider the following hypothetical example of this view of family stress and symptom formation: In the Smith family (mother, father, son, and daughter), there are diffuse (overly open) boundaries surrounding the marital couple. The parents are seldom alone; they permit and perhaps even encourage their children to join them in almost all activities. The family as a whole would be described as enmeshed. Mother and son have a strong stable coalition with a rather rigid boundary around their relationship; father and daughter have a similarly close relationship. All works well within this family until the daughter, who is the elder of the two children, reaches adolescence. At that point her needs change. She wants to separate more from the family and join her peer group. She no longer wants to be "Daddy's girl." Furthermore, society no longer finds the physical intimacy between father and daughter acceptable.

The daughter wants and needs to identify more with her mother at this point in her life, but cannot get close to her because of the rigid boundary around mother and son. As the daughter pulls back from the father and tries in one way or another to disrupt the bond between mother and son so that she may enter, everyone in the family feels the emotional reverberations. The family is in an unstable and emotionally charged state, and one family member is likely to develop a symptom. If the daughter does separate, there will be an increase in stress between the parents. This stress may be defended against by triangling in a third person, perhaps the son, who may suddenly become difficult to control.

Most families negotiate transitions with only temporary and moderate stress. The more rigid the patterns of interaction, the more stressed families will be by the need for change, and the more likely they will be to develop symptoms. Predictable developmental changes are not the only changes that stress family functioning. A move to a new community, a change in career, or a change in economic circumstances—these are but a few examples of the kind of things that can upset a stable family system.

The structural approach does not ask *why* a particular structure has developed. It would not, for instance be concerned with why the parents in the hypothetical example above have sought intimacy from their children rather than from each other. It is not concerned with historical precursors or intrapsychic functioning. Instead, it observes what the structure of the family is and tries to change it so it is more in accord with the way well-functioning families operate. According to the structural view, a well-functioning family should be hierarchically organized, with the parents having more power than the children, with older children having more tasks and privileges than younger ones, and with clear generational boundaries.[5]

Haley, a family therapist who falls somewhere between the structural and strategic approaches (the latter to be described shortly), puts even more emphasis on the importance of hierarchies in the family structure than does Minuchin. According to Haley (1979), symptoms result when an organization has a hierarchical arrangement that is confused. Haley looks at the sequences or patterns of interaction in families. He is particularly interested in coalitons (joint action against a third person) that are taking place across generational lines. Symptoms develop when the coalition across generations is denied or concealed. He is not talking here about occasional cross-generational coalitions, but, rather, coalitons that are repetitive and rigidly held.

An example of Haley's view is his analysis of how to deal with young people who develop severe symptoms (psychotic breaks, drugs, delinquency) at the point at which they would be leaving home. Haley (1979) argues that the young person cannot leave home because his presence as a problem offspring is necessary to stabilize the marital relationship. He states, "Dealing with mad young people over the decades, it has become more evident that madness is an expression of a malfunctioning organization" (p. 19). As the young person becomes more and more troubled, he begins to have more power in the family than the parents.

Haley's starting point, consequently, is to put the parents in control and to strengthen their authority as the parental unit. Since the child is viewed as having developed his symptoms to prevent focus on the marital difficulties, the aim is to get the parents to talk about their difficulties with each other in the presence of the young person. In

---

5. According to L. Hoffman (1981), the structural approach has a normative model against which it compares the malfunctioning family—that is, in normal families the parental subsystem has clear boundaries, the sibling subsytems have clear boundaries, the family is organized hierarchically, and the boundary around the nuclear family is respected by the larger system of which it is a part.

such situations, Haley observes a repetitive cycle in which marital difficulties appear and separation is threatened when the adolescent is behaving normally. Like Minuchin in his work with anorexics, Haley observes that coalitions shift, in that the parents will alternate in how forgiving or angry they are at the problem child.

The Jones family provides a good illustration of concealed coalitions of the sort Haley describes. In this case, the coalition was between the youngest daughter and the father against mother. Whenever mother asked this daughter to do some chore, mother would be met with a contemptuous response. Fights between them would escalate until the daughter ran off in tears. Overtly, father would always support mother, telling daughter to be more cooperative. Privately, however, he shared daughter's belief that mother was demanding, critical, and "a nervous wreck." After an argument, he would say, "You should listen to your mother," but at other times, when mother wasn't home, he would comment on how peaceful it was in her absence. He kept his alliance with his daughter strong by refusing to make parenting decisions or to back his wife fully in the decisions she made.

The fact that the alliance was a "secret" one in that father did not openly disagree with his wife both confused and further enraged the daughter. She would escalate the fight and provoke her mother into increasingly irrational behavior in the hope that father would finally openly criticize mother.

In dealing with this aspect of her history in individual therapy years later, it was helpful for the daughter to recognize more clearly that her mother's irritability was in part a response to feeling the effects of the covert alliance in which she was the disliked intruder. Her further realization that her father was fueling the fire and in a sense using her as a pawn in a battle against mother put the whole history of the mother–daughter conflict into a different perspective. Insight into the system that existed when an individual was growing up can play an important role in freeing that individual from bewildering guilt and anger.

The Strategic View

For strategic therapists, the fabric of psychological difficulties is woven with irony; it is the very efforts that people make to set things right that so often are what keep the problem going. They set into action a repetitive cycle that is both destructive and self-maintaining.

In *Change*, Watzlawick, Weakland, and Fisch (1974) give many examples of how a marital pair may get into a self-perpetuating destructive cycle. For instance, a wife may think that her husband is too secretive. She asks him a lot of questions and checks up on him. This is her attempted solution to the problem. The husband finds this behavior too intrusive; his solution to his wife's intrusiveness is to withhold even trivial information, which of course furthers her worries. The less information he gives, the more persistently she seeks it, and the more she seeks it, the more secretive he becomes. The aim of the strategic therapist is to break the repetitive, self-perpetuating sequence.

This account of the ironic sources of psychological distress has many parallels with perspectives that guide a good deal of work in the individual psychodynamic tradition. Karen Horney's work in particular is strongly characterized by an ironic vision (P. L. Wachtel, 1979b); as she describes it, it is the very efforts to defend oneself against anxiety that create the vulnerabilities the person is plagued by. More recently, a variation of this point of view, under the name "cyclical psychodynamics," has been put forth as a framework for integrating various psychotherapeutic approaches (P. L. Wachtel, 1982, 1985).

Both cyclical psychodynamics and Horney's approach concern themselves with intrapsychic conflict in a way that strategic family therapy, with its sharp focus on manifest interaction patterns, does not. But there is nonetheless considerable overlap between these basically psychodynamic conceptions and that of the strategic approach. The attempted solutions to intrapsychic dilemmas inevitably involve other people, and within these basically interpersonal versions of psychodynamic thought, vicious circles involving the behavior of two or more people are a central concern.

In our work with individuals, we frequently ask questions that focus on how the patient "copes" with conflicts. One man, for example, was plagued by his fear of humiliation by women. At the same time, he had a great need for the security and comfort they offered him. He dealt with this conflict by getting involved with a woman, but being vigilantly on the lookout for signs that she was treating him disrespectfully. If he did notice something, he would deal with his fears of humiliation by taking aside those present and letting them know that the girlfriend's behavior had not gone unnoticed and that the relationship would soon come to an end. In fact, however, he never carried through on such avowals.

Since he was hypersensitive to what he regarded as humiliation, he often would call his friends' attention to minor events that had gone unnoticed. Thus he was frequently in the position of feeling like a bluffer in the view of his friends and of seeming weak in their eyes, since he continued to stay with a woman whose every potential humiliation of him he was calling to their attention. His efforts to detoxify the humiliation he felt with her by showing his friends he was savvy about what was going on ended up increasing the humiliation instead—and fueling the feelings that would lead yet again to the same unfortunate sequence of events.

The Milan Model

The notion of circular causality finds a somewhat different expression in the work of Mara Selvini Palazzoli and her colleagues (Selvini Palazzoli, 1978; Selvini Palazzoli, Cecchin, Prata, & Boscolo, 1978), whose way of conceptualizing and working with family pathology is referred to by some as the "systemic model" and by others simply as the "Milan school" on the basis of the city of its origin.[6] This model has become increasingly prominent in the United States, as well as in Europe where it was first developed. It is based on the hypothesis that "the family is a self-regulating system which controls itself according to rules formed over a period of time through a process of trial and error" (Selvini Palazzoli, Cecchin, Prata, & Boscolo, 1978, p. 6). In searching for the unspoken fundamental rule, out of adherence to which the pathological behavior arises, therapists of the Milan school concentrate on present interactions in both the immediate and the extended family. By focusing on the transactional rules, these therapists hope to avoid thinking in terms of linear causality, in which the behavior of one individual is thought to be the *cause* of the behavior of another.

L. Hoffman (1981), writing on the Milan approach, states that according to Selvini Palazzoli and her colleagues, "the enemy the clinician must attack is not any family member or even the malfunctioning family itself, but what [systemic therapists] call the family 'game'" (p. 288). Systemic therapists approach each dysfunctional family as if they were detectives trying to uncover a mystery. Past and present relationships within both the immediate family and the extended family

6. Some family therapists object to the name "systemic" for the theories deriving from the work of the Milan group, since proponents of competing theories of family therapy also think of themselves as systemic in their orientation.

are explored, as well as recent events within the family that might have strained the family's ability to sustain the rules. The answer to the mystery comes in discovering how the symptom is a solution to a current threat to the family's transactional rules.

The Milan school's concern with a circular conception of causality is evident as well in an intentional departure from traditional linguistic habits in describing psychological difficulties: Rather than saying, for example, that the mother in a family "is depressed," or even that she "gets depressed" in response to a particular situation, they say that she "shows depression." This leads inquiry away from internal factors in the depression and toward the function of the depression in the ongoing system. If one thinks of the mother as "showing" depression, then one begins to ask such questions as *to whom* she shows it, with what consequence, and so forth.

It should be noted that such a perspective does not necessarily imply that the mother is only "pretending" to be depressed, or that she is not "really" depressed; rather, for the Milan school's purposes, it has proven more useful to consider the consequences of "showing" depression and to follow the novel pathways that this way of speaking and thinking leads to. For the individual therapist, an *exclusive* emphasis on this perspective is likely to prove unsatisfactory, but as an additional, complementary way of thinking about what is transpiring, it may be of considerable value.

As an illustration of the Milan school's approach, one might consider a family treated by Selvini Palazzoli and her colleagues (described in L. Hoffman, 1981), in which the 17-year-old daughter, Antonella, had suddenly become anorexic. In exploring the events that had occurred in the months preceding the development of the symptom, it became apparent that Antonella's anorexia was connected to her being forbidden to date a boy of whom the family strongly disapproved. Further exploration revealed that mother was extremely attached to her own mother and seemed to be more concerned about this maternal grandmother's *upset* about the situation than she was about her daughter's "illness." In the family, the unspoken rule to which everybody submitted was that "It is forbidden to make decisions in one's own name." Thus, Antonella expressed herself through "sickness," and both mother and father expressed their wishes by acting out of "respect" for their parents. The family "game" was that "Antonella must forget Franco and must recover in order not to make grandmother suffer. . . . But as happens with every dysfunctional system, no one metacommunicates on the absurdity of such a claim since the level on which this claim is expressed is solely analogic" (Selvini Palazzoli, Boscolo, Cecchin, & Prata, 1978).

In another case involving an anorexic, the symptom arose as a way of adhering to the family rule, now passed down for three generations, that "Whoever speaks *badly* of his relatives is *bad*." In this family, all the brothers, wives, and children worked together and had the reputation of unusual harmony. The myth was that there were no family feuds, no bickering, no jealousy, envy, or competition. When Nora, the 15-year-old who was now anorexic, felt persecuted by her cousin, who seemed to be jealous of Nora's emerging beauty and success, she was faced with the option of either breaking the iron-clad rule or denying her own perception. In becoming anorexic, she preserved the family system (Selvini Palazzoli, 1978).

The strategic and systemic schools of family therapy have developed many innovative techniques to break vicious cycles and to disrupt what Selvini Palazzoli has called these "games without end." Some of these techniques (e.g., reframing, positive connotation, and the use of paradox) can be adapted to work with individuals and are described in Chapter 6 of this book.

Internalized History as the Cause of Family Stress and Symptoms

In the preceding discussion, we have described some of the ways in which the present interactions in the family can lead to stress and dysfunction. In this section, we discuss some theories of family dynamics that emphasize the internalized histories of the family members and the effect of these internalizations on the family system. The theories to be described are *also* interactional, but they include in the interactional equation the individual's intrapsychic realities and psychic structures. Some of these theories have been described as "historical," others as "experiential," and still others as "psychoanalytic." We group them together under the rubric of "internalized history" because they all emphasize current interactions not only as shaping current intrapsychic realities, but as shaped by previous patterns that are stored, transformed, and manifested in the present.

Murray Bowen's theories are a good example of this type. We have already discussed Bowen's concept of triangulation and the fluctuation within and between triangular groupings because of the buildup of stress. According to Bowen (1978), there is more stress in relationships when the individuals have a low level of basic differentiation and are psychologically fused. He sees fusion between the partners as the result of unresolved fusion within the partners' families of origin.

Although, according to Bowen, people with equivalent degrees of togetherness needs are attracted to each other, the desire for fusion leads to difficulties. Poorly differentiated individuals wish for merger with each other, but then become terrified at the loss of self that occurs. The instability and anxiety that result from intense fusion in relationships is resolved through fighting, distancing, the compromised functioning of one partner, or the banding together over concern for a child (Kerr, 1981). Since the fusion that exists in the present family is the result of the husband's and wife's never having fully differentiated from their families of origin, Bowen feels that current family problems can only be resolved by changing the interaction in the original extended family. The aim is to be more differentiated and less overreactive to the emotional forces in that system.

Even where the individuals having difficulty in their relationship seem to have gained considerable distance from their families of origin, Bowen would still point back to the earlier relationships as the source of the difficulty. In families where fusion is particularly threatening and emotional intensity is potentially overwhelming, family members may try to cut off the relationship more or less completely. This, however, simply leaves the various conflictual feelings toward the original family members unresolved, and these unresolved issues show themselves in contemporary relationships with spouse, children, and others.[7]

Bowen's approach to this situation is to coach the individual on how to change his relationships with parents, siblings, aunts and uncles, and other family members. Considerable effort is made to gather a good deal of information about family members; trips back home, as well as letters and phone calls, are utilized to establish a different, more differentiated relationship with the original figures. It is expected that, the family being a powerfully homeostatically functioning system, family members will do a variety of things to undo the individual's efforts to change things. The therapist's task consists largely in "coaching" the individual in order to prevent these efforts to change things from

---

7. Emotional cut-off may be utilized as a means of gaining a measure of relief and control in the new relationship as well. It will again be unsatisfactory, as it does not really deal with the issues which remain unresolved.

being undermined; this requires anticipation of how the other family members are likely to react to the individual's tactical maneuvers. The aim is not for the individual to try to change the other people per se, but to define *himself* differently and more clearly in the system through careful observation and through changing the role he plays in the process of the family system. In pursuing this task, it is inevitable that other participants in the system will change as well, but the focus, though systemic, is squarely on the individual (though, to be sure, on the individual *as he functions in the system*).

Bowen's system, with its emphasis on differentiation, on internalized properties of individuals, and even on the therapist's working with individuals alone (though as part of a system, to be sure), is in some ways reminiscent of traditional individually oriented psychotherapies. The resemblances to psychoanalytically oriented therapies are many; there is even a rough parallel to the training analysis in his training method, which stresses the importance of the therapist's working on his own family and not relying solely on being supervised in work with others. There are striking differences as well, however; the most important of these is probably the attitude toward transference. For Bowen, transference is not a phenomenon to be utilized as part of the therapeutic process, but something to be strictly avoided. Everything possible is done to prevent the person's becoming strongly emotionally involved with the therapist. For Bowen, this represents a displacement onto the therapist of affects that really belong in the family system and that must be worked on there.

Framo (e.g., 1981) presents a different approach to resolving issues with the family of origin. He sees marital and family difficulties as stemming from attempts to master earlier conflicts from the original family. Framo's approach is both intrapsychic and transactional. He sees "intrapsychic conflicts derived from the original family . . . being acted out, replicated, mastered or defended against with the current intimates" (1981, p. 137). Transference distortions can involve both partners and children.

Framo's notions of intrapsychic conflict derive from Fairbairn's (1952) object relations theory. He believes that infants incorporate the frustrating aspects of their relational world and that these internalized objects are retained as introjects. External, real figures are assimilated into the existing bad internalized object. According to Framo, individuals perceive their mates and children in terms of their own needs or as carrying denied split-off traits. One's current intimates, one's spouse and children, are shadowy stand-ins for old ghosts, the embodiments of old introjects (1981, p. 138).

Framo considers factors such as the blurring of generational boundaries or the maintenance of symptoms for system purposes, but he regards unresolved problems with the family of origin as more basic and underlying. For this reason, Framo often conducts family-of-origin sessions, in which the adults bring into therapy their siblings and parents. According to Framo, "[d]ealing with the real external figures loosens the grip of the internalized representatives of these figures and exposes them to current realities" (1981, p. 138).

The essence of the theoretical approaches we are describing does not lie in whether or not the actual family of origin is worked with. It is, rather, an orientation that conceptualizes the current difficulties in terms that include transgenerational transmission of problems. Whereas Bowen sees this transmission as taking place through the individual's failure to differentiate, and Framo sees the transmission to the next generation as mediated through the internalization of significant relationships, still others, such as Norman Paul (1969), Skynner (1981), and Stierlin (1977), think more in terms of the passing on of "repressions" or developmental failures from one generation to the next.

Skynner, for instance, thinks in terms of the general *developmental level* of the family. Parents who have not had proper mothering or fathering "will be likely to behave inappropriately when required to play these roles to which they have not been exposed, and for which they have not internalized an adequate model. Thus families are seen as suffering from characteristic developmental failures over generations, in similar fashion to the idea of 'fixation' on or 'regression' to developmental levels in the Freudian schema" (1981, p. 41). Symptoms develop when there is some stress with which the family cannot cope because it does not have the necessary models or learning experience.

Like Framo, Skynner emphasizes the predominance of projection in marital relationships. For Skynner, however, the projection process derives not from the splitting off of denied aspects of oneself, but from "wanting the other to function in a perpetually gratifying parental role" (1981, p. 43). In order to avoid re-encountering the pain originally experienced at the time of the developmental failure, both partners avoid the straightforward expression of these needs. They may preserve marital harmony by projecting their needs onto a child or outsider. Symptoms develop when an emotion that has been excluded from a family over generations begins to emerge with such intensity that the couple's defenses do not work well enough and the stress is externalized onto another family member through projection.

Intense emotions are stirred as the children in a family pass through developmental stages. Thus the arrival of a child may intensify denied needs for nurturance on the part of one or both parents. Similarly, the child's developing need for autonomy, or his emerging sexuality, may evoke feelings in the parents that they cannot handle directly. For Skynner, the goal of therapy is to identify the projective systems and bring them back from the child to the marriage.

Other theories that emphasize the role of repression and denial in family dysfunction are those of Boszormenyi-Nagy and Spark (1973), Stierlin (1977), and Paul (1969). For Paul, uncovering loss and helping families with the "unresolved mourning process" is the heart of the work with symptomatic families. For him, it is the failure to properly mourn an important death or loss that leads to fusion in a family. Family members may be induced to take on roles that compensate for the unresolved loss. These roles may be comforting to the bereaved, but do not allow for autonomous development on the part of the family members who assume these functions.

Stierlin (1977), expanding on Paul's thesis, explains that loss may be not only of persons but "of ambitions, of ideals, of skills and physical assets" (p. 326). According to Stierlin, "parents who bind and delegate their children ordinarily manage to avoid the very mourning process which they (the parents) should have experienced while they related to, and tried to separate from, *their* parents" (p. 326). He gives an example of a father who, when able to give up an idealized image of his own father and mourn this loss, became much more accepting of his "good-for-nothing" son, whose failure lay, in part, in his having been delegated to meet his father's need for success. "[T]he father here held his son accountable for what *his* father had (or had not) done to him—for the failure to serve as a father and model whom he . . . could respect and love without distorting idealization" (p. 327).

Boszormenyi-Nagy, too, views historical issues as being of central importance to current family functioning. In the book *Invisible Loyalties*, Boszormenyi-Nagy and Spark (1973) describe the importance of what they call the "balance of accounts" or "ledger of merits" in families. Each member of a family has a mental record (often unconscious) in which he keeps accounts of justices and injustices that have been done to him. The "accounts," if not settled, are passed down from one generation to the next and determine the structure of the current nuclear family. "A husband's abusive act toward his wife may have far more dynamic connection to a behavioral sequence of 30 or 60 years ago than to the act of hers that triggered his abuse" (Boszormenyi-Nagy & Ulrich, 1981, p. 162). Boszormenyi-Nagy means by this that the husband may be holding his wife accountable for injustices done to him by his parents. Such displacements of the wish for retribution occur because children feel "invisible loyalties" to parents and prefer not to confront their disappointment or rages.

Boszormenyi-Nagy speaks too of "relational ethics," by which he means "the balance of equitable fairness between people." When "loyalty" to parents is maintained by substitutive blamings, by parentifying a child (who becomes a parent to the parents), or by "failing" as a parent or spouse so as not to do better than one's own parent did, there is a violation of "relational ethics" and "exploitation" of family members.

Boszormenyi-Nagy's notion of "invisible loyalties" as a motivating force for self-destructive behavior leads us directly to perhaps the most important concept in family therapy today—the idea that individuals are often motivated to develop symptoms by a wish to help the family as a whole. In the next section, we examine this concept more fully.

The Symptomatic Family Member

Although family therapists tend to look at the symptomatic individual as expressing a problem of the family as a whole—indeed, Bloch and LaPerriere (1973) have suggested that the essence of the paradigm shift in family therapy involves a movement from a concern with the family *of* the patient to a focus on the family *as* the patient—one can still ask how it is that any particular individual ends up as the one with the symptoms or becomes the identified patient. Many consid- erations are relevant here, with emphasis depending to a substantial degree on the theoretical orientation of the observer. To some extent, it is simply a matter of one person's having been in the wrong place at the wrong time. For example, the youngest child might develop symptoms after the older siblings go to college, in response to the family's need to avoid the empty-nest syndrome.

Similarly, one child may be at a particular developmental stage that lends itself well to the needs of the family at a particular time. In a family in which the mother is extremely distraught at the sudden death of her own mother, for example, a child who happens to be at a developmental stage in which security needs dominate is more likely than his siblings to meet the mother's currently exaggerated need for intense closeness.

Changes in the position of the family vis-à-vis the outside world may affect one child more than the others. Thus, in a family in which economic necessity has forced the mother to find employment, the child who is cared for after school by a grandparent may be the one to express, through symptoms, cross-generational stress.

If one adopts a theoretical viewpoint that focuses predominantly on current interactions, the symptomatic individual would be seen as one who has gotten caught up in a positive feedback loop in which attempts to correct a problem lead to more and more difficulty. From this viewpoint, what could have been a minor transient difficulty inadvertently (without motivation) escalates into a symptom. For example, the attempted solution to a child's "delinquency" may be to be more permissive, which response leads in turn to greater acting out and correspondingly greater supportiveness, until what might have been a temporary stage and expression of a wish for guidance becomes a rigidified symptom.

It is important to note that theorists differ in how active a role they assign to the identified patients themselves in this process. Some family therapists regard the "problem" individual as a scapegoat or a delegate who has been chosen by others (e.g., Ackerman, 1966; Stierlin, 1977). In this view, the child is regarded as more or less a passive victim of the parents' projections. Framo (1981), for example, states that the roles assigned to the child "usually have nothing to do with the inherent nature of the child. Children who are assigned the role of 'the troublemaker,' 'the crazy one' . . . may incorporate and *become* their assigned role" (p. 140). Similarly, Ackerman (1966) states that "a family member may be helplessly sucked up in the swirl of uncontrolled violent conflict in another family pair," and that "one member of the family may save himself from the more injurious aspect of psychopathological contagion by keeping another member of the family sick" (p. 102). A modified version of this view regards the child as playing an active part in the maintenance of a role that he was initially assigned (Kerr, 1981, p. 245).

A number of views have been put forth as to the child's motives in maintaining a symptomatic role. One that has gained increasing acceptance is the idea that the actions of the identified patient are based on a wish to help other family members. Haley (1979), for example, says that "a mad act is . . . a way of doing service to others" (p. 27), and that young people who do not leave home are sacrificing themselves for the good of the family. He states that "It is best to assume that [they are] sacrificing themselves consciously and willingly" (p. 40). Similarly, he states that "underlying most marital problems is a protectiveness that keeps the problem going. It is the benevolence that is often most difficult to change" (1976, p. 157). This view is echoed by family therapists of widely differing theoretical pursuasions. Boszormenyi-Nagy, whose theory of invisible loyalities has little else in common with Haley's view, similarly sees the child's difficulties as arising out of loyalty to the parents. The child, he says, "will tend to feel obligated to save the parents and their marriage from the threat of destruction" (Boszormenyi-Nagy & Ulrich, 1981, p. 169).

Skynner, from the viewpoint of a psychoanalytic family theory based on developmental impairments in families that lead to repression and fixations, sees something similar. He states that although "[t]he 'sick' member is usually chosen because of some special characteristics . . . [t]he individual concerned colludes in the process out of a deep, if unconscious, recognition that he is preserving the parent, the marriage or the family as a whole from disintegration, out of a motive of attachment as well as guilt" (1981, pp. 46–47).

Maintaining symptoms in order to protect other family members is thought to occur not only between parents and children, but between marital partners as well. Acting out a particular role may be part of the implicit marital "contract" (Sager, 1981), in which the partner silently agrees to protect the spouse from conflictual aspects of himself or herself. This is accomplished by "seeing" the partner as he or she needs to be seen, or by acting out the partner's unacceptable traits and thus enabling the partner to say, "This is not me."

The theories described above have thus added to the list of human motivations those of benevolence and protectiveness. Self-sacrifice is regarded not as a rarity, but as a natural concomitant of loyalty and family ties. These theories show an interesting convergence with some psychoanalytic views, such as that of Searles (1958), which similarly stress the child's protectiveness toward the parent.

Other family therapists who have also used these formulations seem to do so more as a technique or effective ploy for bringing about change than out of a belief that this is the real motivation. By positively connoting problem behavior as an attempt to be "helpful," one changes the family members' reactions to the behavior and thereby alters the system that has maintained the symptom. This is often referred to as changing the "punctuation" of events so that a different meaning emerges.

When a group of experts convincingly tells a family, for instance, "This is our opinion about the irresponsible behavior of your daughter: We feel instead that your daughter's is very responsible behavior— that what she has been doing for all these years that you might feel was irresponsible behavior was extremely responsible," it is difficult for the family to continue to play the "game" exactly as before. Furthermore, the identified patient herself may recoil from the notion that she is being helpful or self-sacrificing, and may thereby be induced to give up the troublesome behavior. Although therapists of the Milan school acknowledge that statements such as "X's behavior is necessary for the welfare of the family" do not comport with conceptualizing the problem in circular rather than linear terms (L. Hoffman, 1981, p. 295), they make such statements as a strategy to break up interactional patterns without asking the family to change. In Chapter 6, we discuss in detail the way in which paradox and positive connotation are used by therapists of the Milan school.

If one accepts that children do actually act "disturbed" in order to preserve their parents' marriage, one can speculate as to the way this comes about. Perhaps a child spontaneously behaves a certain way and then notices, consciously or unconsciously, that this behavior has had a temporarily beneficial effect on the parents' relationship. They may, out of worry for their child, have a rare intimate moment. If the child is pleased to see this temporary rapproachement, he may be tempted to bring them together again when the stress between them reaches an ominously high level. Whether or not the child is really consciously deciding to be helpful is not at all clear, but couching the interpretation in terms of choice may enable the child to give up his rescue operation.

One can also speculate that the *parents* notice that a child's problems have a beneficial effect on their relationship. The parents may unconsciously and covertly reinforce the disturbed behavior, leading the child to continue his actions out of a wish to please the parents. This formulation fits better with notions of circular causality, in that both parents and child play a role in the maintenance of the symptom. The child may not be aware that the parents are covertly pleased because the symptom stabilizes the marriage, but nonetheless senses that his symptoms are in some way positively received.

A number of family therapists have noticed that the symptomatic individual often has great power which he may be reluctant to give up. Both Stierlin and Boszormenyi-Nagy have described the power the symptomatic individual may wield in his family. "In . . . living up to his parents' negative attributions, the victim delivers himself as the living proof for his parents' badness and failure as parents—even though he wrecks his life in the process" (Stierlin, 1977, p. 325).

According to Stierlin, the more the family needs the symptomatic individual, the more powerful that person becomes. Thus a "troubled" adolescent may make his parents feel guilty for demands that are age-appropriate. "He can make 'inoperative' these parental expectations by presenting himself as too sick, inept, anxious, nervous, etc. to comply with them. His motivation in continuing to be 'sick' may be not only to punish his parents, but also to "spare himself the painful work of separation and growth" (1977, p. 297). Stierlin believes that the therapist must "erode the victim's powers for inducing guilt." He does this by interpreting the patient's enjoyment of suffering and the sadism that this implies.

Haley (1979) also sees the problem young person as having gained so much power that there is a reversal of the usual hierarchy in which parents have more authority than their children. His therapy with such families begins by putting the family in charge of their child. He states that the more handicapped and helpless the young person becomes, the more he dominates the parents. Thus, although (as we explain above) Haley sees the symptom as a protective and self-sacrificing act, he also notes that this leads to the gaining of a great deal of power.

The motive of "power," like that of "self-sacrifice," can be used primarily as a strategy, regardless of the accuracy of such statements. Minuchin, for example, relabels the anorexic's not eating as an act of defiance rather than of illness. While recognizing that such a formulation may not do justice to the problem, he feels that this maneuver brings about a therapeutically induced crisis from which new transactions may develop.

The account above has been designed to familarize the reader with the chief conceptual tools that have evolved out of the family therapy movement and to organize them in a coherent way. In the next chapters, we look at how these ideas may be applied in the context of individual psychotherapy. We look in addition at a variety of *intervention strategies* that have evolved out of clinical work with families, again with an eye toward the application of these new methods to work with individuals.

Some of the methods to be described follow rather closely from one or more of the conceptual tools just described. Others have evolved only coincidentally within the family therapy branch of the family of psychotherapies and could as readily have developed out of work with individuals. Indeed, some of the methods to be discussed (e.g., the use of paradoxical communications) have simultaneously evolved within various approaches to individual therapy as well. Before one is in a position to intervene, of course, one must first have some idea of the relevant issues. We therefore turn first to a consideration of the kinds of questions that need to be asked in order to obtain relevant information about family systems.

3.   *Asking Questions That Reveal the Family System*

THE WAYS OF THINKING we have outlined thus far have important implications for how one proceeds clinically. The combination of an openness to active intervention into patients' difficulties and a consideration of family systems notions leads to a far wider range of therapeutic strategies that can be considered. In the following chapters, we wish to indicate some of the ways in which the position we are advocating leads to specific changes in how one proceeds clinically.

To begin with, we wish to consider the kinds of questions the therapist needs to ask in order to incorporate a systems perspective into his or her work. Without asking the right questions, the therapist cannot gain access to the kinds of data necessary for systems hypotheses and systems-oriented interventions.

If one hears a case presentation on individual psychotherapy at a first-rate clinical facility, one is likely to be struck by the mass of clinical material that is integrated. If one is seeking to understand the case from a systems perspective, one is likely to be struck as well by what is left out. Despite the welter of information about developmental history, current difficulties, fantasies, and even family background, one is frequently left with the feeling that the crucial data for formulating systemic hypotheses have been omitted.

The lines of questioning described here are designed to elicit the kind of clinical material necessary to include a systemic point of view. Clearly, some of what we are suggesting here overlaps substantially with the explorations of traditional psychodynamic clinicians; not all of the questions noted below are the exclusive province of therapists explicitly committed to including family systems considerations in their work. But for many readers, this chapter will provide a "how-to" guide to a kind of inquiry with which they are not thoroughly familiar, and for others it will provide a useful set of detailed guidelines for an expanded clinical inquiry.

Several lines of inquiry are important in alerting the therapist to essential characteristics of the familial and systemic aspects of patients' difficulties. They can be ordered roughly in terms of how much of the person's context is taken into account.

Some of the crucial questions still retain a basically individual focus, but one designed to enable the therapist to gain a more "circular" perspective on the patient's problems. These questions are designed to elicit how the individual may be perpetuating his problems by the very efforts he makes to solve them. Essentially, they represent an inquiry into the vicious circles that characterize the patient's life. A related line of inquiry (also concerned with vicious circles) focuses more on the reactions of others to the patient's symptoms and to his efforts to cope with his conflicts and problems. It looks at how the important people in the patient's life might inadvertently exacerbate his difficulties, and (importantly) at how they might potentially prove helpful in facilitating resolution of the problem.

Another line of inquiry is more fully systemic. It seeks to place the person's difficulties in the context of the larger system of which he is a part. To some degree, following the lead of the Milan school of family therapy, this line of inquiry concerns itself with ways in which the family as a whole might be seen as *needing* the patient to be symptomatic. What would happen to other family members if this individual were to change? What are the "pulls" in the system? Is this person expressing feelings that someone else is denying? Is he being "helpful" to others by not functioning well? These questions address the idea of what might be thought of as "systemic motivation."

We are interested as well, however, in the *unintended* ways in which the system's operation makes the patient's symptom necessary. Here we are thinking not in terms of what the system "needs," but rather of how the structure of the family interacts with the individual's qualities and inclinations. For example, does the "tightness" of the family structure of the husband's family of origin make it difficult for him to love his wife without feeling disloyal? Are there cross-generational alliances? Is privacy respected? And so on.

The answers to these various questions are not obtained all at once. We are not here talking simply about the kinds of questions one might ask in an intake interview or in the first few sessions of treatment.

Rather, these represent basic orienting ideas as we continuously pursue an exploration of the patient's life and the difficulties he experiences. They are questions rooted in our underlying theoretical assumptions about the interaction between the individual and the context in which he lives. Since few patients think of themselves as part of a system, they are unlikely to volunteer the information needed to answer these questions unless the therapist takes an active role in directing their attention to systemic factors. The questions described in more detail below are designed to bring to the fore these factors, which for cultural and technical reasons have tended to be obscured.

Exploring Vicious Circles

In Chapter 1 we have noted a variety of instances in which the patient's attempts to deal with his problems paradoxically make them worse. Exploration of these vicious circles is aided by questions specifically designed to shed light on them. In this, we have found the work of the strategic family therapists to be of great value. Though there are many ways in which their work differs from ours, both in goals and in point of view, their emphasis on how the problem is enacted and on how "the solution has become the problem" is similar to ours.

Discovering How Patients Perpetuate Problems: Direct Inquiry

In attempting to draw a bead on the pattern of vicious circles that are involved in any patient's problems, we aim to ask questions that convert general statements into descriptions of specific behaviors. Thus if a patient states that he has been feeling "depressed" lately, we ask not only about how he *feels*, but about what he *does* when he is depressed (e.g., "What do you do? Do you stay in bed? Do you go to work?"). Moreover (following the lead of the strategic family therapists), we ask in detail about what the patient does to try to get himself *out* of the depression (e.g., "Do you force yourself to go out with friends? Do you withdraw with the hope that it will pass? Do you tell your spouse? Do you try to talk yourself out of it?"). We then go further and ask for an even more specific description. For example, if the person says he goes out with friends, we might ask about which friends he chooses and why (e.g., cheerful, "up" friends, or friends more depressed than himself). How does he act with these friends? Does he tell them about his upset? Does he exaggerate or minimize his feelings? Does he become "jolly" or drunk? Does he feel and/or act angry with his friends at these times?

This degree of specificity is necessary in order for us to pinpoint how the "solution" might be exacerbating the problem. Suppose, for instance, that the patient tells us he's been depressed because he has accomplished little in his life and gets little comfort or pleasure from family or career. Upon initial inquiry into what he does when he is feeling down, he says that he tells his wife about how he is feeling. Further, more specific questioning, however—for example, "When would you tell her? At night in bed? When you get home? While she is preparing dinner? . . . What exactly do you say? How do you know if you've gotten across?"—reveals that our patient wants to tell his wife but feels he should try to be cheerful. So he "tells" her in as casual and light a way as possible, generally while she is preparing dinner. He might say, for instance, "Oh, I've been feeling down but I'm feeling better now," when in fact he is still feeling quite miserable. He does this both because he feels that if he "works at" being cheerful he will feel better, and because he fears he will alarm and annoy his wife if he starts "crying on her shoulder."

The result, though, is that he is disappointed in her lack of responsiveness to him. Busy with dinner and children, the wife doesn't really notice how upset her husband is. She believes what he says, and consequently does not respond in a way consonant with his high degree of distress. His "solution" to the dilemma of feeling depressed but not believing that revealing how he feels will be acceptable contributes substantially to maintaining his sense of getting very little pleasure or comfort from his family.

One patient, Nancy, reported trouble forming lasting relationships with men because she often felt that men would be extremely controlling and would humiliate her by imposing their will upon her. When she perceived a man as being bossy, particularly when her friends were around, she felt both angry and humiliated. As a result of her therapy experience, she had become aware that she was hypersensitive in regard to the issue of being controlled; she recognized that she had a tendency to perceive men as tyrannical when they had in fact not been. Consequently, when her boyfriend said something that she experienced as controlling and humiliating, she would "check it out" with her friends, rather than confronting him with it and/or asking him to stop. This seemed to her a reasonable way to deal with her hypersensitivity, a "solution," as it were.

Close inquiry as to precisely how she "checked it out," however, revealed that what she would do would be, soon after the "humiliation" had occurred, to say something like "Did you hear what Jim said? That was nasty, wasn't it? I'm not going to put up with this much longer. This relationship is not going to last!"

Since this kind of "checking out" provided her with little of the feedback one might ordinarily expect from friends if one really discussed another's behavior in an open and receptive manner, she would come away from these conversations with little real sense that her perception had been affirmed. Consequently, she would continue to be hesitant to take matters up with her boyfriend, and he would remain unaware that his behavior was a source of distress for her. Moreover, since she was in fact quite emotionally attached to this man and did not want to leave him, the relationship lasted, despite her statements to her friends to the contrary. Her "solution" to her feelings of humiliation thus ended up leading to a much *greater* sense of humiliation, for now her experience was compounded by a feeling that her friends thought she was weak for staying with such an ogre. (Interestingly, further inquiry also revealed that she *only* told her friends how controlling Jim was and seldom discussed the things she liked that made her want to stay with him.)

Another patient, Lucille, a divorced woman with a young son, felt terribly guilty about her resentment of the restrictions that having a young child entailed. In order to ward off her feeling that she was a "monster" for preferring to go out dancing rather than stay at home with her little boy, she proved to herself that she did have normal maternal feelings by being extremely concerned with such things as how well the boy was eating or whether or not he was dressed properly for inclement weather.

Her concern for these sorts of issues was excessive. She would worry, cajole, and finally demand that the boy comply with her protective wishes. Predictably, battles would ensue, since the boy, like many children of his age (and perhaps more so because of the divorce), was very intent on having control and making his own decisions. Her attempts at being "mothering" led to terrible scenes and tantrums on the part of both mother and son. These scenes increased her guilt at what a bad mother she was, as well as her sense that being with her son was a burden and a deprivation.

To be sure, Lucille's conflicted experience with her son was multiply determined and had a history that could be substantially understood in terms of her own childhood and relationship with her mother. But her understanding of how the pattern she was now caught in was perpetuated was greatly aided by seeing how the "solution" to her guilt feelings ironically kept the problem alive: If she wouldn't try quite so hard to be a concerned parent, the boy would probably be less difficult, and she would have a better chance of enjoying her time with him.

A second "solution" for her was to go out less than she really would have liked. Here, too, the results were ironic. By denying her wishes, she not only built up further resentment toward the child, but also allowed her desire for greater freedom to build up out of proportion. Had she acted on the wish to go out, she might very well have begun to enjoy those quiet evenings she did spend at home with her son.

Discovering the Reactions of Others: Role Playing

It is often useful in arriving at a picture of the vicious circles in the patient's life to supplement direct inquiry via questions with the use of exploratory role playing. Typically, for these purposes, the therapist plays the part of some figure with whom the patient interacts; the patient supplies the background material for the therapist's participation by describing the other person and indicating what that person would be likely to say in a particular situation.

As we do the role playing, we ask the patient to correct us if we are not quite capturing the intonation or manner of the character we are playing. Once we are confident that we now can "act" the part, we ask the patient to act the way he generally would if the interaction were the real thing. From this role playing, we often get a much clearer picture of both our patient and the other person. We have found that the other person really comes alive, because the patient, out of necessity, must describe him in great specificity and in action terms if we are to be able to portray this person accurately. Surprisingly few patients say they just can't describe the other person well enough to "direct" our performance. Patients often feel shy, but with encouragement are themselves surprised by how well they can imitate those people who are important to them.

When we observe through the role playing exactly what the patient says, we can often see how the "solution" has become the problem. Later, we discuss using role playing to help the patient develop new ways of interacting, but for now we are focusing only on the *information* we get by making this situation come alive. We often observe, for example, that in the effort to minimize hurt feelings (on his part or the other person's), the patient is considerably more vague than he realizes. This vagueness can lead to confusion on the other person's part, to continuing demands or requests, to further guilt and concern about hurt feelings, and so forth.

In the case of Dora, to be described next, an unnoticed modifying of what she thought was an assertive message undermined and contradicted her intended effect. In the course of role playing, this modifying became apparent in a way that it had not in her previous descriptions.

Dora, who was extremely distressed by her mother's intrusiveness, felt enormously bothered by how often she wished her mother would "disappear." When her mother said, "I'm sorry to bother you, dear, but you know I love you so much and worry about you," Dora—as it became clear through the role playing—would reflexively respond "I love you too, mother" in response to the implied accusation. As it turned out, this remark—pretty much a constant factor in their interaction—tended to override for mother any complaint that might accompany it. Its effect was to reinforce mother for her intrusive behavior, since such a response from her daughter was what she desperately sought. The rest of Dora's message was essentially irrelevant to mother; whatever complaint Dora was making was insignificant, compared to the importance to her of hearing from Dora "I love you too." Thus Dora's almost tic-like use of this phrase had the effect of encouraging her mother's continuing intrusiveness, and therefore of rekindling Dora's need to put distance between them. In circular fashion, it then stirred the need to defend against that forbidden desire by adding another "I love you too" at the end of the next conversation, with the predictable response.

The full implications of this pattern did not in themselves become clear simply from the role playing; what the role playing revealed led to further exploration, which clarified the meaning to mother of Dora's seemingly *pro forma* remark. But it was only through the role playing that the therapist learned at all about the "I love you too" comment and was in a position to explore further. Prior to this enactment, the patient had reported only her attempts at being assertive (e.g., "Mother, please don't call me at this hour"). It was hard to see what kept the interaction going without the opening wedge provided by the discovery of the "I love you too" ending to her efforts at putting her foot down.

Asking Questions That Help Us Locate the Individual's Symptom in the System

In our initial interviews with a patient, we ask questions not only about the patient himself and his developmental history, but also about the people with whom the patient currently lives and about the present situation of the living members of his family of origin. In particular, we ask whether there have been any significant changes in the lives of any of these people.

To illustrate, let us consider a hypothetical case discussed in Chapter 2 (see p. 44). As presented there, a woman's depression is seen to be related to the loss of her role as "nurturant" parent as a result of her husband's becoming more involved with the children. This new involvement with the children is in turn seen as related to the husband's guilt over his angry relationship with his dying father. How would one get the information that could lead to such a hypothesis?

The material would probably be elicited by the kinds of questions we would routinely ask as a consequence of exploring contextual and systemic matters. We might ask, for example, such questions as these: "Tell me about your husband. What does he do? How does he feel about his work? Have there been any changes in his life lately? Are his parents alive? How do they get along? What about his siblings?"

If the response to any of these questions seems possibly significant, we explore further. Thus, in this example, Mrs. D might say that her husband is unhappy with his job. We would than ask, "Why? Is there anything new in that? Is he changing jobs? How does he deal with his unhappiness about his job? How does it affect him? How does it affect the family?"

We are alert to changes that have recently occurred, as well as chronic conditions. If the husband has been chronically dissatisfied with his job, we keep this in mind in assessing the function of the wife's depression in the family system. If, as in our hypothetical example, the wife has only recently become depressed enough to feel a need for professional assistance, we look to see whether something has changed in the system. Thus, if we discover that the husband has been chronically unhappy with his job but that nothing is significantly different in that sphere, we go on to explore other aspects of his life—for example, his family. It is here that we discover that he has never gotten along with his father, who is now critically ill. We inquire into how he has reacted to this illness. We ask the patient what she has noticed about how his father's illness has affected him.

In discussing this line of inquiry with colleagues, some have expressed concern about the patient's reaction to questions that on the surface have little relevance to the matter at hand. We have found that, by and large, patients accept as sensible our explanation that it helps us better understand them if we know something about those with whom they are close. Patients seem to "know" without being fully conscious of it that their feelings and behavior can't be truly separated from the context in which they live. Perhaps they find such a perspective less strange than therapists do, because they have not been as fully trained to think of their problems as wholly within themselves.

In addition to inquiring about changes in the lives of family members, we ask questions that compare the patient to others in the family. These "comparative" questions are aimed at trying to elucidate any interpersonal defenses or collusive processes that may be part of what the symptom is about. For example, if a patient describes rage reactions, we would inquire not only into what may have altered in the system or what stresses the patient may be under, but also how others in the family express anger. "Who else in the family gets angry? How does your husband deal with anger? How do you know when he is mad? How does he react to your anger? Does he know what kind of things trigger you? What is his part in those triggering events?" By asking questions such as these, we are trying to see whether the patient might be being cued to express emotions that are denied by her partner.

We have also adapted from the systemic school the method of "circular questioning" (e.g., Penn, 1982). This technique, when used in family therapy, involves asking different family members a variety of comparative questions, and provides a kind of cross-referencing of information. One family member is asked to comment on the relationship of two others. When adapting the method to work with an individual, we attempt to map out the family system by asking such questions as these: "Who in the family worries most? Who is more assertive, you or your husband? Who is closer to their parents?" And so on. Asking such questions of only one family member does not have the benefit of the *Rashomon* effect, as it does when a number of family members are questioned. Nonetheless, the information gained does help one form hypotheses regarding the possible systemic function of the symptom.

It is important to make the questions asked in this way rather concrete, so that useful relationships between different people's activities can be discerned from the comparisons. One might ask, for example, "If your teenage son is going on a trip, who worries about it, you or your husband? Who makes calls to complain of noise? Who invites over guests? Who complains about feeling ill?"

We are very much interested in what happens on those occasions when the partner acts uncharacteristically—when, for example, a typically calm wife yells at the children, or a typically optimistic husband expresses worry. We want to know, when a man who is usually calm becomes anxious, whether his wife's anxiety increases or decreases. This kind of information is seldom volunteered without direct inquiry, but is relatively easy to obtain via the comparative questioning we are describing here.

Asking Structure-Oriented Questions

Thus far we have been talking about questions that get at something akin to motivational aspects in the interactions. What do people need? How are they using one another to defend against aspects of themselves? How have changes in the system placed greater stress on a particular member who has heretofore served a particular function in the system or has had a particular need met by one or more other members? The second category of systems questions one can ask are those that help define the structure of the family. To get at this, the therapist might ask the patient to describe a typical day. Do both parents get up together? Who attends to the children in the morning? Are the children expected or permitted to make their own breakfast? What is dinner like? Where do people go and what do they do after dinner? Do the children spend the evening with their parents? Do the parents spend time alone? Who is close to whom in the family? How does information travel? (For instance, does a daughter confide in her mother? Who then tells the father? Do the children talk about the parents' "secrets" in front of their grandmother?)

Following a structural analysis of the sort delineated by Minuchin and described in Chapter 2, one can inquire into what may have changed in the structure of the family that is causing difficulties for the individual who is the patient. Has a daughters's departure for college deprived mother of a confidante, with ramifications for everyone in the family? Is this situation exacerbated by an alliance between father and son that excludes mother? Has the spouses' relationship changed with the birth of a child?

Understanding how events in the patient's life change the structure of the family and how this changed structure may be a source of stress helps the therapist to articulate the therapeutic options available. Consider the case of Sara S. Sara and her husband had recently moved to a new city. Since the move, husband and wife spent more time together than they ever had before. Though they had always considered themselves to be close, they both had strong ties to family and friends. The move to the new city meant less contact with others, and greater focus and dependency on each other. The balance of closeness and separateness that had worked up till now was no longer possible to maintain until a new support system was established.

A variety of therapeutic options would be available to the therapist, based on such a picture. He might, for example, work with Sara on issues of intimacy and closeness with regard to her husband or on issues of dependency with regard to her parents. He might explore the anxieties that were preventing her from creating a new support system in the new city, and/or introduce assertiveness training to help her in this regard. He might, alternatively, help her to understand the stresses on her resulting from *her husband's* difficulties in tolerating closeness or in separating from his family or in establishing a new support system. Or, more likely, he could look at how all of these factors were interacting in producing Sara's distress and at how he might help her to extricate herself from the maladaptive pattern she had begun to be caught in since the move.

The various lines of inquiry just described are part of a larger effort to identify and address the dynamics of the individual in the context of his family system. We have highlighted, for the purposes of this presentation, those lines of inquiry that are particularly suited for exploring the family dynamics that are the context for the patient's difficulties. These lines of inquiry are intended by us as a complement to more traditional lines of exploration in individual psychotherapy, not as a replacement. As we indicate from a number of perspectives throughout this book, we do not believe that the advances in family therapy, significant as they are, have made individual psychotherapy obsolete. Rather, in many instances, greater understanding of family systems enables the individual therapist to do his or her job more effectively.[1]

1. This is not to say that there are not many other cases in which the development of methods to work conjointly with a number of members of the family system *has* made such methods the treatment of choice.

4. *The Genogram*

ONE METHOD deriving from family therapy that we have found a particularly useful diagnostic tool in our work with individuals is the construction of a "genogram." The genogram is essentially an emotional family tree. Family relationships going back three generations or more are charted and explored via a structured technique, which we shall describe presently.

For most people, constructing a family tree has a ring of familiarity. Patients often have done some prior exploration into family history, and if not, they generally welcome the idea of doing so. The genogram is both similar to and considerably different from the family tree of the genealogists. The similarities lie in the interest in the significant events and personal histories of ancestors. Like genealogists, we too are interested in the social history of the family and find it invaluable to have a sense of the larger context within which to place the individual. A sense of the family background and social milieu, and particularly the position of our patient's immediate family in the mosaic of the extended family, has been invaluable in our work. Among individual therapists, only Erikson (e.g., 1964) has really explored these matters in depth.

Having a clear sense of the differences and similarities in social background between the maternal and paternal sides of the family has often provided much insight for us into the conflicts and ambivalences of our patients. The emphasis in constructing genograms is on the elucidation of relationships and patterns of interaction. Information is obtained, for example, about distance and closeness between people, power hierarchies, and modes of interaction. Though family therapists differ in exactly how, when, and why they use genograms (differences that we soon discuss), they share a common interest in the transmission of multigenerational patterns and influences that are assumed to be of central importance in understanding people's current difficulties and dilemmas. The emphasis by most family therapists on current interactions and immediate problems is in no way at odds with a concern with the kind of material revealed in the genogram. The apparent contradictions can readily be reconciled when one recognizes that previous patterns are stored, transformed, and manifested in the present (cf. E. F. Wachtel, 1982).

Although the genogram is used by family therapists of almost all schools of thought, it has been written about almost exclusively by those working from the theoretical orientation of Murray Bowen (Carter & Orfanidis, 1976; Guerin & Pendagast, 1976; Pendagast & Sherman, 1977). When used in the context of therapy based on Bowen's theoretical orientation (see Chapter 2), the genogram is thought of as providing the facts that enable the work to begin. "The assumption is that the more facts you know, the better position you are in to evaluate what has happened in your family and thus to understand your own position and to change it if you wish" (Carter & Orfanidis, 1976, p. 206). There is an emphasis on "objectivity" in the writings of these Bowenian therapists. Doing a genogram helps the patient "[shift] the focus from guilt and blame to a more objective researcher position" (Carter & Orfanidis, 1976, p. 205). Genograms are used by Bowenians to help in planning where the patient can begin to change his role in the family system. Family patterns over three generations are examined as data to aid in answering such questions as these: What are the central triangles? What are the patterns of overfunctioning and underfunctioning? What is the importance of sibling position in the family system? How close or distant are family members? What were the stresses on the family at various stages of its history? Pendagast and Sherman's (1977) guide to the genogram is a comprehensive compilation of the wide range of issues that can be elucidated by means of the procedure.

We too use genograms to obtain information about repetitive patterns of interactions and significant events in the family history. For us, though, the "factual" information obtained is less important than the opportunity the genogram gives us to better understand the idiosyncratic world view of our patient. We regard the genogram as an unusually good vehicle for obtaining information about the individual's unconscious assumptions, wishes, fears, and values. One need not limit the genogram to an explication of "facts" or even to hypotheses about family patterns. For us, it is a map to the unconscious as much as it is a map of manifest family patterns. Like some projective tests (e.g., the TAT), the genogram requires a certain amount of attention to reality considerations, while at the same time leaving a good deal of room for the expression of the individual's idiosyncratic concerns.

Since we see the genogram as providing us with highly subjective information as well as objective facts, our means of obtaining a genogram are both similar to and different from the standard method. It seems useful, therefore, before discussing cases and the clinical inferences one can make from the material obtained, to review in some detail just how we proceed.

Doing a Genogram: The Basic Procedure

We regard the *process* of doing the genogram with the patient as of equal importance to the content. For this reason, we do not have the patient do it at home and bring it in, even if he makes this suggestion. Generally, we start the genogram in our third or fourth meeting, after we have established some sense of a personal connection with the patient and have an understanding of why he is coming to see us. We then state that we find it useful to get a sense of his family background in some detail in the form of an emotional family tree. We sometimes do the genogram in an earlier session if the patient has spontaneously begun to talk about his family, in which case we introduce the genogram as the format through which we like to get information.

We begin by asking which side of the family the patient knows better and start by working on that side of the family. That question alone provides useful clues to the family structure. A number of factors might account for knowing one side of the family better than the other—physical proximity, one parent's being dominant, greater liking for or identification with that side of the family, and so on. A patient might say, for instance, that although he saw his mother's family much more often than his father's, he liked his father's family better.

Starting with the side of the family the patient knows better, we begin by asking for some factual information about each grandparent: name; data of birth; illnesses; age at death (if deceased) and cause of death; where grandparent came from; when and where grandparent met spouse; age of grandparent (if living); when spouse died (if deceased); religion; remarriage (if any); with whom grandparent lived; how supported; occupation; number of children; and so forth. Since we are interested in the impact of events on the individual with whom we are working, we also ask (or compute) the age of *our patient* at the time these various events occurred.

Once we have obtained this basic factual information, we ask for a description of each grandparent. Often we are told that the grandparent was not personally known by the patient. We then ask for descriptions based on how the patient pictures the grandparent, based on the bits and pieces of information he has picked up over the years. Some patients can readily say how they imagine people to have been, while others have a difficult time with fantasy. Either way, we learn something about the individual by the way he handles our inquiry.

In cases where little or nothing is known about important relatives, we also wonder out loud about this lack of information. We might, for instance, ask our patient why he thinks it is that his mother never talked about her father.

Once we have descriptions of each grandparent, we then go on to ask about the grandmother and grandfather's relationship. We ask such questions as these: "How and when did they meet? How did your grandparents get along? What do you think they got from each other?" Who was the leader, or more powerful person in the relationship? Who was the more sociable or outgoing one?" It is often the case that little is known about the relationship. Once again we encourage speculation and fantasies, and regard this information as perhaps even more important than the "reality."

If only one of the grandparents on one side of the family is still alive, or if both have died but one outlived the other by a number of years, it is useful to inquire about how the surviving grandparent dealt with the death. Did the survivor live alone? Remarry? Move in with one of the children? Seem depressed for a long period of time, or resume an active involvement in life after a brief interval? Such questions are often quite revealing.

Lastly, we ask for one or two "stories" that the patient has heard about his grandparents, and prod for such stories if they are not easily forthcoming. We are usually able to elicit some stories by making it clear that the stories we are interested in do not have to be colorful tales. The "boring" and the "mundane" are equally useful. For our purposes, "Grandma went East to college, despite everyone in the family thinking it was foolish" is a "story." So too is "Grandpa did fairly well during the 1920s, but then lost most of his money in the Depression soon after he got married."

When we have gotten as much information as we can about grandparents, we proceed to the next generation, our patient's aunts and uncles. We ask how many children the grandparents had, including children from other marriages. We then chart them in order of age, marking with a prominent asterisk the sibling who is the parent of our patient. We are sure to include children who died in infancy or early childhood—a fact that the patient may omit unless instructed otherwise.

Once we have charted the names and ages of all siblings, we go back and fill in the details. We ask about all the aunts and uncles such questions as these: Did they marry? Are they still married? To whom? Children? How many? Occupation? Socioeconomic status? Place of residence? We then ask for adjectives that describe each aunt and uncle's personality or character. As with grandparents, if an aunt or uncle was not personally known, we ask for a description based on what has been pieced together from what has been heard, and for stories that may make the descriptions more vivid.

We then inquire into the uncle or aunt's relationship with his or her partner. What is the spouse like? Do they have children? What are their ages? Although we do not go into as much detail about the children (our patient's cousins), we do indicate a general interest in information about anything that might be noteworthy. This information is usually volunteered when we ask for their names and ages; it generally doesn't require structured questioning. Thus a patient might say, "Yes, Uncle John and Aunt Mary have three children. Janey, the oldest, is my age; Bob is 32; and Sue is 28. Janey is married and living in Cleveland. Bob is a very prominent lawyer, and Sue lives at home still. She's always had problems, has been hospitalized a number of times."

If there has been some traumatic event or unusual situation with a child (e.g., chronic illness, death, drug abuse), we ask how this situation was handled. In doing this, we often get a good deal of information about the opinions and values of the patient.

When we have gone through all the aunts and uncles on one side, saving the parent for last, we then inquire directly into the relationships between the parent and the parent's siblings. By this point we almost certainly have a good deal of information about these relationships, since they will have been talked about directly and indirectly in the context of descriptions of people and family stories. Here, though, we look more specifically at, for example, which of the siblings was closest to the grandparents and which of the siblings are closest to each other.

Such an inquiry reveals not just who was close to whom, but also how closeness tends to be expressed in the family and how our patient evaluates closeness—whether by physical proximity, working together, socializing, or whatever. A grandparent, for example, may be described as living with and being dependent upon a child with whom she is continuously fighting, and as worshipping (from afar) a more distant and independent child.

In general, inferences are drawn not just from what is said, but from the accompanying affect. We listen carefully to the tone of voice and observe facial expressions. Is the story told with pride? Contempt? Dismay? Whenever we are uncertain about the personal meaning to our patient of a description, we ask for clarification. We might say, for example, "How was he generous? Could you give me an example?" Or, "What do you mean by 'generous'?" With regard to family stories, we ask, "From whom did you hear this story?" and "How is it usually told? With anger, say, or humor, or pride?"

Asking the patient about the source of various stories or impressions can spark extremely valuable reflections and can help him become aware of where he has unwittingly accepted notions that do not really jibe with his own experience. It can help him become aware as well of instances where he has incorporated one version of the family mythology while screening out another. ("I guess my impression of Grandpa Steven as an unusually good man comes from my mother. She always described him that way. But come to think of it, my father didn't seem to see him that way.")

Reexamination of the sources of impressions about family members can help the patient clarify his assumptions about the consequences of various action sequences and revise his ideas about role models. As the patient begins to wonder where one did get certain ideas after all, he can also begin to question them. Maybe Aunt Edna *didn't* really suffer for marrying a man who didn't work so hard. Maybe Grandpa Brown's business failed because he wasn't that bright, and not because his children demanded too much of his time. Questions like this arise frequently once the patient begins to become more focally aware of the background assumptions he has picked up in the process of growing up in a particular family. Perhaps for the first time he is applying adult understanding and judgment to certain key ideas that have been taken on faith and, without awareness, have become a template for later judgments and decisions. To realize for the first time that Cousin Warren wasn't really inconsiderate, but had just been called that by his mother because he married while still in medical school instead of waiting as his mother had wanted; or that Aunt Tillie wasn't quiet and dull, but was just more reflective and intellectual than the other members of a rather insensitive and boorish family group, can stimulate a great deal of further reexamination and questioning. Recognizing that he has for years thought of someone as bright or kind or selfish who upon any reflection does not seem that way to him can be a very striking experience for a patient.

Since we like to get a good many details, it usually takes a full session or more to complete one side of the family. When that is completed, we repeat the process for the other side of the family. A useful description of the symbols and other notational devices that can aid in putting down the information obtained in taking a genogram can be found in Pendagast and Sherman (1977); these authors also provide an excellent check list of the type of factual information one wants to be sure to obtain. We would add, on the topic of getting it all down on paper, that "neatness doesn't count." It is often very difficult to get all the information down as the patient begins to get into relating his genogram. Both the amount of time available and the size of the piece of paper can seem insufficient. Expect to scribble and to have rich information rather than a neat-looking chart.

While we are doing the genogram, we are continuously giving the patient feedback regarding the inferences we are drawing from the material collected. We discuss later in the chapter how and why we give this feedback.

The Clinical Yield of the Genogram

Genograms provide so much material that the creative clinician is sure to discover uses that we have neglected. As a general guide, however, one can look at the material in terms of three basic categories of information: significant facts or events, patterns and systems in the family, and the idiosyncratic world view of the patient.

Significant Facts or Events

Factual information, obtained in the course of doing the genogram, has often given us an important perspective on the patient's difficulties. Patients often do not regard as particularly relevant to their problems significant events (both historical and current) that we, upon hearing about them during the taking of a genogram, find of "obvious" importance. Generally when we share our perception of these events, the patient says, "Yes, of course," but makes it clear he would not have thought to volunteer the information. Though we have no way of knowing this for sure, it has seemed to us on a number of occasions that such information, which seems to the patient irrelevant and unconnected to his problems, would have taken many months or years to emerge without the structured questioning of the genogram.

Of particular importance in this regard is the history of both mental and physical illness in the family. For example, Albert, a 40-year-old man who described himself as having a "midlife" crisis, did not consciously connect his depression with the fact that there was a history of early death and incapacitating illness in males on both sides of his family. He viewed his problem not as fear of aging, but, rather, as reevaluation of the choices he had made in his life regarding career and commitments.

He did spontaneously mention early in the therapy that his father had died of a stroke caused by high blood pressure at age 42, but he said he was not consciously concerned about this, since medical advances made such an event extremely unlikely in his case. In doing the genogram, it was revealed—he had not spontaneously mentioned it prior to the structured questioning—that his mother's brother had died of cancer at age 53 and that his father's older brother, who had recently died at the age of 76, had suffered from increasingly debilitating Parkinson's disease from the age of 51.

Though these facts do not "explain" the midlife crisis, Albert's unconscious expectations as to what life held in store for him certainly seemed relevant to his reevaluation of his life. Hearing this familial pattern of death and disease at midlife at one sitting had an impact that would have been unlikely if each event had been reported separately, as an association to some experience or another over a period of weeks or months. The genogram, with its structured questioning, put facts into a pattern that might otherwise never have emerged. Since Albert was not particularly close to his uncles, it was unlikely that he would have spontaneously reported his uncle's recent death and debilitating illness, nor would he have been likely to mention that when he was 12 another uncle had died of cancer at age 53. Events such as these can imprint themselves on the young child and, in unrecognized ways, shape his philosophy of life.

Consideration by the patient of the possible impact of familial events that were never consciously articulated as a pattern can enable the patient to reexamine some of the assumptions by which (not necessarily consciously) he has been living. Events themselves, after all, do not lead to one inevitable conclusion. Albert's sense of how much "good" time he had left, for example, derived from how he had processed and dealt with the deaths and illnesses just noted. Since the impact of events varies from person to person, the "factual" information simply gives us some hypotheses, which we then explore further. "Make the most of your life because you never know what will happen," "Conscientiously guard your health to prevent illness," and "What's the use? I'll die soon anyway" are very different attitudes one can have toward the same pattern of events.

Many times we have found that a history of mental illness in the extended family is a black cloud that hovers ominously, if unconsciously, over our patients. For example, Estelle F consulted us because she was extremely depressed after the break-up of her marriage. Though she certainly needed help in handling her feelings of abandonment and rage, her depression was made worse by her fear that she was going crazy and would end up institutionalized. This fear become explicit when we did her genogram.

Both her parents were the "well" children in families in which there was a good deal of alcoholism and depression. Estelle had identified with the "health" of her parents and had rarely allowed herself to feel depressed or sad. Though her response to the divorce was not such an unusual one, "depression" had been a taboo emotion in her family, and it evoked anxiety out of proportion to the distress she was experiencing (thereby, of course, increasing the distress). Her feelings in response to her marital crisis triggered fears that she hadn't known existed.

Sometimes one event rather than a pattern of happenings has profoundly affected and shaped the personality development of a child. Cyril was a man in his late 20s who had, at this young age, already earned his first million dollars. He was a generous young man who derived a good deal of satisfaction out of helping his less fortunate family members. In doing a genogram, it was revealed that his father's older brother had behaved much like Cyril. He too had made his fortune in his youth and was revered by his family for his generosity. Tragedy struck the family when this uncle suddenly died of a heart attack at age 35. Cyril, who was 10 at the time of his uncle's death, felt that the mantle was being passed to him in order that he carry on in his uncle's footsteps. His father saw in his young son the idealized brother whose loss he mourned. Cyril's identification with his uncle was quite conscious and surely would have come out sooner or later in a less structured inquiry. Getting this information sooner rather than later, however, proved to be quite important in this case.

At the time Cyril entered treatment, he was in a highly distressed state over the break-up of his marriage. He would drive long hours to "escape" from his feelings of jealousy and torment. Discussing his uncle led to the revelation that Cyril had always assumed that he too would die a tragic death in his late 30s. By inquiring further into his "escape" driving, his therapist soon learned that he was speeding and driving recklessly. Though he had not initially thought Cyril to be suicidal, his assessment of the suicide risk changed on the basis of this information about his uncle.

Another kind of factual information that we find quite useful but that is unlikely to be reported spontaneously is information about events in the lives of first cousins. Of particular significance is the death of a cousin's father or mother (the patient's aunt or uncle). Particularly in families where the extended family is very close and where the cousins are raised together almost as if they were siblings, tragic events in a cousin's life may have a powerful impact because of the identification with the cousin as well as the closeness in the parental generation.

Charla, a woman in her late 20s, was extremely inhibited about asserting herself. She remembered clearly that as a young child she was terribly fearful of incurring the displeasure of her father and feared that if she were "bad" he would no longer love her. As an adult, she imagined terrible repercussions if she in any way alienated someone by asserting herself.

In doing her genogram, Charla reported that her aunt's husband had died of cancer at an early age. As the genogram also revealed,

Charla's mother and her sister had been very close. They lived in the same neighborhood and had daughters very close in age. Charla and her cousin Sandy were closest friends in early childhood and played together almost every day. Charla was 5 when Sandy's father died. Given the closeness between the two cousins and their mothers, one can assume that this death had a profound impact on Charla. Though she herself was not close to the uncle and did not suffer a direct loss, she very likely registered, at some level, that relationships with loved ones can be cruelly and suddenly terminated.

Speculations about the importance of such events are based in part on assumptions about the developmental tasks and issues for children at specific ages. At age 5, Charla was at an age when children often begin to think about mortality. Perhaps when her father yelled at her, she was terrified of her own anger and loss of love for him. Temporary extreme rage at a parent is a feeling that most children can handle, though it distresses them. For Charla, however, the vicarious experience of loss may well have contributed to her fear of asserting herself; she had, after all, real knowledge that parents can die, leaving their children bereft and adrift. It is interesting to note that Charla stated that she probably would not have thought to mention this event in "her cousin's" life—she had not registered it as an event that had had a significant impact on her own life—except for the structured questioning of the genogram.

Patterns and Systems

In addition to examining the "facts" that emerge in the genogram, we focus on the patterns of relationships in the extended family, assessing the impact of the larger system on the individual. To begin with, we notice the positions of the patient's immediate family in relation to each parent's extended family. Was this family less or more well off financially than the extended family? Did they work for, or were they taken care of by, family members? Were they, in contrast, the providers and caretakers? Which parent's family was more successful or powerful, and how was this dealt with by the couple? Did one partner "adopt" the other's closer or more powerful family? Were in-laws incorporated into the family or did they remain "outsiders"? Were there loyalty conflicts between devotion to the family of origin and devotion to the nuclear family? The answers to such questions often help us more fully understand the conflicts and ambivalence of the individual. Although descriptions of the parents and their relationship alone will undoubtedly contain this information to a considerable degree, the genogram greatly enriches our understanding of the balances and imbalances in the system.

Harold, for example, came to therapy because he was suffering from anxiety attacks and felt quite incompetent to handle the ordinary tasks of living. It soon became clear that he had been "claimed" by his mother in a profound conflict with the father and had never allowed himself to identify with his father's strength and competence. Had we confined ourselves only to information about the immediate family situation, we certainly would have gained some understanding of Harold's place in the system. In elucidating the relationships, however, the genogram enriched our understanding of the parents' relationship and the consequent strength of the pulls on Harold.

We saw in the genogram that Harold's father was extremely close to his older sisters, who doted upon him and with whom he spoke almost daily, and that he had been the pride and joy of his mother. He was a very successful Wall Street lawyer, and the "good son" who excelled at everything and was loyal to the family (unlike his father, who had left the family and moved to Colorado).

Harold's father never seemed to have been as involved with his wife as he was with his sisters and mother. He was, however, involved with the children and wanted to pass on his abilities to them. Harold's mother, of course, played a part in her husband's unwillingness to devote himself to her the way he did to his original family. Although his family might have felt very threatened by sharing their "golden boy" with his wife, he might have been able to resist the pull of his system had his wife been able to offer him some of the same kind of gratification that his family of origin offered. Harold's mother, however, came from an impoverished family in which she and her mother had been abandoned by her father, an alcoholic, when she was 7. We can speculate that at the first signs of "abandonment" by her husband, Harold's mother reacted with anger, expressing her readily elicited rage at such behavior by undermining her husband to her son. She would put him down as a fraud, all bluff and bravado and no substance. Harold's father seems to have made peace with his wife by giving her this son instead of himself and focusing his attention on the older boys.

How one might use such information depends, of course, on the model from which one is working. At the very least, the information and speculation derived from the genogram open up new pathways of exploration and provide insights that in themselves may be useful. In our own work, we find as well that we can often use the genogram as a guide to active interventions, such as predicting system pulls and setbacks, or reframing and coaching in how to alter the system.

In addition to looking at the relationship between the nuclear family and the extended family, we use the genogram to see whether there are relationship patterns that may be serving as models (probably unconscious) for our patient. For instance, we look at the relationships between husbands and wives, mothers and daughters, brothers and sisters to see if we can discern a predominant pattern. But we concern ourselves as well with the ambiguities and divergences in the pattern. There are always the uncles or aunts who are the exception to the rule and who have forged a marriage or chosen a path that is uncharacteristic of the family as a whole. Thus the genogram can provide a basis for discerning viable alternatives for the patient, as well as for highlighting presently dominant attitudes and identifications.

An illustration of the relevance of the genogram in this context is provided by Kathleen, a woman in her late 20s who had recently married for the second time. During the 2 years they had dated and lived together prior to marrying, Kathleen and her boyfriend had had much fun together. Their relationship was characterized by a lot of laughter and good times. The couple would often go out together for a drink at a neighborhood bar. Kathleen and Stephen were "pals" as well as lovers, sharing many a drink and escapade. By the time they had been married a little over a year, however, Kathleen was feeling depressed and abused. It had evolved that Stephen now stayed out late with his buddies, while Kathleen seethed and sulked at home. Doing a genogram revealed that almost all the married women on her mother's side of the family (the side she seemed to identify with most strongly) were martyred caretakers who "suffered" from the irresponsibility and drunkenness of their men. Real "men" were unruly "boys" who had to be scolded and whom one had to put up with. Though Kathleen could readily see similarities between her marriage and her parents', the genogram made it clear just how pervasive a pattern this was and how much Kathleen associated this kind of relationship with being grown up and a proper woman.

The information obtained in doing the genogram led to a discussion of how Kathleen had felt looked down upon by her family for having divorced her first husband. The unspoken family rule was that women were expected to put up with bad marriages. Working, raising a child as a single parent, and having "fun" at the same time were all additional negatives in this very traditional family. Insight into the family system led to Kathleen's understanding of how she had actively participated in transforming her relationship with her husband into one that would ironically gain her self-esteem but not happiness.

Of particular significance are patterns that the genogram may reveal with respect to the resolution of conflict. In some families, aunts, uncles, and grandparents feud but remain connected. In other families there are one or more "cut-offs" in which the tie between a family member and his parents or siblings is completely severed. Some families are forgiving, while others hold grudges. Do family members reconcile, or do they go to their deaths with rage? Such information is extremely important, for example, in assessing the "reality" aspect of the individual's fear of incurring the disapproval of his parents.

Thus an adult child in a family where the mother has not spoken to her older brother in 15 years because he committed some act of disloyalty might be justified in his apprehension about stepping out of his assigned role as the "good son." In contrast, some families speak in a disapproving, but fond, forgiving, and even respectful way of the nonconformist in the family. Highlighting such an attitude may help the patient gain the courage needed to "buck the system."

The genogram may also provide insight into the motivations and feelings of the patient's parents. The perspective provided in this way may aid in reframing events in the past so that they are viewed differently and perhaps with less anger. A parent's tightness with money, for example, might, depending on the information obtained through the genogram, be seen as an attempt to promote independence or self-sufficiency. Or, as in the case of Andrew, an intolerance for the expression of feelings may be seen as the parent's attempt to prevent the dreaded emergence of serious emotional disorder. Andrew's mother came from a family in which an older brother had had serious bouts with depression. The family's explanation for this was that the brother's feelings had been excessively indulged as a child. Though this explanation may not make logical sense, it was an assumption that surely affected the mother's child-rearing practices. Andrew's genogram thus provided material that helped make his mother's behavior more understandable.

In the case of Tony, understanding of the father's feelings gained through the genogram helped in understanding an otherwise puzzling pattern in the patient. Though obviously quite intelligent, Tony always prevented himself from becoming successful in the corporate world. Each success would be followed by anxiety and by behavior that would undo the good impression he had made. He seemed to find recognition for his achievements intolerable, and would "inadvertently" sabotage his own achievements. Ultimately, he would always withdraw from the competition.

Although his therapist suspected that Tony's inhibitions in regard to assertiveness, competition, and success had something to do with being afraid of outdoing his Italian immigrant father, his portrayal of relationships in his immediate family did not seem enough to justify such a strong renunciation of competitive striving. In doing a genogram, the therapist learned that though Tony's father was the youngest child in the family, he was not the one who was babied or indulged. The father was described as being greatly resentful of the extreme favoritism showed to his older brother Vinny. The story went that Vinny, with the help of the mother, had become an extremely successful businessman, while Tony's father could barely make ends meet. Vinny then went on to flaunt his wealth, and regarded Tony's family as the poor relations. In relating this family history, Tony expressed considerable empathy for his father.

At one point, while describing his father's feelings about Vinny, Tony suddenly remembered that frequently his father would slip and call him (Tony) Vinny. It became clear that Tony's father had unconsciously transferred to his son his feelings toward the young competitor from his family of origin. Appreciation of the exacerbating influence of the father's family history gave an added dimension to the therapist's understanding of the intensity of Tony's conflict over competitive strivings.

An added dimension is also provided by understanding the patient's place not just in the family of origin, but in the extended family as well. It tells us where the patient stands in relation to his relatives. Is he more or less conventional, rich, successful, intellectual, emotionally stable? Is he pleased or distressed by the comparisons? Do the parents feel pride or embarrassment about this child in relation to their siblings' children?

Consider, for example, the case of Lucia. Lucia was very close to her mother's family. Lucia's mother was by far the most striving and upwardly mobile of the five children in her family. Lucia described her mother as undoubtedly the most intelligent and genteel. Everyone expected that her husband and children would be outstanding. Despite her being different from her brothers and sisters, however, Lucia's mother remained quite close to her family. She was their pride and joy.

In doing the genogram, it became clear that Lucia felt she was regarded by aunts, uncles, and cousins on both sides of the large extended family as "special." Her interest in books and her decision to go to medical school gave her great status in this largely working-class family. She was the "gifted" daughter of the shining light in the family.

This picture of Lucia's place in the extended family was quite helpful in understanding her terrible sense of disappointment in herself. Though by objective standards she was doing quite well, she never felt as "special" in the world of high-achieving adults as she did as a child in the world of her extended family.

Similar feelings are often encountered by individuals who were the first child in a close and doting family. We also often see only children whose feelings of specialness were threatened not by a sibling, but by the success of a younger first cousin. The genogram can give us a good sense of the individual's earliest reference group, often providing important information that does not ordinarily come out in individual therapy; cultural biases (cf. P. L. Wachtel, 1983) and patients' understanding of what therapists are "after" can truncate associations, pointing them rather exclusively to the patient's "own" family and away from exploration of the impact of the larger world of uncles, cousins, and aunts.

The Idiosyncratic World View:
The Genogram as a Projective Technique

Thus far we have discussed the importance of facts and events revealed through the genogram, the elucidation of family patterns, and the impact of both of these on the individual. Perhaps the most interesting use of the genogram is its potential for use as something akin to a projective technique. Descriptions of family members, and the "family stories" remembered and transformed in the telling, act as a map to the unconscious. Like some projective tests (e.g., the TAT), the genogram involves a mixture of reality and fantasy. Intermixed with a description of facts and family patterns are many clues to the unspoken and perhaps unconscious fears, wishes, and values of the individual.

Using the genogram in this way involves "interpreting" or drawing inferences from family stories, as well as attending carefully to "incidental" information. The affect with which stories are told is extremely important in assessing the values and wishes of the individual. Thus, for example, an uncle may be described with a smile as "the black sheep because he stowed away on a ship to Argentina at the age of 16, not to be heard of again for 10 years, when he made his fortune." The fact that the patient remembers this particular story and tells it with a smile suggests that he identifies with or longs for such behavior in some way.

One patient, when asked to tell a story about her grandmother, described her as someone who would walk across the street with the assumption that cars would stop for her. This story was *not* told fondly. We can deduce from this that the patient disliked or at least was in conflict about the aggressive assertion of self.

Often family stories seem to have been swallowed whole during youth and to have remained undigested by the adult. Such stories can have a powerful effect because they have never been examined by mature, critical intelligence. Mr. Kent, for instance, described his father as having had a stroke because he "worked too hard to support his ailing mother, wife, and three children." This was the family story heard when he was age 9 and never questioned. Now, at age 39, Mr. Kent believed this story as thoroughly as he had during his childhood. He had never questioned the assumption that his father's stroke was directly caused by overwork. Recognition of the lesson learned in childhood that "domestic responsibilities can kill you" provided an important insight into his apprehension about the prospect of having a child. The belief that domestic responsibility might literally mean death was unconscious until brought to the surface by the genogram.

Descriptions of family members, like family stories, also provide clues to the individual's concerns. For example, the first thing Ella G said about her mother was that she had lost her father when she was only 7, and that it had been a great hardship to her mother to have lost a parent at such a young age. She chose this story of loss as the most salient fact about her mother, reflecting not only how she perceived her but also, one might hypothesize, that she was deeply concerned about issues of abandonment. Further discussion indeed revealed that she equated her wish to return to work with an abandonment of her own child.

Another patient described her mother as a "stepchild," since the mother's mother had died when she was 13 and her father had remarried soon thereafter. This led to a discussion of the patient's perception of her mother as needy and in need of mothering—a perception that had resulted in the denial of the patient's own dependency needs.

Numerous other examples could be given. The point is that in any description people select from a myriad of facts what they feel is most important. This selection makes the description as revealing of the describer as of the person being described. One's inferences in this regard must be viewed as tentative hypotheses requiring further confirmation, but if one makes note of them while proceeding with the genogram, this "projective" orientation will be richly rewarded.[1]

Even "neutral" or "benign" information can provide useful clinical hypotheses. For example, some women, when asked their mother's name, will give the maiden name too. Hearing this, one might wonder and eventually inquire about such issues as maintaining one's identity, differentiating from one's spouse, or failure to separate from one's family of origin.

By focusing on the dimensions along which family members are evaluated, the therapist learns more about the patient's values and concerns than the patient could disclose consciously. Craig, for instance, described all the women in his family (on both sides) in terms of how competent or incompetent they were. "Aunt Sarah never learned how to drive a car" or "Lucy was quick with numbers" were the kinds of statements he would make. On the other hand, the men in the family were described in terms of whether they were kind or good-hearted.

---

1. As in most inferences made in the course of therapy, it is not necessary that the patient's view be erroneous or distorted for it to be appropriate to make something of it. To be sure, each of these patients was reporting a "fact" that was "real," not a figment of their imagination or a "transference distortion." But there were countless other facts that the patients also could have reported. It is the fact that each one *chose* this particular aspect of the mother or other relative to report on that is significant.

Craig was surprised when the therapist pointed out what he seemed to value in each sex, and upon reflection agreed that although he had not been conscious of this, it was a valid description of his feelings.

One patient gave detailed descriptions of the physical appearance of family members. Height, weight, hair style, and coloring were among the first details offered. Descriptions of this sort are, in our experience, quite unusual. This observation led to a discussion of the fact that although both men and women in this family were of relatively small stature, this was never regarded as a deficit. On the contrary, the family as a whole had an image as "very attractive, fashionable, and highly competent." Though parents, aunts, and uncles, as well as siblings, noticed and picked at every detail of one another's dress, this was done as a form of "primping" one another rather than as criticism.

Another patient categorized family members according to hair coloring. There were the "redheads" and the "brunettes." The "redheads" were not as pretty but were more passionately self-determined. The patient, herself a "brunette," was poignantly expressing, through these descriptions, her sense of being stuck with a definition of herself that she no longer found gratifying. Though we would most likely have gotten to this material in another manner, the genogram helped to highlight early how rigidly typecast members of this family were.

By pointing out to the patient the dimensions along which he describes people and the implicit concerns and assumptions reflected therein, the therapist provides the patient with an opportunity to reflect upon just how much he actually is governed by these inherited family values. Jerry, for instance, described uncles on both sides of his family as having married for money, not love. The fact that these marriages were now of 30 to 40 years' duration in no way altered the stigma attached to their being conceived out of convenience rather than romance. The characterization of marriages along the dimension of "love" versus "convenience" proved to be an extremely relevant issue for Jerry. His family placed a very high value on the importance of love in marriages, and the articulation of this as a family value helped Jerry come to terms with a recent divorce.

The genogram is also helpful in noticing the special meaning that particular words may have for the patient. It helps the therapist learn what words to use and which to avoid. An awareness of the emotional meaning of particular words can help the therapist couch his statements in the language that has the most impact and is least likely to mobilize resistance. One may notice, for example, that words such as "fun-loving," "gruff," or "self-centered" are used many times in the description of family members. One may then surmise that these particular words are highly charged and not to be used casually. Often such words have a "special" meaning quite distinct from their common usage. For this reason, it is important to inquire about the meaning of any adjective that seems to be used repeatedly.

The "special" meaning that particular words may have can be seen in Mary's description of numerous family members as "crazy." Mary had unthinkingly adopted her mother's description of relatives on her own. Her mother described as "insane," "demented," or "crazy" anyone she intensely disliked, and Mary continued this tradition. Saying someone was "crazy" was meant in that family as venomous cursing. Whereas for Mary "crazy" meant "contemptible," for Samantha the same word really meant "zany" and "delightfully free from conventional restraints."

Descriptions of relatives in the genogram can provide useful clues about conflicted impulses. Alex, for example, described a number of uncles in terms of how much or how little fun they had in life. By noticing his smile and animated expression as he was describing one "fun-loving" uncle in particular, the therapist was able to point out to him that he seemed to long to be a bit more that way himself. Generally Alex tended to get extremely angry at his wife's "irresponsible" and "frivolous" behavior. But in talking about these relatives while doing the genogram, Alex was able to recognize his own longings, which he had heretofore renounced; he began to see that his anger at his wife served as a defense against his own longed-for but unacceptable "outrageous" behavior.

If we listen with an ear attuned to the latent meanings, we often get a sense not only of what the patient admires in other people and how he or she would like to change, but also of some previously unarticulated fantasies about how the patient's partner could help with that change. For example, Mrs. Wright, who acknowledged that she was often quite domineering, described an aunt and uncle of whom she was particularly fond in the following way: "My aunt is stubborn and difficult, but she is married to a warm man who knows how to handle her. When she is angry and brooding, he just tells her to 'cut it out' in a forceful way, and she relaxes. He doesn't let her push him around and really brings her out of her moods."

A response such as this provides an extremely useful clue for all concerned as to how the difficulties between a patient and spouse might be resolved. It can help to make certain provocative behavior more explicable, and can suggest to the therapist that it might be useful to encourage or even coach the patient in getting the spouse to behave in this helpful way. Especially when viewed from the transactionally oriented cyclical psychodynamic approach we have advocated, such material from the genogram is of great practical value.

Why Do Genograms?

Some readers may find themselves thinking that much of the information we have described will emerge sooner or later without the aid of such a structured inquiry. Though this may well be the case in many instances, we see the genogram as having certain properties that make it uniquely suitable to a form of therapy emphasizing the interaction between the individual and the system.

There is a prevalent myth among psychotherapists that patients' associations are spontaneous upwellings of inner springs, and that if the therapist is patient enough and sensitive enough, the data that are required will inevitably emerge. It is our belief that associations, like all behavior, are socially shaped. The pathways of association certainly reflect the individual's unique psychological structure, but they are also determined in crucially important ways by socially shared assumptions about causality. The patient's ideas about what is "relevant" to the therapeutic process inevitably influence his associations, no matter how hard he tries to suspend such judgments. We have already noted how "incidental" information about cousins and other relatives might throw light on the patient's difficulties. Left to his own devices, the patient might well never report such information; thinking along individualistic lines, he is unlikely to regard such information as "relevant," and thus it is unlikely to "occur" to him.

Introducing the genogram is a way of altering the individualistic assumptions typically shared by patient and therapist and of thereby widening the context within which the individual's difficulties are examined. The patient is likely to think of himself as having difficulties of a one-to-one nature in relation to one or both parents. He usually does not see himself and his parents as part of a larger system, and is thus unlikely spontaneously to offer data relevant to that system. The genogram can help to broaden the field of inquiry and bring into focus material that otherwise might not come forth.

Furthermore, even if all the information about relatives *were* to emerge without the structure of the genogram (a highly unlikely possibility), it would be difficult without the structure of the genogram to organize the material into patterns. The genogram helps us see people and relationships in juxtaposition to other relationships. When events and family patterns are charted, new ways of thinking about the patient's difficulties begin to emerge.

Because the genogram asks for descriptions of many people, repetitive themes can become apparent quite quickly. Though a knowledge of the patient's values, longings, and personal language would readily be learned by individual therapists without using the genogram, the genogram gives information about assumptions, values, and longings in *relationships*. Since our orientation is to see the individual in context, and our goal is in part to help the individual shape his context so as to meet his needs better, the genogram has a special utility in that the "projective" material and latent meanings are often about self in relation to others. The data it provides consist of transactions between and among people, in addition to the individual characteristics of family members. Again, the individual therapist will spontaneously get some of this information, but the genogram particularly pulls for interactional data and fantasies about relationships.

The genogram can have a certain mystique for patients as well, which gives extra weight to conclusions drawn from it. When interventions are made that require the active participation of the patient in his daily life (see Chapter 6), the genogram can lend weight to the therapist's suggestions and strengthen the rationale for therapeutic tasks.

Ultimately, the strengths of the genogram derive from the same source as the strengths of other projective tests and other therapeutic procedures. They depend on the sensitivity of the clinician and on the quality of the therapeutic relationship. The genogram per se does not magically give us useful information. It provides us with a context or format for using our skills in clinical inference; it also provides us with data that we might not ordinarily have, or that might not ordinarily be highlighted in the same way, thereby giving our skills a greater opportunity to be potentiated. There is no substitute for clinical sensitivity. The value of the ideas and methods described in this book is in aiding and directing that sensitivity. Sharp vision in a tunnel is still tunnel vision; when one can see the surround, one's vision is both clearer and fuller.

5. *Systems and Interpretations*

A NUMBER of prominent family therapists have made the claim that understanding plays little or no part in therapeutic change and that interpretations aimed at promoting understanding have no therapeutic value. We do not agree. Although we do feel that traditional approaches to individual therapy have placed an excessive emphasis on insight and interpretation, there is a clear and important role for such considerations in our approach. Not surprisingly, the interpretations we make follow readily from the kinds of questions we ask, as described in Chapter 3. This is apparent in the material to be presented here.

Structural Interpretations

Structural family therapists make insightful observations about the workings of families and develop clear pictures of how the family needs to change. They tend not to convey these impressions directly to the family, however, preferring to achieve the desired change via "structural moves"—actions by the therapist designed to shift those aspects of the family structure thought to be problematic. Direct statements by the therapist as to how the family functions and why certain features create problems are thought to be ineffective, if not actually antitherapeutic.

In part, this assessment is based on the assumption of massive resistance by family members, which can only be overcome by essentially covert maneuvers by the therapist. This is an assumption that is certainly rooted in clinical experience, but that we feel needs to be tempered by other considerations equally consistent with what one can observe in clinical work. There is no question that there are families—and individuals—whose anxiety about change is such that they have difficulty in making good use of descriptive comments about how they function. It is understandable that the powerful interpersonal maneuvers of the structural family therapists should have developed and been brought to bear in such instances.

In our own work, however, we prefer to proceed initially on the assumption that the patient can benefit from an enhanced understanding of the issues in his life. Included very importantly among the matters into which we find insight is useful are considerations of the sort emphasized by the structural family therapists. We wish to indicate here how some of these notions can be applied in communicating interpretative comments to patients.

An analysis of the family structure puts the patient's difficulties in a larger framework. It translates what the patient may regard as entirely intrapsychic into the interpersonal realm. Consider, for example, the case of Helene.

Helene was an extremely intelligent woman in her early 30s who had a history of "failing" just at the point when recognition and success were imminent. She did this by delaying so long in completing assignments that the praise due her for the excellent quality of her work was tempered with reservations. Her need to fail was obviously connected to a fear of competition with her father. During Helene's adolescence, her father had become severely depressed over his own failure to achieve what he had hoped for in his career. For many years, father and daughter had fought bitterly. It seemed to Helene that her father couldn't tolerate her intellectual independence, and that he fought viciously to maintain his superiority in the intellectual realm.

After a number of years, Helene and her father were reconciled, and at the time of the treatment they were unusually close and "lovey-dovey" with each other. There was a strong bond between them, a bond that did not seem to exist elsewhere in the family. Helene's brother (her only sibling) had moved to California. Her mother spent a good deal of time traveling with her sister and close women friends, while father stayed at home content in quiet retirement. Helene and her mother were pleasant to each other but not close. With her father, on the other hand, Helene felt both cared for and supportive. When mother was traveling, father often joined Helene and her husband for dinner. In turn, father often provided a sympathetic ear for Helene's upsets about her marriage and other related issues.

It was pointed out to Helene that, given the family structure, a rift between Helene and her father would have serious and far-reaching consequences. As long as the two of them stayed close, father could tolerate an extremely distant relationship with his wife. If, however, Helene's success really did put a big strain on the relationship, this would upset the whole family arrangement.

To be sure, this analysis of the family system cut both ways, in that, given the existing structure of the family, father had more of a stake than ever in remaining on good terms with his daughter and overcoming his competetive feelings. Our point here, however, is that understanding of the factors involved in Helene's fears of surpassing her father was amplified by considering how the dyadic relationship between her and her father affected other relationships, such as father's relationship to mother, and how this larger set of forces in the family bore on the patient herself, adding additional pressures that might not have been considered without such a structural analysis.

An analysis of family structure can be applied not only to the current system, but to the state of affairs that existed in the patient's family of origin when he was growing up. Such historical reconstruction often helps to alleviate guilt and self-recrimination.

Deborah, for example, was always a "good" girl; she never gave her parents a moment's trouble. Looking back on her childhood, Deborah was upset by just how conforming she had been. As an adult, she felt that the need to please sometimes interfered with her judgment. Though, by and large, she had become a fairly independent woman, Deborah remained oversensitive to her mother's feelings.

Generally, Deborah tried to avoid hurting mother by expressing opinions she would find unobjectionable. She did not want mother to feel upset by their differences when it came to such value-laden issues as religion, politics, and family. Confrontations, or even real engagements, were therefore avoided.

This avoidance of conflict seemed due more to Deborah's fear of "upsetting" her mother than to anxiety about her mother's becoming angry. When mother was upset, Deborah felt terrible. Consequently, she avoided telling mother about anything that might make her worry or be unhappy. This included such issues as Deborah's job dissatisfaction, as well as some very serious medical difficulties she was having. An analysis of Deborah's early years in terms of the family structure that existed at the time helped explain the intensity of these feelings.

Shortly after Deborah's birth, her father, with his wife's encouragement, had started graduate school at night. Between work, school, and studying, father was seldom available. Mother did not mind this so much, since she was tremendously involved with her daughter.[1] Two years later, a baby brother was born; he had several serious illnesses, which required a number of hospitalizations. Throughout this period, father continued to hold a full-time job as well as to attend graduate school. Mother felt at her wits' end. She was determined, however, to manage by herself, and thus asked for and got very little help from her family.

Given this family structure, one could now understand the push for Deborah to be a joyful, good child who couldn't risk upsetting her mother. The excessive sense of responsibility for her mother that still plagued her had its origin in a family structure in which mother had needed a relationship with her daughter as a replacement for the tenuous relationship with her husband. As things stood then, Deborah, at age 2, had been her mother's main support. Understanding this gave her a new perspective on her present experience in her relationship with her mother, and contributed to her ability to change her attitude and begin to establish a different kind of relationship.

The Significance of the Patient's Problems for the System

The interpretations to be discussed next deal with such questions as these: How might the family as a whole be benefiting from the patient's symptom? Is the patient expressing something that some other family member is feeling but cannot acknowledge? Is the symptom deflecting attention away from some other problem in the family?

There is, of course, a good deal of overlap between this category of interpretation and the structural analysis just described. In order to understand the meaning of a symptom, one must understand the structure of the family in which it exists. The emphasis in these interpretations, however, is more on the *meaning* of the symptom in interpersonal terms than on the structure that may have made such a symptom necessary.

1. This information came out in a meeting with Deborah and her mother. A detailed description of how and when we use such meetings is presented in Chapter 7.

Kara described herself as getting so upset during fights with her husband that she would writhe on the floor quite hysterically. Sobbing, shouting, banging her head on the floor, Kara would become quite "crazy." Her husband would respond to this behavior by becoming extremely rational. He regarded her as very disturbed and helpless.

Much as described in the preceding section, the work with Kara included asking many questions about what was going on in the lives of other family members. In this case, we discovered that Kara's husband was going through a particularly difficult period in his life. He was a Vietnam veteran who could continue to get 100% disability payments as long as he was unable to work. At the time of Kara's treatment, he had just finished graduate school and was interviewing for jobs. Giving up the support of the VA and making it on his own was something he very much wanted to do, but he was frightened about finally being self-sufficient.

This information, combined with the sympathetic tone (despite her anger at him) with which Kara described her husband's anxiety, led us to hypothesize that her "crazy" tantrums were related to her husband's dilemma. They seemed capable of being understood both as an attempt to encourage his self-confidence (since he reacted to them by feeling strong and competent in contrast) and as expressing for him a feeling he could not tolerate expressing overtly himself— namely, "I'm a child, I don't want to grow up."

This interpretation did not, of course, preclude other reasons for Kara's outbursts; symptoms are multidetermined. But one important feature of this interpretation in particular was that it cast what had seemed to be pathological behavior (the tantrums) in a positive light. As we discuss more fully in the next chapter, such "reframing" can itself be of considerable therapeutic value. Among the several possible interpretations of behavior that are consistent with the clinical material presented at any point, we attempt to choose the one that seems most likely to provide useful therapeutic leverage and to lead to further development in a therapeutic direction.

Paula, a 32-year-old married woman with a 4-year-old child, had a great deal of difficulty dealing with being close to her husband. She felt that she loved him, but after a week or two of closeness she would pull away and become flirtatious with other men. Paula described her mother as communicating to both husband and daughter that she regarded marriage as a plebeian institution. The mother was a "closet Bohemian" who longed for a more exciting and glamorous life.

It was clear to Paula that she was modeling her own marriage along the lines of her mother's assumptions. What were not clear to her were the loyalty issues involved in such modeling. Questioning revealed that Paula never gave her mother a glimpse of those periods when she was feeling close to her husband. She never was physically affectionate toward her husband in her mother's presence. Though Paula was quite open with her mother about the problems in the marriage, she would never tell her about the times in which there was warmth and closeness.

An interpretation was made that perhaps her discomfort with a good deal of closeness stemmed from a feeling that this would constitute disloyalty to her mother. Again, this was only one of a number of possible levels of explanation, but it was a potentially useful one, and was not readily derivable from more traditional therapeutic stances.[2]

Amy, a young woman concerned about her ability to have a monogamous relationship, felt guilty and frightened by her extreme promiscuity as an adolescent and felt that she needed to come to terms with her history if she were ever going to be able to trust her feelings of commitment to her current boyfriend. Though it had been several years since she had been promiscuous, she still felt that the explanation she had given herself for her past did not really make sense. She was extremely bothered by how easy her parents made it to lie to them. They seemed determined to close their eyes to what was happening.

An exploration of the family dynamics revealed that the parents had an extremely "liberal" attitude toward sex but were themselves fairly inhibited. The suggestion that perhaps her parents got some vicarious gratification from her promiscuity was a simple but rather welcome change of perspective. Rather than asking why Amy needed to do this and what she got out of it, we investigated instead why *others* in her family might have needed her to behave in this way.

Roberta, a woman in her mid-30s, was married to a powerful, dynamic, and energetic young superstar. When he was angry at her for some major or minor offense, she became completely preoccupied with worry about just how angry he was and whether and when they would be reconciled. In describing this upset, she stated that though she had always been extremely anxious about work or school, those

2. But see the interesting work of Searles (1958) and Weiss, Sampson, and The Mount Zion Psychotherapy Research Group (in press) for important (though not exclusive) exceptions.

kinds of anxieties had almost totally disappeared since her marriage 5 years ago. During these 5 years, she had completed graduate school and had begun her career with relatively little distress.

When Roberta was in the midst of a disagreement with her husband, she barely gave a thought to anxiety about her performance in her career. In fact, periods of great stress between them often served to remind her of how inconsequential her ordinary daily concerns actually were; if she was beginning to worry about her job performance, one fight with her husband would restore what she regarded as her sense of priorities.

One day during a period of calm in the stormy sea of her marriage, Roberta reported feeling greatly worried (and even beginning to develop a migraine headache) about a prospective confrontation with her supervisor. Her therapist suggested that had she been fighting with her husband, she would not have been bothered by the difficulty with her supervisor nearly as much, since she would have told herself, "Who cares? What's really important is reconciling with Jack." A further interpretation was made that the instability in her marriage very likely helped her contain anxiety about other things as well. The therapist then explored with her the possible consequences to her defensive system if her marriage were to become a stable and peaceful one.

Systems interpretations can serve to shift attention both from the intrapsychic to the interpersonal and vice versa. In the case of Kara, for example, her hysterical reactions were seen as having an interpersonal meaning, in that they did something for her husband. On the other hand, in the case of Roberta, a problem that was defined by the patient as an interpersonal one was also seen to be understandable as a defense against her own individual issues concerning performance.

A fairly common interpretation of this sort is one in which fighting with family members is seen as warding off depression. The "start" of this interpretation depends, of course, on which family member the therapist is working with. One might say, "You help your spouse ward off depression by fighting with him," or, conversely, "You fight with your spouse rather than experience your own depression."

A related type of interpretation is one that emphasizes the collusive defense mechanisms that may exist in a relationship. A very dependent woman married to an extremely aggressive man may be involved in a system in which each partner expresses the unacceptable aspects of the self for the other. Similarly, a person who is always berating his or her spouse for the impulsive or inconsiderate things the spouse has done may be colluding in a mutual defensive system in which one person is "id" and the other is "superego."

Interpretations Based on Vicious Circles

Thus far, we have discussed interpretations that are based on a structural analysis of the family system and those that look at the *meaning* of the symptom in the context of the systemic relationships. A third category of interpretation that is relevant to our main themes consists of those that emphasize the vicious circles, or the "solution becoming the problem" aspects of the interaction. Here we are looking at how the individual's attempt to deal with personal conflicts and anxieties inadvertently makes things worse, as well as at how the attempt to solve problems of an interpersonal nature may be leading to greater difficulties.

An example of the solution exacerbating the problem that is probably familiar to all therapists is the common case of the individual who so fears being aggressive that he overcompensates with excessive niceness. This "reaction formation" to anger very frequently has the ironic result of generating even more anger. In trying so hard to be anything but hostile or aggressive, to be particularly cooperative, pleasant, considerate, and inoffensive, such a person tends to sacrifice or give short shrift to his own needs. The result is likely to be resentment, deriving from frustration and deprivation and from a sense that others are getting what he is not and/or ignoring his needs. But because this resentment is not acceptable to him, he cannot allow it to become conscious, and in warding it off he calls into play his familiar technique of accentuating opposite behaviors to bolster his disavowal. The result is to repeat the same cycle, again generating the very feelings he is trying to ward off and again dealing with it in the same counterproductive way.

The dynamic is a common one between parents and children. Parents' excessive sacrifice of their own needs for the sake of the children leads to resentment. Guilt over these resentful feelings leads the parents to disregard their own needs still further, which in turn again fuels the unacceptable resentment. Somewhere along the line the spiral gets out of control, and a symptom or crisis is precipitated in the parents and/or the children.

In some instances where the solution has become the problem, the main ironic effect is the *prevention* of experiences that could have led to modification of old and maladaptive assumptions. The person protects himself so well from anticipated dangers that he never can learn that circumstances have changed and that the danger no longer exists or is so imminent.

Selena, for example, a business consultant in her early 30s, would become extremely anxious about making mistakes. Fearing that small slip-ups could lead to disaster, Selana checked and double-checked her work so as to be sure nothing would go wrong. She could not delegate to her secretary even minor jobs. Though she had never consciously articulated it prior to therapy, it seemed to her that the world was peopled by harsh and punitive judges.

Feeling in control of what happened to her was a central concern with Selena. Fearing the negative consequences of mistakes as intensely as she did, Selena at a very early age became quite adept at covering her tracks. As an adult she tried excessively to avoid any errors at all; not surprisingly, this anxious overconcern in itself sometimes led to errors. When this happened, she would run herself ragged to correct such errors before her clients ever found out about them, or would bluff and cover them over.

Many disturbing events in Selena's childhood contributed to Selena'a anxiety and the assumption that the world is a hostile and intolerant place. But as she came to realize in therapy, it was her very skill in preventing others from knowing she had erred that kept her assumptions about the world alive. Since she never, or at best rarely, had the experience of her errors being discovered and responded to by others, she had no opportunity to observe more sympathetic responses than she had early come to expect, and therefore no basis on which to alter her assumptions.

Craig was a successful businessman who confessed to the therapist that, despite his success, he had a large number of anxieties that exercised a great deal of influence on his actions. He was particularly anxious about new situations where he didn't know the ropes well. Fearing the feeling of inadequacy and humiliation that came from looking ignorant, Craig would either avoid new situations or would spend a good deal of time preparing in advance for what might happen. If business required him to travel to a new city, for example, he would be sure to know before he left the fastest route from the airport to the hotel, so as to be able to give the taxi driver instructions. Spontaneous travel was avoided, since he felt humiliated by having to ask about good accommodations and restaurants. Like Selena, Craig was so good at protecting himself from feared negative consequences that he never had a chance to learn that not knowing every last detail in advance need not lead to humiliation. The combination of avoidance and preparation had made his assumptions impervious to change. The interpretations required in both cases were ones that conveyed an understanding of circular causality and made clear to the patients the vicious circles that their defensive efforts got them caught in.

Max complained that his wife's extreme anxiety was intolerable. Worry of one sort or another seemed to be at the center of their every conversation. Finding her worries and preoccupations "boring" and excessive, Max responded to his wife by constantly communicating that she was making a mountain out of a molehill. Her reaction to his attempts to minimize what to her seemed like valid concerns was to further her efforts at proving to him that her worries were in fact realistic.

The problem was further exacerbated by the fact that Max could not accept his own anxieties. When he was upset about something, he would deny his worry and act confident and manly. This stance of unflagging strength and unflappability encouraged his wife to lean on him by revealing her worries. Moreover, when her fears resonated with his own denied concerns, he would further his defensive efforts by exaggerating still further his posture of calm confidence and certainty that all was well. This would further encourage his wife both to try to persuade him that she was right to worry, and to feel that he was a rock she could lean on. Only when interpretations helped him to see how he contributed to the behavior on his wife's part that he thought he had been combating could he begin to seek a different strategy, as well as to understand more of the needs in him that had led him to get caught in this self-defeating circle.

Ralph was concerned that his wife didn't really love him. For him, love and dependence were inseparable. He thus tried to get her to "love" him more by doing things that would foster her feeling of dependency. Fearing that if she had a good job or was more attractive, she would no longer need him, Ralph subtly undermined his wife's feelings of competence. When some household project needed to be done, he would give his wife detailed instructions rather than letting her use her own judgment. He would also express concern about her ability to handle a career and children. Similarly, he was "accepting" of her appearance, although she was significantly overweight.

When the therapist inquired about his wife's reaction to these "concerned" and "supportive" statements, it became clear that they made her angry. She experienced Ralph as being overly controlling. Thus his attempt to make her dependent (and, by his logic, therefore, to love him) backfired; it in fact led to resentment and alienation, as he gradually came to recognize.

It should be noted that the interpretations being described here have consisted largely in explicating interactional dynamics, rather than uncovering repressed or split-off parts of oneself. Such a perspective, however, is in no way incompatible with the more typical focus of psychodynamic interpretations. In a number of the examples above, it is evident that examination of the interpersonal consequences and mutual interaction sequences was closely woven into a consideration of the feelings and experiences that the patients were warding off. Moreover, systems interpretations that focus on mutual or collusive defense mechanisms do implicitly deal with aspects of the self that are denied. Emphasis is placed in these interpretations, however, on the interactional aspects of the defense mechanisms, rather than on the impulses per se.

Whatever the focus of our interpretations, we always ask ourselves how this insight into the patient's unconscious feelings can ultimately be used by him. What is the range of manifestations of what we have discovered? How does it influence his behavior? How could he act differently so as to alter the unconscious feelings that have now been brought to light?

Regardless of how "true" the insight might be, we wish to explore with the patient as well how it can be used to provide the basis for a change in the patient's life. We do not generally regard it as a useless resistance when patients ask about an interpretation, "So what do I do about it?" Many of the examples of vicious circles discussed in this book became clear as we tried to respond to just such a question.

Educating the Patient about Others' Motives

As we have indicated in numerous places throughout this book, our approach to psychodynamics is a contextual one. We believe that it is essential in understanding the patient to understand how his experiences, his conflicts, and his anxieties are responsive to the actions and messages of those around him. Consequently, we believe it is important for the patient not only to achieve insight into what experiences, thoughts, or feelings he is warding off, but also to appreciate his impact on others and to improve his ability to understand others' perceptions and experiences. We see our responsibility as including assuring that the patient has a sound understanding of the key other people in his life.

We thus do not share the assumption of some therapists that one should not "educate" the patient. As we have elaborated in numerous ways throughout this book, we do not believe that providing advice, information, or perspectives on interpersonal events implies that the therapist knows more about life than the patient; it merely suggests that his areas of ignorance or incompetence are not likely to be identical to those of the patient. The structure of the therapeutic situation is, moreover, one designed to enable the therapist to see events more clearly than he does in his own life, where his own conflicts and anxieties can more readily come to the fore.

Comments to patients about others may be based on an intrapsychically oriented analysis as well as on a systemic understanding. For example, on the basis of a patient's description, we might say something like this: "Given all that you've told me about your husband, he seems to get angry with you for the very things he himself is afraid of." Or we might say, "Based on how ambivalent you've been and all you've told me about your girlfriend, she might be pulling away from you in order to protect herself." Or, "Perhaps your wife is really expressing her own feelings of neglect by you when she complains that you do not spend enough time with the children."

We suspect that most therapists make statements of this sort, even if their theoretical assumptions may at times make them feel uneasy about doing so. Since we believe that the main job of the therapist is to help patients change crippling patterns of interaction, we do not hesitate to make such statements if they will facilitate change. To be sure, our comments about others are inevitably more speculative than those about the patient, with whom we have spent a good deal of time. But it is nonetheless frequently possible to make a fairly good guess about what is going on—one that proves to be helpful to the patient in seeing how to break out of the repeated bind he has been in.[3]

3. It should be noted that our speculations about the dynamics and characteristics of significant others in the patient's life are not always based solely on the patient's descriptions. As described in Chapters 7 and 8, part of our emphasis on the importance of understanding the systems of interaction in which the patient participates includes a readiness to invite significant others into occasional sessions, in order to be able to observe firsthand the cast of characters in the patient's life and how he interacts with them.

Our cyclical and transactional model also leads us to regard it as useful to educate the patient in other ways as well. Since the patient's difficulties are in substantial degree a reflection of ongoing events in his life (filtered and translated, of course, by his personal cognitive and motivational schemas), interventions that help to change the pattern of those events can contribute significantly to changing both the internal state and the overt behavior patterns that are the objects of the patient's complaint. In the right circumstances, for example, it would be perfectly consistent with our approach to discuss theories of child rearing with the patient if we felt that such a didactic and intellectual approach would be effective. Similarly, we have found that many of our adult patients welcome some basic sex education. We sometimes recommend books or articles on this topic if we think it will facilitate changes in attitude and behavior.

Wording of Interpretations and Being Supportive

We come now to a set of considerations that may not at first seem particularly germane to the importation of family therapy notions into the arena of individual therapy. We believe that what follows is none-theless so important for *any* kind of therapeutic progress that we include it here. Moreover, since our initial exploration of these matters (e.g., P. L. Wachtel, 1977a, Chap. 11; 1980), we have come to see ways in which the contributions of family therapists—particularly with regard to connotation and reframing—dovetail with and can enhance the considerations that have mainly guided our efforts.

Family therapists tend to organize their clinical work around building on the strengths of the people who consult them. Many of their strategies and techniques emphasize the positive, and reinterpret various actions and feelings in order to do so. We discuss the specific methods utilized in this regard later. Here, our concern is with how this general orientation can aid the effort to make interpretations more capable of registering and promoting change.

Whatever the particular focus of our interpretive comments to the patient, we are concerned about how to couch our comments so as to maximize the chance that the patient will hear them and will be helped by them. A critical aspect of this task is to be aware of the surplus meanings that interpretations or any other comments made to patients will inevitably have. In particular, it is essential to recognize that comments about feelings, thoughts, or intentions that the patient has not fully admitted into consciousness are likely to be experienced in some way as either permissions or rebukes; they will convey either that perhaps what has been fearfully avoided is more acceptable than the patient has thought, or that the patient has been "caught" doing or thinking something he shouldn't (or, as noted below, that he has been caught *avoiding* thinking something, which by the ground rules of therapy is also perceived as "bad").

These connotations of acceptance or criticism are, to be sure, very substantially a function of the patient's transference. The patient's experience of the therapist and his attitudes is hardly an objective matter. But it is a mistake to attribute all of these connotations to transference. A good deal of the variance in how the therapist's remarks are experienced lies in the remarks themselves. There are a variety of ways of conveying basically the same denotative message to the patient, and their differences are crucial.

Most good interpretations are permission-oriented. They address an aspect of the patient's experience that he has disavowed or obscured, and convey the message that it is all right to be more accepting toward that experience. They expand the patient's sense of entitlement with regard to conflicted aspects of his psychic life. They point out to the patient in one way or another that he has been afraid to acknowledge something about himself, and that perhaps this anxiety is no longer necessary.

Not infrequently, however, if one looks closely at how an interpretation is actually worded, one finds that it contains an implicit rebuke. Something like "You pretend not to feel such and such, but really you do" is the tacit message.

In the great majority of clinical situations, we attempt to couch our remarks in a context of permission and to avoid forms of expression that are more readily experienced as critical; in our supervisory work with students, we do this as well. We find that beginning students frequently phrase their comments in such forms as "You are trying to hide . . . ," "You are avoiding . . . ," "You're denying how . . . you are," "You're really very . . . ," ". . . is a cover for . . . ," and so on. Experienced therapists, one expects, do so far less frequently, but we have found even in listening to tapes of experienced therapists (including ourselves, we must confess) that such comments are not really so rare. When we have alerted various friends and colleagues to these issues, they have tended to be surprised at how common such remarks are in their own clinical work. These are, as it were, the unwanted tics of our profession.

The main cure for these "tics" is the firm possession of a set of alternative forms of expression, particularly of ways of framing comments that convey permission to reappropriate previously warded-off feelings. Here are some examples: "You seem rather harsh with yourself when you sense any hint of sexual feelings." "You seem to expect something terrible to happen to you if you have any wish to be taken care of." "I have the sense you're angry at your mother but think it's awful of you to feel that." "I think you're feeling critical of Susan because you're afraid if you get too close to her you'll get 'mushy' and she won't think you're a man; maybe that kind of caution isn't really necessary."

Reinforcement and Shaping

These matters can be further elaborated in terms of the behavior therapists' notions of reinforcement and shaping. Whatever else interpretations may convey, they also always function as positive or negative reinforcements. This occurs whether or not the therapist intends to reinforce the patient and regardless of whether he conceives of his task as one of being "neutral." Therefore, it behooves the therapist who is able to acknowledge this not to leave the reinforcement value of his comments to chance, but rather to pay careful attention to this dimension of what is going on between patient and therapist, as he does to other critical dimensions.

Crucial to the effective use of the reinforcement dimension is recognition of the variation in people's behavior, even in behavior that is part of a rather entrenched pattern. No one is ever *always* anxious, angry, seductive, irritable, or tendentious. There are always degrees of such behavior even when it is useful and substantially accurate to describe someone as "hostile," "resistant," "timid," or what have you. By knowing how to ride those variations, as it were, the therapist can enormously increase his therapeutic power.

We recall, for example, an instance when a student, attempting to be empathically responsive to a patient's difficulties, said to her, "You have difficulty talking." Much to the therapist's surprise, the patient responded by withdrawing still further into silence. The statement, it became clear, had left her feeling labeled as a noncommunicative person, with a despairing sense that that was just who she "was."[4] We suggested to the therapist that next time he try a variation on this message that did not convey to the patient such a static picture of characterological entrenchment: "Sometimes you talk more easily than at other times." Such a comment conveys that there are variations to build on, rather than calling up a picture of fixed attributes that are simply "what I am like." It also is more likely to elicit curiosity about the differences between the times when communication is relatively free and those when it is difficult (i.e., curiosity about the "meaning" of the communication difficulties).

The patient's behavior can always be seen as momentarily just a little bit better or a little bit worse with regard to his therapeutic goals. At any given moment, he is almost inevitably at least a trifle more or less resistant, more or less anxious, more or less affectively accessible, and so forth than he was a moment before. If the therapist's comments to him take this into account, they can help to influence the further direction of the patient's movement and make it more likely that the movement is in a therapeutically helpful direction.

The concept of "shaping," so central to the work of reinforcement theorists, provides a useful clue to how to do this in a way that facilitates therapeutic growth and change. Central to their efforts is attention to progressive approximations to the behavior that is eventually desired.[5] The individual is not always able initially to respond in the way that is sought; from the perspective of fully effective functioning, he falls short. But he can be helped to move closer to the desired goal if he is rewarded (encouraged) for beginning efforts in the right general direction. Then, as he becomes able to approximate more closely the

4. Here again, it is certainly important to be alert to the transference aspects of such a reaction by the patient. But it is essential to be alert as well to the ways in which particular ways of putting things to patients increase the likelihood of one or another kind of reaction. Transferences are powerful, but they are not inexorable; *which* of the numerous possible transference reactions consistent with the patient's history and personality structure will come into play depends on many features of what actually transpires (see Gill, 1982; I. Hoffman, 1983; P. L. Wachtel, 1981a, 1982).

5. "Desired by whom?" is an important question that may be a disquieting one for some readers. It is unfortunately the case that reinforcement considerations are sometimes paired with a manipulative orientation, in which the goals pursued by the reinforcing agent are not those of the subject. This is by no means intrinsic to considerations of reinforcement, however, nor is it endemic to all those who utilize such a perspective. We hope it is clear that in our own approach it is the attainment of *the patient's* goals that is paramount (cf. P. L. Wachtel, 1977a, especially Chapters 11 and 12).

desired patterns of behavior, encouragement is offered only for his better efforts. What could not have been achieved in the beginning is now readily within his reach and becomes the base from which to launch a new effort. Thus, in contrast to not uncommon stereotypes about the behavioral point of view, this perspective helps assure a more humane approach when used properly. For it emphasizes very centrally not expecting of someone more than he is at that point capable of, nor assuming that what he is capable of now is indicative of what he will be capable of later. It gives greater weight to a step in the right direction than to the distance that still must be traveled.

From the point of view of reinforcement and shaping, one might consider the following general rule: When the patient makes any slight movement in a therapeutic direction, the therapist responds positively. This encourages the patient to do more of the same—to shift his behavior in the direction of greater openness, of less hostile rejection of whatever one is saying, or whatever. When, however, his movement is in the opposite direction—just a bit *less* open or *more* oppositional— one withholds the positive response and/or "interprets the defense."

What we are suggesting here is not a mechanical kind of "conditioning." Nor need it be "manipulative," as it might seem at first to the reader who is unfamiliar or uncomfortable with ideas of reinforcement, or who regards them as concepts solely applicable to rats in Skinner boxes. The basic thrust of what we are describing can be understood in terms of imparting information to an intelligent, sentient human who is able to choose just how to use the information he receives. It has been a source of considerable fallacious theorizing— ironically, shared by both Skinner and his most vociferous opponents— to regard reinforcements as inexorable forces that "control" behavior (see P. L. Wachtel, 1977a, Chap. 11, for more on this). One can as readily view them, especially when they are social reinforcements delivered to humans rather than biological reinforcements delivered to animals, as simply guidelines indicating whether the person is going in the right direction; these guidelines, if they are consistent with the goals and with the basic perceptions of the patient, are for that reason likely to be taken seriously. When a therapist indicates to a patient that he is doing something that is apt to prove helpful to him, it is not surprising that this communication is likely to have an impact. There is nothing sinister about this.[6]

6. For further discussion of the problems in thinking in terms of either neutrality or unconditional positive regard, see P. L. Wachtel (1979a, 1982).

Reinforcement considerations suggest that one must often modify the general clinical rule of interpreting defenses first. Let us imagine that one is working with a patient who is very obsessional, hedging every statement with qualifiers and approaching his own experience in a highly intellectualized fashion that cuts him off from his own affective life. Such a patient is also inevitably going to be more obsessional some times than others. But since he is *generally* rather obsessional, even on the occasions when this tendency is a bit less, the therapist is still likely to be struck by it.

Suppose, for example, that the patient comes in to one session acknowledging more than he previously had that he enjoys irritating his wife with his excessive neatness. It is likely that he also will do so in a still obsessional manner. For instance, he might say (we exaggerate here for purposes of exposition): "It occurred to me that I had under-estimated the probability that your comment yesterday about the possible hostile intentions of my actions had some truth to it." It may be very easy for the therapist to pay more attention to the continuing intel-lectualization than to the fact that the patient is at least considering in a way that he previously hasn't that his behavior might be hostile. This can lead the therapist to call attention to phrases such as "under-estimated the probability," instead of responding to the content.

Such tactics by the therapist are designed to bring to greater awareness (and eventually make ego-dystonic) the obsessional defen-siveness that hedges the experience even as it is seemingly being ex-pressed. The effect of such a comment, however, will probably be to drive the patient's budding awareness of his hostility back underground (except insofar as he is able to recognize his anger at the *therapist* for his putdown). The patient may feel hurt and inadequate, his self-esteem damaged by a comment all too consonant with the kind of parental contingencies that probably have led to obsessional defenses in the first place—an implicit demand for a degree of effectiveness that is at that point beyond the person's capability. Such a comment from the therapist carries the connotative message that what the patient has offered (a somewhat greater acknowledgment of his hostile inten-tions) is not good enough and that all that is noticed was how it falls short (it is too obsessional).

In contrast, a comment that focuses instead on the movement itself, on the fact that the patient has acknowledged more than he previously has, should serve not only as a reinforcement (making further movement in the same direction more likely), but should also help firm up the patient's self-esteem instead of further undermining it. As a result, though not directly addressing the obsessional defensive system, the comment will actually be contributing to its diminution, since it will be contributing to diminishing the perfectionistic demands that are one of the important sources of the obsessionalism.

Such a comment—on the order of "You seem more in touch with what you're feeling today" or "You're more open today to considering what I've been saying"—can be understood from a number of perspectives. It bears an interesting similarity to what goes on in biofeedback. There, the individual is helped (by the aid of biological monitoring and amplification) to notice variations that he would ordinarily be unable to discriminate. Biofeedback can enable someone to learn to control skin temperature or blood pressure, because it enables him to notice when his skin temperature or blood pressure has gone up or down—something he otherwise could not detect. Once he is able to become aware of these variations, he is in a position to alter them voluntarily in accordance with his overarching intentions. Similarly, calling attention to the patient's diminished defensiveness also enables him to notice a variation he might otherwise miss, and thereby to have an opportunity for some degree of voluntary control. Particularly with obsessionals, the inability to notice variations in their functioning— everything is reduced to equivalency as being less than perfect—is a major contributor to their difficulties.

Reframing and Positive Connotation

Much of the foregoing can usefully be understood as well from the perspective of reframing, which is central in the work of many family therapists. As Watzlawick *et al.* (1974) have noted, our conception of what is "really" the case in any situation we encounter is not a simple matter of what is "out there," but rather is very much a function of how we define and make sense of what occurs. The way in which experiences are interpreted and construed in most therapeutic paradigms has a decidedly negative tone; finding hidden pathology rather than finding hidden strengths is the primary direction (cf. Wile, 1981, 1984). The strategy implicit in what has just been described is designed to enable the patient to gain a new perspective on the choices and possibilities that confront him. Like the new perspectives offered in much family systems work, it frequently provides a more positive connotation than is typical of more traditional therapeutic approaches.

As Frank (1973) has noted in summarizing the results of decades of psychotherapy research, perhaps the most crucial task of psychotherapy is helping the patient to overcome his sense of demoralization. For this purpose, a focus on the positive is obviously useful. This is not to advocate a Pollyannaish vision, but merely to recognize that "truth" is never fully captured in any interpretation or formulation and that some versions of the truth—some of the partial approximations that are all we are ever privy to—are more capable of producing change than others.[7]

Addressing Behavior outside the Therapy Hour

Most of what has been addressed thus far in this chapter deals with the patient's behavior in the therapy sessions: openness to new experiences, readiness to hear what the therapist is saying, and so forth. But a great deal of what is therapeutic about psychotherapy occurs *outside* of the therapy sessions. It is in the *application* of the insights gained in therapy that significant change is most likely to be generated. A central premise of the point of view guiding this book is that psychological difficulties are maintained primarily by the cycles of interaction in which the person repeatedly engages. Internal states, unconscious motives, and intrapsychic conflicts are crucial in this, but are themselves also understandable in terms of the circle of causes that interaction patterns both reflect and generate.

Consequently, the considerations noted above (reinforcement, shaping, positive connotation, etc.) are applied as well to the patient's outside behavior. Steps that he takes to change troubling patterns of behavior or to confront some feared situation or experience are primarily addressed with a concern for whether what is reported is a step forward, rather than in terms of whether regressive or conflictual material can be discerned.[8]

7. Other applications of the notions of reframing and positive connotation are presented in the next chapter.

8. Given our psychodynamic background, such evidence of conflict or of developmentally significant distortions is certainly noted by us. We keep such observations in the back of our minds, both in order to anticipate and better understand potential blockages and resistances, and to help us formulate the direction of the therapy and the exact nature of therapeutic tasks and comments in the most effective fashion. At some point in the course of the therapy, most of these observations are brought explicitly into the work and discussed with the patient. But it is frequently countertherapeutic to address these observations explicitly at the time they are first noticed by the therapist.

Just what constitutes a step forward is, of course, a complex question. It is certainly not something for the therapist to determine unilaterally. Rather, the determination is based on the patient's own goals as they are revealed in the exploratory process of the therapy, as well as on the understanding that the therapist reaches of how the patient has been blocked in the pursuit and even the recognition of his aspirations.

Therapy from this perspective can be thought of as consisting of two stages, though these stages are more frequently overlapping and simultaneous than sequential. The first stage consists of helping the patient articulate what is bothering him and how he would like to change. It is in this first stage that something like neutrality is required. It is not our business to set the goals for the patient (though it certainly is to help him to clarify his goals, which includes examination of how he may have been deceiving himself about just what his real goals are).

Once the patient has achieved some clarification of what he really wants and feels, however, it is ethically appropriate and therapeutically useful to exercise influence in the service of helping the patient reach his goals. We see as our mandate to do what we can do to facilitate change in the direction that the patient decides to go in (with the important proviso that the methods to be used do not violate the patient's sense of dignity or themselves contravene the patient's aspirations).

There are some patients—for example, those striving to extricate themselves from the consequences of parental efforts to program their every move and feeling, and/or to deny that there could be any differences between the feelings of the parent and the child—for whom one must be especially careful about providing direction or overemphasizing approval and disapproval.[9] But it is our impression that it is more often a problem that therapists, in their effort to avoid being

---

Often they must take a back seat to the need to encourage the patient to continue his forward efforts and to value them. The more complex and conflictual aspects of his experience are frequently best left for later.

9. Even here, though, it is important to recognize that strict neutrality is simply not possible. Reinforcements can no more be ruled out of the consulting room by fiat than can the law of gravity. It is in the very nature of the work we do as therapists that we will inevitably see some actions by the patient as more in his interests than others, and some as more defensive and counterproductive. And this is true notwithstanding the fact that there are also many other instances in which we genuinely do not know whether something is in the patient's best interests or not.

directive, unwittingly encourage the patient to be "stuck" in his ambivalences.

In line with the strategies outlined above, one way to help the patient change in his desired direction is to underline and call attention to those times when he is doing things differently. One might say, for instance, "I'm struck by how you handled this issue. You seemed to be more able to discuss the matter openly, even though you were feeling anxious." Or, "You may not have noticed the change, but I can see that in the past few months you've been much more determined to shake off your depression quickly."

Such statements not only call attention to change and encourage it further; they also attribute to the patient characteristics and inclinations in terms of which he has hesitated to think about himself. In our experience, one's self-characterizations are enormously important in determining one's sense of possibilities. Believing that change is possible is a necessary precursor to actually trying something new.

6. *Active Interventions*

THE CLINICAL activities discussed thus far are mainly designed to clarify—for patient and for therapist—just what the issues are in the patient's life: What are the dimensions of experience that are muted or warded off? What thoughts, affects, or motivations are unacceptable? What are the reactions of others and how do they help to maintain the problem? And so on. Even here, to be sure, our orientation leads us to be concerned with the action implications of the insights that may be attained; we have already noted that we do not believe that a question or an interpretation can ever be "neutral." In this chapter, however, we present more explicit interventions designed to aid the patient in taking active steps to reverse the maladaptive patterns in which he is enmeshed.

Not all the active interventions explored in this chapter derive directly from what are usually thought of as systemic views. Some are methods that have developed elsewhere. (Paradoxical methods, for example, have been given a systemic rationale—and sometimes interestingly and distinctively systemic foci—by family therapists, but were independently developed by therapists from other orientations as well.) Some are methods whose origins do not lie in the family therapy movement at all, but which (as the reader will see) are quite consonant with the overall thrust of what we are presenting here— either because they embody an active approach to reversing maladaptive patterns, or because they derive from a view that sees people's difficulties as intimately related to the ongoing transactions in which they participate (usually both).

Giving Tasks

Some effort to actively encourage the patient to engage in particular behaviors is useful in almost every therapy. Depending on the patient's personality and on the dynamics of the patient–therapist relationship, the proposal may be couched as a strongly encouraged "suggestion" or as a directive akin to "homework." The goal is to help the patient take steps that will facilitate a new subjective experience of himself or others.

Individual and Systems-Oriented Tasks

We have elsewhere discussed the general issue of the use of therapeutic tasks and assignments and how this can be compatible with a more traditional psychodynamic approach (e.g., P. L. Wachtel, 1977a, 1985). Understanding of the overall rationale for such tasks and of how to present them is essential for any more active approach. Here, however, in keeping with the specific purpose of this book, we focus primarily on the interpersonal and systemic aspects of the use of such tasks.

One important change when one thinks of tasks in terms of systems, instead of from a strictly individual perspective, is that the therapist is led to greater consideration of the interests and reactions of other people in the patient's life. Traditional perspectives on clinical work frequently lead inadvertently to the "blaming" of others in the effort to be empathically on the side of the patient (see E. F. Wachtel, 1979). Taking a systemic perspective leads the therapist to be more sympathetic toward the patient's parents, friends, and relatives.

To be sure, there is something extremely valuable in the dedication and commitment to the patient's welfare and to seeing things through the patient's eyes that characterizes most traditional individual therapies. But, as we have noted in a variety of places, there are complex ethical and conceptual issues that have been obscured by the individualistic bias so prevalent in our society. Much of the time, in fact, a more comprehensive understanding even of the welfare of the individual patient requires taking into account the welfare of the other people who are significant in his life (including those who are initially presented as adversaries or irritants). Moreover, the ethics of committing oneself solely to the welfare of one person without consideration of the impact on others is questionable.

Our conceptualizations of the causes of patients' problems are based on both individual and interpersonal–systemic models, and consequently so too are the tasks we have used. If, in a particular case (or at a particular point in a given case), this understanding is largely based on such individual concepts as anxiety, split-off aspects of one's self, or irrational assumptions about the world, the task will be aimed at influencing these aspects of the self. For example, a patient who has come to realize that his arrogant behavior is a defense against a dread of looking foolish might be requested to purposely ask a foolish question daily. Or a patient who now "knows" that his perception of his boss is distorted because he is relating to him as if he were "father" might be asked to keep a daily list of observed ways in which this person differs from his father.

When the problem seems to be a more interpersonal one, the patient might be directed to behave in an uncharacteristic way that will disrupt the pernicious system. For example, a man who always responds reassuringly to his anxious wife might be encouraged to be more upset than she, as a way of disrupting a system that results in his being both contemptuous and resentful of his wife's "fragility."

Though tasks can be devised that are paradoxical, in that the hope is that the patient will "rebel" against doing what is asked, the tasks that we are describing in this section are straightforward extensions of our understanding of the problem. Later in the chapter we discuss the possible use of paradoxical statements and tasks, but, for now, we are focusing on more direct efforts on the part of the therapist to make a bridge between insight and action.

Sometimes helping patients to translate what they have learned in therapy into changes in their way of being in the world requires simply directing the patient's attention to the action implications of what we have come to understand. Other patients need more direction, and for these patients assigned tasks are often quite helpful. In more traditional therapies, this help is sometimes withheld because—ironically, in the name of "neutrality" or the *non*imposition of values— therapists impose on patients their own values and expectations regarding autonomy. Though it is true that therapists do not know how to live any better than anyone else, therapists do have an expertise in understanding feelings and unconscious motivations (both in the patient and in others he relates to) and in understanding the consequences to the individual of particular ways of behaving. As a result of their training, therapists know (or should know) a good deal about the kinds of actions and patterns of interaction that help to overcome anxiety and the kinds that maintain it; about the effects of negative and positive reinforcement; about some of the behavior patterns that are likely to have ironic consequences; and about the likely effects of one person's behavior on the systems of interaction between and among people.

Giving therapeutic tasks need not be thought of as antithetical to an interpretive orientation to patients' difficulties. Suggestions or prescriptions regarding actions can make the import of an interpretation clearer and more powerfully grasped. Consider, for example, a man whose anger at his stepdaughter is seen by his therapist as deriving from his fear of openly expressing his dependency—something that she does rather readily and that therefore makes him uncomfortable. Real appreciation of the relevance of this dynamic for him requires more than just an acknowledgment of the therapist's comment as one that seems to make sense; what is needed to make the insight really vivid and affectively meaningful is to experience the anxiety and resistance that are generated when the seemingly straightforward implications are put into practice. Just talking about it does not readily bring this about. But consider instead the impact of suggesting to this patient that he ask his wife to baby him in some way. Here he encounters rather immediately his discomfort and powerful reluctance; the idea becomes alive, an emotional experience that transcends mere words.

Further Examples

In the case of Myra, anxieties about her body persisted, despite a good deal of psychodynamic exploration of the meaning and origins of the anxieties. The thought that people were also "bodies" was extremely disturbing to her, and on an emotional level it was almost inconceivable to her that her friends or business associates had sex. She of course "knew" that they did, but she could only imagine them with clothes on, not as "bodies."[1]

Not surprisingly, Myra's sex life was extremely limited and unfulfilling. Though quite attractive and personable, she went out on dates only rarely. Men seemed to sense her discomfort with things of the flesh and tended to have friendly or cordial relations with her, but to avoid approaching her with any romantic intentions. She had no ongoing relationship in which sensate focus exercises with a partner (see Kaplan, 1974; Masters & Johnson, 1970) could be attempted.

Myra was asked to make a study of how and when other people called attention to their bodies. Clothing, makeup, ways of walking

---

1. It will come as no surprise to most readers that Myra was aware that it was particularly hard for her to imagine *her parents* having sex. Considerable primal scene imagery was explored, and this seemed to help some; however, prior to the introduction of the therapeutic task, her inhibitions remained unusually powerful.

and holding oneself, and verbal references to parts of the body or to bodily experiences all became foci for Myra's notebook. She was asked not to try to change anything about her own behavior at this point, but simply to become a student of "people as bodies."

As is frequently the case, this kind of observational emphasis, shorn of the pressure to do something about what one observes, in itself had a noticeable impact. When Myra felt comfortable enough to try to call attention to her own body, a number of tasks were worked out; some came from suggestions by the therapist, and some were spontaneously thought of by Myra.

She changed her hairdo and makeup style, and (a harder step for her) began to discuss this with other people "Do you think this darker lipstick goes with my complexion?"). Out of one discussion of anxiety-arousing situations, Myra resolved to wear intentionally a pair of stockings with a run in them and to say to a few people, each time as if she were noticing it for the first time, "Oh, my stocking has a run." This was frightening to her at first, but she felt exhilarated when she could do it and by the third time got a real kick out of her "naughty" behavior. She also found a way to get into a discussion of menstrual cycles with a friend, something that had seemed impossible for her previously. Gradually, her quality of inhabiting her body as if it were occupied territory diminished. Men seemed to notice the difference and started responding to her in a different way. Much other work was still needed, but the tasks seemed to her to have made a significant difference.

Eleanore came to therapy because of a great deal of difficulty in separating from her family. She had recently gotten engaged, but as the wedding date approached she became increasingly apprehensive about taking this big step. She feared that the marriage would lead to a rift with her parents and that she could not tolerate the envisaged separation from them. The "gulf" she anticipated would arise not because she wouldn't be seeing her parents, but because her parents would feel distance from her if she was no longer emotionally dependent on them. Feeling both guilty that she was growing away and fearful that her growth would mean the loss of her mother's love, Eleanore maintained the deep connection by secretly visiting home and falling apart emotionally during these visits. She would tell her parents that she was uncertain about her feelings for her boyfriend and did not think that she could go through with the marriage.

When Eleanore said these things, she truly believed them; in the service of dealing with her anxieties about disruption of the relationship with her parents, she would focus on every trait of her boyfriend's that was less than perfect and would thereby generate very real anxiety about her future with him.

As a further effort to deal with her conflicts and (according to a highly idiosyncratic logic) to show her loyalty to the family, Eleanore tried as much as possible to minimize contact between the subjects of her divided loyalty. She did not tell her parents that she had definitely decided to marry Bill until a few weeks before the date they had set, and because of this she had to content herself with the prospect of a very minimal sort of wedding.

From a very early age, closeness between Eleanore and her parents was expressed through her being upset and their giving her reassurance. Thus Eleanore's fear that there would be a big gulf between them if she were no longer needy was not entirely unfounded. Up to that point, Eleanore had not given her parents any other basis on which to feel close to her. The entrenched pattern between them of her never sharing with her parents her triumphs, joys, and plans for the future left them feeling isolated from their daughter, except when she came to them with a problem and seemed emotionally fragile. Nevertheless, though there was some basis in fact for Eleanore's feelings that a gulf would exist once she was married, her fear that they would no longer love her since she would no longer be dependent seemed quite excessive. Her anxiety about contact between her boyfriend and family was clearly phobic, since on the few occasions they had met, things had gone fine.

Like any phobia, Eleanore's anxiety had persisted because exposures to the feared event were few and far between. Eleanore's fear of differentiating from her family was dealt with by attempting to keep her parents from seeing her in the role of successful adult with a loving mate, and by being visibly and ostentatiously upset in the presence of her family so as to feel their warmth and affection for her. Her anxiety had never been mastered, and new ways of interacting had not developed, because the "solution" to the problem had been avoidance.

Though Eleanore had gained some awareness of this dynamic in the course of the therapy, little had actually changed, and it was felt that she needed to be encouraged to take specific steps which could remedy the situation. She was asked to begin to give her parents something to substitute for their loss of a dependent child by sharing with them some information each day about something that was making her happy. For instance, she might tell them about something she and her boyfriend had done that had been enjoyable. She was asked to say just one positive thing a day until she gradually became more and more comfortable with this new kind of involvement with them. She was cautioned to take small steps so that both she and her parents could learn to incorporate a new way of relating. (Recall the discussion of gradualism and mastery in Chapter 1.)

Eleanore was also asked to arrange for brief but frequent occasions at which her parents and boyfriend would meet in the weeks remaining before the wedding date. She was encouraged to explain her feelings to her boyfriend, who had in the past been very supportive and empathic. It was suggested that she indicate to him that it would be helpful to her if he would make overtures to her parents, which he had already expressed a willingness to do. She was also encouraged to respond very positively to any moves he spontaneously made toward becoming closer to them.

The aim in all these suggestions was to help the patient find a new basis for feeling close to her parents and to help her give them something to substitute for what might indeed have felt like a loss to them. Such a strategy of helping patients find alternate routes to satisfy in new ways both their own needs and those of others who are important to them is one that is frequently of considerable value.[2]

Claire felt tremendously insecure about sustaining men's attention. She felt that she needed to be devoted and cooperative at all times, or she would incur the wrath of the man she was dating. Having been left by many, many men, Claire was desperate to make her present relationship work. Therefore, she tried even harder than usual to form a strong bond by showing how devoted she was. On the basis of a detailed exploration of her other relationships, the therapist hypothesized that her "caring" and devotion overwhelmed men and made her seem empty and lacking in self-respect. In fact, Claire was not at all an empty person. She had many interests and an active social life when she was not involved with a man. Feeling that men required

---

2. It is important to note that, as obvious as these steps may seem to the reader, they were not obvious to Eleanore. By seeing her parents alone, she had felt she was being loyal to them, while in fact she was sustaining the system in which getting married would have the meaning of betrayal.

complete devotion, however, she molded herself to what she perceived as their needs.

Having gained some understanding of this pattern, but sensing that her appreciation of it was still largely intellectual, Claire initiated, with the therapist's assistance, a series of experiments designed to test out in a new way her fears and ideas regarding what would make her boyfriend angry. For instance, she decided not to take time off from work in order to drive him to the airport. With Claire, the therapist's role was mainly limited to being encouraging and to helping assure she would make reasonable moves rather than drastic moves that could backfire.

Andrew was chronically disappointed in people. No one ever fulfilled his expectations. Most of all, he was disappointed in his wife and children. He complained that his wife was not emotionally available to him and that he might as well be living alone. She seemed to prefer doing things without him, and when they did have intimate discussions, he said, she was always critical.

Andrew was not manifestly defensive. He was more than willing to explore his feelings and loved figuring out their origin. An understanding of Andrew's background made it fairly clear why he was always prone to want more and to feel cheated by how little he got. This understanding in no way changed his feeling, however, that in fact his wife gave him very little.

On the basis of all he had heard, the therapist suspected that Andrew's feeling of deprivation was in fact probably based on a relatively realistic appraisal of what was going on between him and his wife. A pattern had developed in which Andrew would complain and his wife would withdraw, furthering his feeling that he was being cheated. Andrew saw this but could not seem to stop his part in the cycle. He needed something to help him feel less deprived. When the therapist explored with him whether there were some times that felt better between them, he discovered that in fact, when forced to focus on it, Andrew was able to notice positive aspects of the relationship. He had developed a negative selective perception that tended strongly toward confirming his multidetermined assumption that people were disappointing.

Because Andrew had a precise, somewhat obsessive cognitive style, the therapist asked him to notice and jot down each day ways in which his wife was nice to him. He was *not* to write down negative observations, but only positive ones. Assigning such a task helped change Andrew's perceptions, which in turn made him less critical. As was hoped, his wife, feeling less oppressed by his criticism and disappointment, withdrew less and gave him more positive behaviors to add to his list. The same technique proved useful in regard to his children. Andrew was ready to give up being chronically disappointed, and the task gave him a vehicle compatible with his style with which to make the shift. For many months, he spent half his session time reading his lists to the therapist. The rest of each session was spent exploring what he could do for himself to get more gratification out of his life.

Patients' Reactions to Tasks and Assignments

As one would expect, patients' reactions to the assignment or suggestion of a task vary greatly. Some patients feel very much cared for by the active stance the therapist is taking. Others, on the other hand, may feel pushed, controlled, or guilty about their failure to perform as instructed. These reactions are not necessarily indications that the interventions have been a therapeutic error. They are, rather, as the saying goes, grist for the analytic mill.

By and large, it seems to be the case that if the therapist indicates right from the start that he will be active in trying to help the patient reach his goals, the transference reactions are lessened. In general, our emphasis on knowing the real people in the patient's life and on understanding his actual daily interactions leads us to rely less exclusively on the analysis of the trasference than do many dynamically trained therapists.[3] Nonetheless, it is crucial that the therapist understand how the patient is experiencing any action or intervention by the therapist; if this is not taken into account, the work is greatly impeded.

Often, it is at the point of giving tasks that much useful transference exploration goes on. One patient, Michael, for instance, always seemed very interested and cooperative when concrete suggestions were set forth. It was noted, however, that he never spontaneously brought up a discussion of the task, and in fact frequently "forgot" or totally

3. One of us (PLW) tends to rely more on the transference in his work than the other (EFW). Perhaps this reflects the latter's extensive training and experience in family therapy, in contrast to the former's more exclusive focus on work with individuals, albeit with a strong emphasis on cyclical and systems considerations of the sort discussed in this book.

ignored that part of the preceding session. An exploration of this tendency revealed that this was precisely how he dealt with both his mother and his wife. Rarely openly disagreeing, Michael would simply be pleasant and cooperative, but would never actually do what had been asked of him. His reaction to therapeutic tasks led to a much better understanding of his feelings about being controlled and the ramifications of his attempt to deal with those feelings.

On the other hand, one young woman, Anita, who seemed to be extremely self-sufficient, was surprisingly pleased to get some concrete tasks. She scrupulously performed the tasks and called between sessions to get clarification on precisely what was to be done. Her approach to the tasks was quite revealing to the therapist. He had not quite realized how much she desired assistance, since she was unusually adept at covering dependency needs. In the acceptable context of a task, Anita was able to enact and express what had been impermissible elsewhere.

How one presents a task, or what one says if it is not carried out, is something that varies from patient to patient. Giving tasks is part of the total process of therapy and must be presented and dealt with on the basis of the particular conflicts and characteristics of the individual patient. The only firm guidelines we suggest is that if a task is given, it should be followed up on. It is important for the patient to know that the therapist has not "forgotten" and that the task is regarded by him as important. Just how one follows through and conveys that it is important will vary according to the style and needs of both patient and therapist.

Developing Interpersonal Skills

Despite a good deal of understanding of themselves and the system of which they are a part, many patients are unable to change because they have failed to develop the requisite skills needed for new ways of interacting. Systems of interaction are sustained by the interpersonal consequences they repeatedly generate. When a patient's efforts to initiate a new way of acting do not show sufficient skill, the feedback is likely to be other than what was hoped for, and the result can be to confirm rather than to challenge old patterns.

The procedures that together have come to be known as "assertiveness training" provide a useful way to help patients to develop effective system-changing behavior. In this sense, though a method originally deriving from the behavioral rather than the family systems orientation, assertiveness training is an important therapeutic tool for the therapist desiring to incorporate systemic considerations into his work.

The skills that the patient may need to develop include more than just those that might first come to mind under the rubric of assertiveness—the ability to say no, for example, or to request assistance or express annoyance. Just as crucial, and just as often missing, are the ability to express affection, to say one is afraid, or to give a compliment.

The term "assertiveness training" is probably a bit misleading, given the range of affects and inclinations we wish here to address. "Expressiveness training" or "communication training" would probably be better. But since there is by now a substantial clinical tradition (together with a large literature) that goes under the name of "assertiveness training," and that includes basically the procedures we wish to discuss here, we have chosen to use that term, while at the same time offering the caveat above. That many behavior therapists have also expanded the meaning of assertiveness to include such actions as expressing love or feelings of dependency adds to the reasonableness of such a choice.

Several key elements contribute to the general therapeutic strategy to be described in this section. Graduated risks and difficulty, role playing and role reversal, modeling, and simply talking with the patient about what might be done in a particular situation or class of situations and what the likely result of various alternative ways of expressing oneself might be all contribute to the effectiveness of the overall approach. Ultimately it is the assignments in the patient's daily life that have the most significant impact, but the work within sessions can make the difference between a successful or unsuccessful effort by the patient.

Gradualism

Gradualism and an appropriate level of difficulty are particularly important. If one is attempting to help the patient to experience new feedback from others, it is essential that he not undertake a challenge for which he is not yet prepared; the result will probably be an experience of defeat or humiliation that will have antitherapeutic results.

Thus a patient who must ultimately renegotiate boundaries with an intrusive mother may find, if he attempts it prematurely, either that he is ineffectual (thus confirming for his mother that he needs her supervision and assistance, and strengthening for both of them the preexisting pattern of interaction), or that he is so aggressive and unreasonable in his efforts that he feels guilty and retreats (again strengthening the old pattern—most likely not only by his own retreat, but by further persuading his mother that he is not yet "grown up").

Such a patient should be encouraged to approach his ultimate task of dealing with his mother only gradually. First he might be encouraged to choose some other authority figure who may be easier to deal with, or, if he is to make an early attempt with his mother, to do so in regard to some relatively easy or benign issue rather than an issue that is at the center of their conflicts.

Not all patients require quite the same degree of gradualism. There are certainly people who are very close to being able to deal with an important person in their life, and who just need a little encouragement, prodding, or practice. It would be ritualistic to hold them up in the same way as the patient who is in real danger of counterproductive results unless he sticks to a carefully graduated regimen. The important point is to tailor the treatment to the particular patient, going neither too fast nor too slow, and staying sensitive to the feedback provided by the patient in his descriptions of his interactions with others.

Role Playing and Role Reversal

Not all patients require elaborate work in the sessions; some need just a bit of conversation and some help in determining what challenges to take on. But for many the various techniques that together comprise the approach of assertiveness training are extremely valuable. Of particular significance in this regard is the use of role playing. Role playing enables the patient to "try on" new behaviors in a nonthreatening situation—one that nonetheless gives him the feel of what it would be like to act in certain ways and the opportunity to bring forth his creativity in generating new responses to potentially difficult situations.

Often one of the main problems for the patient is that in the actual situation his anxiety is so strong that he cannot think of what to say, or at least cannot think of anything effective. As a consequence, he has an experience of frustration or defeat, leading to a continuation of the anxiety and hence to the same pattern of ineffectiveness all over again.

Role playing can be approached either directly (with the patient playing himself, trying out new behavior vis-à-vis the other, as played by the therapist) or through role reversal. In the latter case, it is initially the *therapist* who plays the role of the patient, and the patient plays the person with whom he wants to practice interacting. We find that it is frequently useful to begin with role reversal, and then later to switch roles and ask the patient to assimilate into his repertoire the new possibilities he has learned from the prior role-reversal activities and from other aspects of the therapeutic process (including trying things out in his daily life and observing the consequences).

One advantage of beginning with role reversal is that the patient often feels less pressure that way, and, perhaps surprisingly, frequently feels less self-conscious playing someone else than playing himself. This is because there is less performance pressure for him to "get it right" this way, and also because he feels less exposed. One great advantage of role playing is that it conveys what the person is like in a particular situation far more vividly than his telling us *about* what he is like[4]; but that is also a *dis*advantage, at least from the short-run experiential perspective of the patient, since it makes it harder for him to hide, as it were.

The role reversal serves another purpose as well, which also provides a convenient way of introducing the procedure: It enables the therapist to get a clearer picture of the person with whom the patient must interact.[5] Often we introduce role playing by saying to the patient something like "I'd like to get a good idea of what you're up against. Perhaps you could play the role of your mother so I could get a feel

4. This is, of course, also the case for observations made of the patient's transference reactions. But as we have indicated in a number of contexts, the transference, despite its enormous utility, is not a sufficient substitute for knowledge about how the patient is with *others*. Interactions with the therapist simply cannot exhaust the range of interpersonal transactions that are significant in the person's life.

5. A still clearer picture is provided, of course, by actually meeting the other person. In Chapters 7 and 8, we discuss procedures and rationales for meeting the cast of characters in the patient's life—something we believe is of considerable therapeutic value, for a variety of reasons.

for how she would react if you asked her to stop reading your mail. I'll be you and you be your mother." The role playing can then begin with the therapist (in the role of the patient) telling the mother how he feels about the reading of his mail. This enables the patient to join in after the therapist has initiated the role playing.

Modeling

Role reversal also enables the therapist to model appropriate behavior, which the patient can later adapt if he wishes. Doing the modeling in this way tends to feel less like telling the patient what to do. It has more the quality of providing the patient an opportunity to observe almost "incidentally" another way of doing things. This is, after all, how we learn much of what we know about how to act in various social situations. Our social behavior is derived in large part from countless observations of how other people act—observations that are often incidental and/or out of awareness, but that form the templates from which we fashion our own version of how to be an effective member of our culture.

The hesitance of many therapists to give advice or provide models of effective behavior is unfortunate. Although the motive behind such forebearance is often a desire to respect the patient's innate adaptive skills and foster his autonomy, in fact such a policy tends to *underestimate* people's adaptive capacities; it assumes that people are so dependent and sponge-like that they will helplessly swallow the therapist's suggestions hook, line, and sinker, with little selectivity or ability to work them over and adapt them to their own style, purpose, and values. In our experience this is rarely the case, the power of the transference notwithstanding. The reluctance of therapists to instruct or provide models seems to us another instance of the unwitting incorporation of individualistic assumptions that have their origins more in values unwittingly drawn from our economic system than in careful observations of interpersonal behavior (cf. P. L. Wachtel, 1977a, Chap. 12; 1983).

In modeling behavior for the patient, as in making explicit suggestions about how the patient might handle a particular situation, the sensitive therapist gears his suggestions around what he senses is the person's own inclination or style. Though the patient will in any event work over any suggestions made by the therapist (explicitly or implicitly),[6] it does make a difference if the therapist's suggestion is consonant with the patient's own way of doing things. The danger in the therapist's pushing for things to be done *his* way is less one of the patient's passively adopting it *in toto* than of the patient's ignoring it; if the therapist's suggestions are not in line with the patient's inclinations they are simply not helpful.

Suggestive Interpretations

In this regard, it is useful to think of modeling or of the other aspects of this approach to social skill development—as well as of the other interventions described in this chapter—as akin to interpretations, but interpretations with a closer link to action than is typical. If the behavior the therapist suggests—whether by modeling it in the course of role playing, or by indicating in any other way that he thinks it would be a useful thing for the patient to do—is to be helpful to the patient, it should be something the patient himself is more or less inclined to do but is somehow inhibited about carrying through. Viewed from a slightly different perspective, it is like the preconscious idea or inclination that the analytically oriented therapist discerns in the patient's associations and brings forth with an interpretation. Good interpretations do not address material that is still alien to the patient's consciousness, but rather material almost—but not quite—accessible. Similarly, to ask people to engage in a program of assertiveness training that does not make sense to them, or to demonstrate a way of handling a situation that does not feel at all comfortable to them, is not productive. The ideas or suggestions the therapist presents must be *a bit* beyond where the patient has already ventured—otherwise, they are not a contribution to the person's effort to change—but they cannot feel alien.[7]

6. The issue is not really whether or not to make suggestions, but whether to do so explicitly. Regardless of orientation or of how hard he tries not to, the therapist cannot in fact refrain from being a suggestive model (cf. P. L. Wachtel, 1977a, in press, as well as various discussions of the issue of "neutrality" throughout this book).

7. An exception of sorts would seem to be the use of paradoxical procedures, to be discussed next. But these procedures, too, are based on the therapist's understanding of the patient's wishes and what he is ready to experience. They are utilized in instances where a particular inhibition or immersion in a seemingly intractable interpersonal pattern makes it difficult for the patient to make the conceptual leap from how he sees things now to how he might see things if he moved just a fraction of an inch off center. The therapist in such instances tries to make dead center a little more difficult a position to occupy, in order to facilitate the patient's gaining a new perspective. But here too the patient will only make a shift that is consonant with his values and sense of self.

Often, in our work, the statement that provides the direction for the assertiveness tasks the patient is to undertake has a form that lies midway between that of an interpretation and that of a suggestion or assignment. A typical such statement might be this: "It sounds like you'd like to tell your husband that you enjoy spending time with him and wish he'd come home from work a little earlier, but you're afraid it will come out sounding like you're just being critical and wanting something from him." Such a statement has the kernel of what the patient might actually work toward saying to her husband, while at the same time acknowledging the anxiety and conflict that have prevented her from doing so thus far (and, in most such instances, from quite articulating it to herself in this way either). At the same time, it provides models of how the message could be communicated in a way that is more likely to be effective (emphasizing that her request derives from *liking* spending time with him) and of how it could be experienced negatively (emphasizing that he is letting her down, not treating her right, etc.).[8]

Essentially, this kind of statement by the therapist addresses the patient's not quite formulated inclination and aims both to make it clearer and more conscious and to help structure it in a way that will be interpersonally effective. Unlike more traditional interpretations, it does not aim at insight alone, but incorporates as a crucial element the necessity for effective interpersonal communication if one is to achieve gratification of one's wishes. In making an interpretive comment within the framework of assertiveness training, the therapist is concerned not just with helping the patient to be aware of what he is wanting or feeling, but also with helping him learn to give shape to his thoughts in an effective way. A central assumption is that the very inability to imagine *how* to express his thoughts in an appropriate way is a key element in maintaining the patient's ignorance of *what* his thoughts and feelings really are; it is (by the time one is an adult) the fear that one will say things in either a weak and hesitant way or a gross and hostile way that in very large measure is the operative anxiety motivating defenses. Combining interpretation with training in social effectiveness addresses the patient's anxieties on two complementary levels and

8. It is of course the case that sometimes it is necessary for the patient to be "tough," to call a spade a spade and state unequivocally that the other person is wrong, unfair, or the like. But generally the strategy most commonly used in assertiveness training is to begin with statements that give the other the benefit of the doubt and/or stress the *common* advantage of the behavior desired, holding in reserve the possibility of later asserting one's wishes more aggressively.

increases the likelihood of his feeling able to relinquish some of his defenses.

In the course of role playing, the therapist is able to help the patient anticipate problems that may arise in trying to interact differently with others. After the patient has gained some initial idea of how he would like to address some issue with another person, the therapist can then raise (or the patient may himself spontaneously raise) questions on the order of "What if your mother were to say such and such in response?" They can then go through various scenarios in the relative safety of the role-playing situation, where weak or foolish responses by the patient need not be the beginning of a disastrous unraveling, but simply the occasion for patient and therapist to "take it from the top," try to understand why the patient responded in that way, and consider alternative responses before trying the same scenario again. As the patient builds confidence and skills in this way, the twin sources of his inadequate responses (anxiety and the inexperience deriving from avoidance) are both addressed. He can enter an interpersonal encounter both better prepared and less likely to fall apart if he nonetheless fails to get the response from the other person he had been hoping for.

Paradox

As every therapist knows, such straightforward efforts to change for the better an individual's patterns of interaction with others are not always successful. In many instances, something else is required. Paradoxical interventions can be of great value in such instances, and can be utilized in a way that is quite compatible with a psychodynamic approach to individual psychotherapy. Paradoxical methods are, of course, very central in the work of many family therapists, but they are not exclusively associated with that orientation. They were a key innovation of Victor Frankl's (1959) logotherapy and are utilized not infrequently in the practice of behavior therapy (e.g., Chambless & Goldstein, 1980; Fay, 1978).

A major purpose for using paradox is to help the patient put aside efforts to make things better that themselves have had paradoxical consequences. Throughout this book, we have noted how an attempted solution to a problem may in time become a problem in its own right and/or keep the original problem going longer than it otherwise would.

Thus, on a simple level, "trying" to fall asleep will almost certainly result in wakefulness for the insomniac. Similarly, "forcing" oneself to make small talk may inadvertently increase one's feeling of social ineptness. Sometimes the most helpful thing the therapist can do is to ask the patient to do something that will interfere with his trying so hard. In many such instances, this specifically entails the use of paradox.

Paradoxical interventions can be introduced with varying degrees of collaboration between patient and therapist. Although at times therapists using paradox seem to evince an attitude of manipulation, deception, and acting upon the patient, there are a variety of ways of introducing a paradoxical task that embody a more collaborative attitude. Common to the more collaborative uses of paradox is an initial clear and frank discussion of the failure of efforts to interrupt the problematic behavior by straightforward efforts at "self-control" or "trying." It is made clear to the patient that the harder he tries to stop, the less success he seems to have. Once he understands this, he will be more receptive to the "crazy" or counterintuitive suggestion that the therapist may make.

In some instances, what may be stressed is the need for closer observation in order to understand what is causing the problematic behavior. If the patient can't seem to stop some troubling way of acting, the tack is taken that perhaps we can at least gain some useful information from this behavior. He is asked not to try to reduce the behavior, but to use it as an opportunity to observe.

Sometimes this is all that is suggested. That is, the patient is not particularly asked to increase the behavior (as in most other paradoxical interventions), but simply not to try to reduce it. Rather, he is to keep a list of each time the behavior occurs, what it feels like, and what was going on prior to its initiation. This accomplishes some of the same purposes as the more elaborate paradoxical methods—namely, giving the person something other to do than "trying," which has served him so poorly in the past. As Fisch, Weakland, and Segal (1982) have noted, it is almost impossible for people to simply "not do" something; they must have something else to do in its place. It is, of course, useful in its own right to observe carefully, and sometimes important clinical data emerge from this effort. But what makes it paradoxical is the expectation that keeping careful track of the behavior (and even valuing it as an opportunity to observe) very frequently results in a reduction of that same behavior.

This approach of simple substitution of observation can be particularly useful with procrastinators. Procrastination is a problem *par excellence* for some kinds of paradox; if there is anything procrastinators are good at, it is "trying," and anything that interrupts the continued cycle of preoccupied trying and preparing is a step in the right direction. Once a procrastinator has come to some recognition that further resolutions will be broken as readily as those in the past, he may be receptive to the idea of trying to understand the procrastination better by not trying to overcome it, but simply becoming aware of how it operates.

When a procrastinator is asked not to try to accomplish more in the day, but simply to record the various ways he wastes time and how long each of them takes, the usual set is broken. In principle, he could then procrastinate in this task too, planning to do a better job of recording tomorrow. But in our experience this is atypical. More commonly, one of two things happens. Sometimes this change of set leads simply to a reduction of the procrastination; the patient comes in reporting that there was little to observe this week, because he simply got his work done. On other occasions, the patient does come in with a list, and this too is valuable. First of all, it can provide him with better insight into just how he does go about wasting time and can, at least in a mild case, aid him in making more realistic efforts to overcome the procrastination. Moreover, it can help to pinpoint the anxieties and clarify just what it is that the person is avoiding. Sometimes an elaborate and undifferentiated pattern of procrastination is based on the avoidance of just one or two things. If these are properly identified, the person can either avoid them explicitly, without having to avoid a host of other things along the way, or can work to understand and overcome these more specific anxieties now that they have been identified more precisely.

Interestingly, making a list in the fashion just described can at times also be useful in making it clear to a person that he is not really a procrastinator at all, but rather someone who is overdemanding and perfectionistic. It can be rather startling to hear in detail what some "procrastinators" accomplish in a day. Their distress is not really due to putting things off per se, but to taking on too much and expecting to accomplish more than is humanly possible. Tracking their hourly activities in this kind of detail can help to make this clear.

For many patients, it does not seem sufficient simply to ask them to observe the problematic behavior; this request must be combined with a request that they *increase* the very behavior they wish to eliminate.

This is particularly the case where considerable anxiety is involved. Agoraphobics, for example, are so afraid of the anxiety they might encounter that they usually cannot just go forth and keep track of it. Oddly, though, they may be able to accomplish this if it is combined with the request that they increase the anxiety still further. The reason for this is probably that in the effort to increase the anxiety, they are putting themselves in a position of controlling it instead of being the passive victims, running constantly from an experience of which they are terrified.

With one patient, for example, who could not bring herself to venture even a step out of her house because of the severe anxiety she would experience, the therapist inquired into just how bad the anxiety would be. When she indicated that even one step out of the door would be at a level of 50 on a scale of 0–100, the therapist asked whether it would be possible for her to try to increase it to 60 or 70 so that he could study it better. When she came to the next session, she was apologetic about her "failure" to accomplish the assigned task. Hard as she had tried, she could not get her anxiety above 20. She seemed to have no insight into the implications of this, evincing clear embarrassment at her inability to follow the therapist's directive.

The therapist gave no indication of the humor in her dilemma and simply suggested that perhaps if she ventured further next time, she might be able to achieve the requisite level of anxiety. By means of this procedure, she was before long taking two buses by herself to come to the therapist's office. (Previously she had not been able to go anywhere without being accompanied.) It seemed to come as a great shock to her when one day, toward the end of this series, she said, "My God, maybe I'm cured."[9]

With more sophisticated patients with a greater degree of reflectiveness, it is often useful to introduce paradoxical methods with some discussion of the complexities of control. The general thrust of such discussions is that the patient has had little success in trying to prevent the unwanted behavior from occurring altogether; in continually *trying* to prevent it, he has always been in the position of running away and

9. The treatment included other elements as well, including, very centrally, both psychodynamic exploration and assertiveness training. It will probably be no surprise to the reader that (the genuineness of the patient's fear notwithstanding) the requirement that she always be accompanied, and her inability to do any chores that required her to go out of the house by herself, served some function in the struggle for control between her and her husband. When she could be more directly and effectively assertive, the need for this more indirect and passive form of achieving some kind of parity was diminished.

being caught from behind, as it were. When he intentionally engages in it, at least it is in his control: If he can't not be anxious or not procrastinate or not bite his nails or whatever, at least he can *decide* to do it instead of berating himself or fearfully waiting for the other shoe to fall. And at the same time, this intentional engaging in the behavior provides an opportunity to observe it and understand it better.

In large measure, such a message is straightforward. What makes it paradoxical is the hope that this very effort to produce the behavior intentionally *will* in fact diminish it in a way that *trying* to diminish it will not; and, further, that in order for this to happen, the patient must not be thinking that he is doing it for this reason. This means that a key element of what is being attempted must essentially remain unspoken. The structure of the situation thus requires the cultivation of a kind of double consciousness, in which the patient both knows and doesn't know at the same time.

Paradoxical interventions can also alter the personal significance of a patient's symptoms and the structure of motives that sustains them. Roger, for example, had failed in every effort at slowing down or altering his "Type A" behavior. His strategy for altering this pattern had been to try to do less, to try to relax, and so forth; neither his unaided efforts nor efforts with other therapists, including traditional insight therapy, the introduction of relaxation, meditation, and other techniques, had seemed to help. Finally he was instructed to *increase* his running around, to spend even less time at home and sleep even less. In his case, a central motivation of this behavior had been that he experienced it as manly. When it became part of an assignment, something that he was doing to please the therapist, it made him feel too much like a "good little boy," and it quickly lost its allure. He soon found himself spending an unaccustomed amount of time relaxing or "hanging out." (Naturally, the complex motives for Roger's behavior were also explored, along with their other ramifications in his life.)

Types of Paradox

Weeks and L'Abate (1982) have attempted to organize and describe the various ways in which paradox can be used. They distinguish between paradoxes directed at the individual level and those directed at the system. Either kind of paradox can take two forms—"prescriptive" or "descriptive." Prescriptive paradoxes ask the patient to do something. Descriptive paradoxes, on the other hand, simply describe what the person is doing and relabel it as positive. For example, with an excessively self-observant patient, a prescriptive paradox might ask him to take detailed notes on what he observes and to make sure he has at least 25 items on the list. A descriptive paradox might simply indicate to the patient that there is something very useful in his ability to observe himself in detail, leaving it to the patient to represent the side of change. In such instances, the patient is in effect given a clear field to take a stand on the change-oriented side of his ambivalence, which has theretofore been undermined by people's efforts to "talk him out of" his bad habits.

Paradoxes directed at the individual level involve the patient's attempted solutions to what he perceives to be his *own* problem. For example, a patient who tries to hide his anxiety may be asked to reveal rather than hide his symptom. Watzlawick *et al.* (1974) call this type of paradox "revealing rather than concealing." A similar approach is used for symptoms that the patient experiences as uncontrollable, such as compulsions, tics, or bed-wetting, where the patient is asked to do precisely what he has been trying so hard to stop doing.

These individually oriented paradoxical prescriptions need not be exclusively focused on overt behaviors. We have found it useful to use paradoxical prescriptions for defensive avoidances as well. Russell, for example, was perplexed and bothered by his inability to stick with his sculpture, a hobby that he thought gave him great satisfaction. He would work on the sculpture for a few days and then not touch it for months. When the causes and meanings behind this repeated sudden loss of interest were explored, it became clear that working on his sculpture stirred in Russell sensual feelings and desires for a wilder, more Bohemian life that were very threatening to him. Insight into the reasons behind his avoidance seemed to have little impact, however, and the pattern of avoidance, coupled with frustration and self-deprecation over his failure to follow through, continued. Moreover, his avoidance prevented him from having an opportunity to work through the distressing feelings.[10]

---

10. These feelings were not, of course, exclusively associated with sculpting. The conflict was one that played a role in much of his life. But the sculpting was a useful focus, both because it was a matter of great concern to the patient himself and because it did provide an opportunity to flush out, as it were, the threatening inclinations and affects and to introduce the possibility of working them through.

Consequently, it was suggested to Russell that since he seemed to have difficulty handling the emotional distress involved in sculpting, perhaps it would be best if he did not pursue this hobby. Although the comment was stated in a sympathetic manner, it was expected, based on what the therapist knew about him, that Russell might well hear it as essentially conveying the message, "I don't think you can handle this, and I think you'll just have to resign yourself to the fact that sculpting is something your particular psychological makeup will not allow you to do." This was a message he was likely to resist.

As expected, the therapist's apparent stand on one side of Russell's ambivalence strengthened the desire to sculpt, which stood in opposition to his wish to avoid upsetting thoughts and feelings. In line with the importance of following through on paradoxical interventions (see below), when Russell insisted that he did want to sculpt even if it meant facing distressing issues, the therapist issued a descriptive paradox by saying, "You will know it's too distressing for you if you find yourself bored after a day or two of sculpting." Russell did in fact begin to stick more with his sculpting, and this enabled the therapy to address more fully and focally the feelings that had lain behind his avoidance.

The case of Russell illustrates the use of paradox with what might be thought of as an intrapsychic conflict. Another example of this is the case of Sally, who could not tolerate what she experienced as grandiose feelings. Days when she felt particularly proud of herself were always followed by self-inflicted scathing attacks and eating binges that left her feeling disgusted with herself. Interpretive efforts to address Sally's strong need to punish herself for thinking she was special seemed largely ineffective. Finally, she was told that perhaps the best thing she could do at this point was not to go against her "psychology," but rather to put this pattern more within her control by consciously and intentionally being self-critical rather than allowing it to just overcome her. "Now that we have seen how your problems are related to feelings of success and 'grandiose' fantasies of achievement, it would be best to engage in a kind of prophylactic 'self-criticism session' whenever you feel particularly good about yourself." The patient was perplexed by this suggestion, but said she "sort of" followed the logic and would try to do it. As was hoped, she found it very hard to binge or be self-critical *on demand*.

This strategy of asking the patient to intentionally bring on the very behavior that distresses him has wide applicability and can be understood in a rather straightforward way as well as in terms of paradox. It has considerable overlap with notions of stimulus control and scheduling, which are used frequently by behavior therapists. Frequently, when a patient is struggling with some behavior that he cannot seem to help, we ask him whether he could choose a particular time and place to do it. Sometimes this is done with paradoxical overtones, but at other times it is explained to the patient as a way of giving the behavior a particular (and restricted) role in his life rather than being a pervasive presence throughout his waking hours.

One patient, Cal, who was plagued by reveries about his supposed failures that were frequent unbidden companions, was asked whether he could clear the time from 6:00 to 6:30 P.M. each day for an undistracted and concentrated session of self-deprecation. If such thoughts occurred to him at other times of the day, he should not try to banish them altogether or to try to counter them in the manner of a defense attorney on his behalf as he usually did, but simply to tell himself that this would be good material to develop that evening. He was encouraged to be as unfairly and savagely critical of himself during those half-hour sessions as he could possibly be.

Although there was a good deal of confused laughter on Cal's part when this was first discussed, and the whole communication between patient and therapist was laden with ambiguity and paradox, the final rationale, after Cal saw that the therapist was serious about this, was rather straightforward: Cal really seemed unable at this point simply to stop these reveries, but perhaps they could at least be contained. If he knew that he had a time and place for them, that they would get their due, it would be easier, if not to eliminate them altogether, at least to postpone them until their "proper" time. It was essential that Cal really carry through on the self-criticism at the appointed time and that it always take place in the same location as well (thus associating it not just with a particular time, but with a particular place as well—and thereby, the therapist hoped, cutting its links to other times and places).

Cal found that, in contrast to the failure of his earlier efforts to "stop" thinking such thoughts or to tell himself he was being unrealistic, he could in fact postpone the accusatory reveries to the appointed time. Some measure of "stimulus control" was thus achieved. But he found as well that his bottomless pit of self-loathing tended to run dry when he had to make a deliberate effort to berate himself. Moreover, he found himself laughing at what he was doing, and reported that he gained a kind of perspective in doing this that all the years of trying to argue himself out of being so self-critical had not provided.

This kind of approach is a first cousin of the fairly common approach to problems of insomnia, in which the patient is requested not to lie in bed "trying" to fall asleep. As soon as he finds he is having difficulty in sleeping, he is to get up and go into another room to be awake. Only if he feels rather sleepy is he to go back to bed, and if he again finds himself lying awake he is to get up once more. In this way the bed becomes a place for sleeping rather than, as it has become, a place for lying awake and feeling distressed. This approach to insomnia does not incorporate as many complexly overlapping perspectives as some of the other examples cited, but it helps to highlight the aspect of stimulus control that is so often an element of paradoxical procedures.

Paradoxical prescriptions can readily be employed in addressing interactional dynamics as well as intrapsychic ones. A patient might be told, for instance, that he should find something to criticize in his wife whenever they have had an unusually close time with each other, since closeness seems otherwise difficult for him to tolerate; straightforward closeness without the criticism might produce withdrawal symptoms. In response to such a directive, the patient's critical feelings, which have previously felt spontaneous and have effectively substituted despair over his poor choice of mate for the earlier affectionate feelings that rapidly faded from awareness, can begin to seem absurd and to be *experienced* as a defensive maneuver in response to feelings of closeness. Humor and insight are thereby brought to bear on a pattern that has been pursued with blind and deadly seriousness.

Sticking with Paradox

Many therapists make a paradoxical intervention, but then do not continue with it once it has worked. If a patient comes in and says, "I couldn't get myself to be depressed," or "I didn't react the way you thought I would when my mother expressed disappointment," the therapist should not abruptly reverse himself by being pleased or congratulatory. Too rapid relinquishing of the paradoxical stance may lead to a reversal of the progress by the next session.

Maintaining the paradox is often very difficult to do, but it is an essential aspect of this technique. The aim is to help the patient maintain the new behavior (even if by artificial means) long enough so that a self-sustaining corrective cycle has a chance to take hold. Generally, it takes some time for the consequences of changed behavior to be noticeable to patients. The therapist can facilitate the patient's noticing of new reactions in response to his changes by asking questions about other people's reactions to this unexpected behavior on the patient's part.

In working to sustain the paradoxical situation for a time, it is essential that the therapist not immediately indicate pleasure at the change reflected in the patient's "failure" to produce the behavior about which he has for so long complained. An ambiguous response or an expression of surprise and bewilderment are usually more useful. If the therapist, for example, has prescribed a particular symptom and the patient has not done what was prescribed (e.g., has maintained a good mood or has not berated himself for the entire week), the therapist could say, "I'm glad that you felt better, but I am concerned about your not having followed through with what we talked about. I still think it's really important that you take control by making the symptom happen."

If the patient has performed the task but says that he really had difficulty doing it (i.e., couldn't readily produce his usual symptom) or doesn't think it's necessary, the therapist can emphasize the importance of moving slowly. The task should be modified, but not totally abandoned. When finally it is no longer possible to maintain the paradox, the therapist can admit that things don't seem to be happening the way he expected, but he's not really sure why.

Reversals: Teaching Patients to Use Paradox Themselves

Patients often describe situations with important people in their lives that leave them feeling frustrated and at a loss as to what to do to alleviate the difficulty. For instance, a woman may feel upset because her husband is going through a midlife crisis and mopes around the house in his underwear. Or a parent may be locked in a power struggle with an adolescent in which the parent behaves in ways he later regrets. Often, exploring patients' feelings about the others' behavior with a view toward helping them see what they may be contributing to these situations does not seem to be enough.

Fisch *et al.* (1982) have pointed out that frequently it is insufficient (even if it is possible) simply to stop performing one's part in an interaction; the absence of old behavior patterns may not be noticed by the other party to the transaction. In such instances, adopting a role opposite to the one generally assumed often has the effect of disrupting the entrenched pattern, thereby allowing new interactions to occur. In the family therapy literature, this is called "reversal."

In one case where this approach was tried, Mrs. Daniels was at a loss to know how to deal with her adolescent daughter, who from time to time became despondent and withdrawn. It was clear to both the therapist and the patient that she had a low tolerance for depression in those with whom she was close, and that these feelings stemmed from her own need to ward off dysphoric feelings. She found it very difficult, however, to change this typical pattern of response to her daughter's behavior. Acutely bothered by her daughter's melancholy mood, she would try hard, to no avail, to cheer her up. Then, feeling that she would be neglectful simply to ignore her daughter, she would try instead to be stern and assertive about how her daughter's withdrawal displeased her. This only resulted in further withdrawal and sulkiness. Frustrated as well as worried about her daughter's mental state, Mrs. Daniels very much wanted some advice about what she should do.

It was suggested that she explore the situation further by trying out paradoxical role reversals. For instance, when Mrs. Daniels noticed that her daughter was starting to mope, she might lie down on the couch and stare into space. If asked about this behavior, she could say she was in a bad mood and didn't feel much like doing anything. This would be such uncharacteristic behavior for this energetic, action-oriented woman that it would be likely to catch the attention of her daughter. Whenever her daughter was in a bad mood, she could adopt some variation of this approach. The point was not simply to stop trying to cheer the daughter up, but to allow the daughter to be in the position of the consoling, more cheerful and active party.

In another case, Marla K complained that when she visited her family, her mother heaped food on her plate despite her protests and insisted that she take home bags of groceries and other household goods. Distressed by the fact that her mother spent all her nonworking time cleaning and cooking, and wore a ragged housecoat at home even when she came to dinner, Marla had tried for a long time to convince her mother that it was not necessary for her to fuss over her so much.

For years Marla had also been upset by the constricted way her parents lived, despite the fact that they had plenty of money. She would try to get them to go to good restaurants and would buy them tickets to plays, which they would reluctantly and unenthusiastically attend. It seemed that the more she tried, the more they asserted that they were simple people who liked living the way they did. Though she had by now given up her attempt at cultural conversion, she still found it almost impossible to visit her parents without becoming infuriated by her mother's mixture of subservience and overbearingness. Annoyed by her mother's gifts of underwear, toilet paper, and cans of tuna, Marla would protest and rage against this behavior but would in the end relent.

Suggestions that Marla try being more assertive were met with resistance. She felt that her attempts at assertiveness in the past (e.g., throwing the food in the garbage, threatening not to visit) had only made matters worse.[11] The therapist noted that, except with her parents, Marla was adept at using humor to defuse tense situations, and wondered out loud what would happen if Marla stopped resisting her mother's behavior but instead became more demanding. Perhaps she could ask why her mother had made so little food or request something that she had not already prepared. When mother gave Marla bags of groceries, she could criticize her choice of items and tell her to buy higher-quality items in the future. Instead of the elegant gifts she brought, Marla could bring socks and unattractive but serviceable housecoats. The hope, of course, was that her mother would be taken aback by such behavior and would in turn relent in her "giving."

In utilizing this kind of approach, at times we have noticed some interesting reactions not usually described in the strategic therapy literature. For one, many patients find the very thought of such outrageous behavior a relief. Once they are thinking along the lines of "reversals," they recall instances where they spontaneously behaved in an uncharacteristic way, with a surprisingly beneficial outcome. For instance, one woman remembered that when she was unusually disorganized for some reason, her teenage son behaved in a surprisingly

11. Such behavior is not, of course, what the proponent of assertiveness training would describe as "assertive." Patients often confuse behavior deriving from impotent rage with assertiveness. This is one of the differentiations that they must learn if assertiveness training is to be effective.

responsible manner. Or a man who generally felt he had to give pep talks to his anxious wife, and resented this state of affairs, recalled that the roles were reversed on one occasion when he was feeling uncharacteristically depressed. We have been surprised at how readily people recognize the validity of what we are proposing. Once they get the idea, they not only remember instances when it happened spontaneously, but offer their own creative embellishments on role reversals.[12]

We have observed as well that sometimes simply discussing the option of reversing roles seems to have a therapeutic effect in itself, regardless of whether the plan is actually carried out. This first became apparent when we noticed that some patients did not follow through on the plan, even when they seemingly wholeheartedly and enthusiastically endorsed the idea. Sometimes this lack of follow-through may be the result of anxiety about changing roles that have served some purpose, or it may derive from fear of negative consequences that has not been stilled by the therapist's explanation of the paradoxical effect of role reversals. But in a number of instances among our patients, what became apparent was that they did not do what was planned because the situation seemed to change spontaneously and they therefore didn't have an opportunity to put it into effect. Further inquiry into this curious state of affairs revealed that though the patients did not enact the elaborate reversals planned in the therapy session, they did put the idea into practice in more modest ways.

For instance, Mrs. Daniels, described above, who always worked hard to get her daughter out of states of withdrawal, did not actually lie down and complain about depression as planned. She did, however, modify her behavior toward her daughter in other ways. Where she had previously encouraged her to get out and have fun, she now made no attempts to force her to have a good time, and even went so far as to suggest on occasion that it would be best if she stayed home and did her homework. Perhaps it is small changes like this, the modest residue of more elaborate plans, that cause the seemingly spontaneous amelioration of the difficulties. Or perhaps the patient is responding differently in ways that are extremely subtle and hard to identify, simply because he feels he has options if he chooses to use them. The

12. The discussion between therapist and patient concerning a planned reversal frequently tends to be quite humorous. It is important, however, that the actual performance of the reversals be undertaken with as much seriousness as the patient can muster.

humorous scenario in his head may give him enough distance from the immediate situation that he can subtly alter his response and thereby break the cycle.

Many patients are concerned that the person they are trying this new tack with will "catch on." Actually, there are some situations in which it would not matter, and perhaps would even be beneficial, if the recipient of the new behavior had a sense of the irony in what was taking place. Particularly in a case where the other person has a good sense of humor, he may finally "understand" when roles are reversed. Generally, however, it is better if the patient can be subtle enough so that the other person experiences the new behavior as genuine.

Often patients will experience such behavior as "deceptive" or "phony" and may feel unable to carry out the role. For this reason, it is important to explore with the patient what role reversals will feel most genuine. By and large, the reason such a course of action can work is that the participants in a system frequently divide up between or among themselves the various possible affects and attitudes, each expressing for another the side of himself that is being denied. One is optimistic and the other pessimistic; one is impulsive and the other is cautious; and so forth. If the patient can be helped to appreciate this, at least to some degree, the behavior acted out in a role may be recognized as not quite as phony as it initially felt. Indeed, acting out a "contrived" role in this way can at times be an effective way for the patient to begin to get more in touch with a side of himself he has tended to deny and avoid.

It is important for the therapist to get a clear sense of exactly what the patient intends to say and do. Often patients will misunderstand and think that they should act in a hostile and sarcastic manner. Though their words may now be different, such a manner can easily be perceived by the other as "more of the same" rather than as a true reversal of position. For example, a suggestion by the therapist that the patient say something like "I wish you'd do my shopping for me" (in the case of someone who has always resented his mother's offer of help) might be processed by the patient as suggesting a sarcastic statement like "Why don't you do my shopping for me, too, while you're at it?" The therapist may think the patient has gotten the idea, but only with a concrete example of what the patient plans to say can the therapist be sure that the paradoxical nature of the role reversal has really been absorbed.

Resistance and Paradox

Though anxiety underlies all resistance, resistance manifests itself in many forms, and often the patient's anxiety is not at all apparent. One form of resistance that is quite difficult to work with is what might be called "oppositional" or "negativistic" resistance; no matter what the therapist says, the patient finds a way to devalue and dismiss its import. We have all had the experience of having a patient talk about all the previous therapists who have not been able to help. Though the patient may profess to be discouraged and frustrated by this experience, one readily can detect a sense of pride in being able to stump the experts. Dealing with this kind of resistance through interpretations or analysis of the transference often proves to be futile; no matter how the interpretation is worded, the therapist is still behaving as the patient expects, in that the very act of interpreting or explaining the patient's behavior implicitly communicates the expectation that perhaps with *this* understanding the patient will be able to let therapy help. Though anxiety underlies the patient's negativism, the interpersonal form the resistance takes poses a serious therapeutic problem.

It is extremely difficult to help the patient with his anxiety or to create a safe environment for the patient to explore and master his fears unless his initial negativism can be temporarily put aside. We have found that patients can only really hear interpretations regarding their oppositional resistance during those periods when they are not actually behaving that way. For this reason, it is frequently useful with these very resistant patients for the therapist to take care not to play the expected role.

It is now common knowledge among family therapists that there is little to be gained by "pursuing a distancer" (Fogarty, 1979), whether the pursuer be the spouse or the therapist. Watzlawick *et al.* (1974) give a number of examples of the therapist's taking the paradoxical role of the pessimist. Thus, if a patient states that he is unhappy but doesn't seem to be able to change, the therapist might reflect aloud that perhaps it may be just as well if he doesn't change; there must be something important about the unwanted behavior, or it would not have persisted so long. The therapist might point out particular benefits in the patient's way of being and question whether it would make sense to change. It seems that with resistance that manifests itself in oppositional behavior, it is frequently better to avoid being encouraging or seeming too unambiguously an agent of change.

Certainly part of the effectiveness of this approach with oppositional patients is that it harnesses their oppositionalism in the service of change instead of its being in opposition to change as it was previously. It might therefore be argued that this strategy does not really address the oppositionalism but leaves it intact, merely finding another direction for the person's infantile reactive behavior. The thinking behind the approach described here, however, is that by the very nature of the new ways of thinking and relating that the patient's oppositionalism now drives him into, he will encounter experiences of a sort he has consistently managed to avoid, and will therefore for the first time have a chance genuinely to grow and change. It is these experiences, however much they may have originally been brought about merely as the result of his oppositional tendencies, that can eventually help to modify those very tendencies.

The effectiveness of pessimistic statements by the therapist in such cases can also be understood in another way that is in a sense more straightforward. Even if the patient doesn't reactively oppose them, the statements can reduce his anxiety about the imminence of change, and can thereby help him to be less oppositional. Statements by the therapist such as "I think change should be slow," or "It's not necessary or wise to change too much just yet," help alleviate the patient's anxiety.

It is important to note that paradoxical statements aimed at utilizing negative motivation and resistance to the therapist are not appropriate with most patients. Most patients do not "resist" the therapist. When they spin their wheels and do not seem to progress, it is not because they do not want to conform or to give the therapist the satisfaction of having helped them, but because they feel afraid or feel they do not have the skills they need to behave differently. Patients are often profoundly ambivalent about change. They are unhappy with the status quo, but fear the unknown prospects change may bring. Many of the interventions described earlier in this chapter are aimed at diminishing some of the anxiety and thus at helping the patient resolve some of this ambivalence.

Even with these essentially nonoppositional patients, there are times when a paradoxical communication can be useful. The aim in such cases, however, is not to harness the patient's reactive negativism, but rather to help him resolve his ambivalence. In these instances, the therapist temporarily comes out in favor of the status quo; however, the paradoxical antichange message is directed not at the interpersonal level (the patient's oppositionalism vis-à-vis the therapist), but rather at the intrapsychic conflict that is hampering the patient's efforts to change. The aim is to create an imbalance in the internalized conflict so that the patient gets unstuck.

The paradoxical approach to resistance is sometimes discussed in terms of "joining the resistance." The term derives from the observation that sometimes direct efforts to interpret resistances are ineffective, whereas the therapist's apparent acceptance, or even welcoming, of the resistance seems to undermine the resistive tendency.

Suppose, for example, that the therapist interprets the patient's desire to cut down the frequency of his sessions as a form of resistance to some feeling that is arising in the sessions. Not infrequently in such circumstances, the patient states that he understands and accepts the interpretation, but still feels that his desire to cut down on sessions is valid and is based on other factors as well. Understanding does not seem to affect the desire. Indeed, by opposing the patient's wish,[13] the therapist inadvertently strengthens the resistance.

If instead, the therapist *joins with* the patient's conscious wishes, the patient is no longer engaged in a struggle with external opposition and may be more likely to face his own ambivalence. Without supporting something he doesn't believe in, the therapist can nonetheless still say, "I think your desire to stop may be based in part on a need to withdraw from the feelings evoked in these sessions, but even if that is the case, perhaps you need some distance." In saying this, the therapist is not accepting the patient's explanation; yet his communications no longer seem to have the implication of telling the patient not to do something.

Having witnessed innumerable power struggles between family members, family therapists are perhaps more aware than others that one cannot win in such an encounter. Joining with the resistance is but one of many ways to avoid getting into fruitless power struggles. Other ways include taking a "one-down position" (e.g., "I may be off the mark here, but . . . "); preempting the patient's criticism ("This will sound ridiculous"); admitting one's powerlessness ("I probably won't be able to convince you, but . . . "); or being confused (e.g., "I'm not sure what is going on here"). Such stances by the therapist make it much less likely that the nature of the engagement between patient

13. Usually the therapist does not *directly* or *explicitly* oppose the patient's wish; his official stance, as it were, is one of neutrality, of simply observing what is going on and leaving it up to the patient how he will make use of the observation. But it does not take an extraordinarily perceptive patient to sense that the typical interpretation has the implication that he should therefore continue with the present number of sessions, however much the therapist claims to disavow such an intent to persuade.

and therapist will be one that elicits a direct clash of wills. Subtle struggles will of course continue, and can be dealt with like any other transference manifestations. But some of the grosser difficulties in communication—the sort that make it virtually impossible for the patient to "hear" the therapist at all—can be diminished considerably.

Predicting a Relapse

Most patients change by taking two steps forward and one step backward. They revert to old patterns, both because of the pull of the system and because anxiety tends to recur spontaneously with time and lack of continuity of exposure to the source of discomfort. Predicting a relapse is a family therapy technique that is very effective in dealing with this fact of life in therapeutic work.

There are several ways to utilize this approach. One way that we find particularly effective is to ask the patient to think about what events, behaviors, or circumstances might lead him to relapse into old interactional patterns. We assist in his speculations by suggesting some hypothetical situations that we sense might evoke conflicts that have only recently been resolved.

One young woman, Mary Ann, had recently begun to separate from her mother. She had recognized how anxious and guilty she felt when she acted in a way that made her mother feel disappointed or sad, and had begun to find ways nonetheless to develop her independence and live more expansively. The therapist had explored her feelings on three fronts: the intrapsychic, the interpersonal (what went on between mother and daughter), and the systemic (the role of the mother–daughter interaction in the larger system). In trying to ferret out what might contribute to a relapse, it was important to consider possible causes from all three perspectives.

To begin with, the therapist asked Mary Ann to imagine herself becoming very anxious about her separateness from her mother. How would she attempt to relieve that anxiety? Would she start a fight with her boyfriend? Would she placate her mother? What would make her feel anxious? What if her mother didn't call her? What if her mother was cold? How might the other family members induce her to return to her old role vis-à-vis her mother? What if her father told her that her mother had been depressed lately? What kinds of changes in the family system might reevoke the old patterns? What if her parents began to argue a lot? What if her brother left home? What would happen when her grandmother died?

Exploring such possibilities as these concretizes the factors that could lead to relapse, and it leaves the patient forewarned. The therapist can go a step further and ask the patient what he thinks might help prevent a return to the old pattern. "What could you do when you are feeling anxious? Would it help to speak to a friend? Would it help to remind yourself of what is triggering the anxiety?"

This way of proceeding is straightforward and collaborative. Operating on the assumption that forewarned is forearmed, the therapist's stance is that slippage is possible but by no means inevitable. One must be careful, however, not to make the patient feel that he will have failed if he succumbs to his anxiety or to the pull of the system. Thus, while exploring possible ways to prevent a relapse, the therapist must also communicate that relapses are to be expected as part of the process, and that their occurrence should not be taken as an indication that no progress has been made.

With some patients, particularly those who seem to respond well to paradox, the possibility of relapse can be addressed via paradoxical directives. If the therapist thinks that a relapse is likely, he might ask the patient to relapse on purpose. He might say, for example, "It's important for change to be slow if it is to be really solid. I'm concerned that you are changing too rapidly. I'd like you to force yourself to behave and feel just the way you used to, so that we have more of a chance to fully observe and understand what has been going on." Or the therapist might say that relapses are not uncommon and that the best way for the patient to deal with this possibility is to put it within his own control by making it happen rather than passively letting it happen to him. The patient might be asked to take control by setting aside time each day in which he will think about upsetting things and/ or produce his former symptom on cue. The responses to such suggestions by the therapist, and the ways in which they in fact help secure a more enduring change, are similar to those discussed above for other uses of paradox.

Reframing, Relabeling, and Positive Connotation

Traditional psychodynamic therapies center on interpretations designed to reintroduce the patient to aspects of himself that he has been unable to accept. Interpretations are aimed at elucidating to the patient the "truth" about himself, and usually this truth is at least subjectively an unpleasant one. Family therapists tend to have a more relativistic notion of truth, emphasizing that experiences can be interpreted in a variety of ways and that each of these interpretations has consequences. Many of the difficulties patients encounter derive from the significance they give to actions and events, and often the path to a solution lies in seeing a different meaning with different implications.

To be sure, it often is necessary for the patient to face unpleasant truths about his personality, the warding off of which has distorted his development. And frequently, with the reexamination that becomes possible when the "unacceptable" is looked at more closely, the reality is revealed as far more complex than it seemed when desperate emergency measures were undertaken to cast out the offending thought or feeling; it turns out that the rejected impulse can, with some modification, find a respectable place in the economy of the personality. Nonetheless, there is a weighting toward the negative in much therapeutic work that is far from optimal for the promotion of growth and change.

Here the methods and perspectives of the family therapist can make a very useful contribution. A proclivity to build on positive factors wherever possible is a distinguishing feature of the work of many family therapists and is evident in a wide range of interventions and formulations. Reframing, relabeling, and positive connotation are closely related methods based on the foregoing considerations. They often have a form similar to interpretations, but are designed to induce the patient to take a different perspective on the interpersonal events in which he participates—usually one in which either he or the other person (or both) are seen in a more positive light.

The aim here is not a simple Pollyanna-ish denial flying in the face of reality. Rather, this approach is rooted in a pragmatic view of interpersonal reality that recognizes many possible ways of making sense out of the events that transpire between people. What gets people into trouble is not so much that they operate on a false rather than a true picture of interpersonal events, but that, from the variety of partially true constructions that can be achieved (partial truths being the best we can hope to achieve in this complex and imperfect world), they have chosen those that keep their problems going. What is sought is not a superficial gloss, but a version of the truth that works better.

Familiar images, such as the blind man describing the elephant or the glass that can be seen as half full or half empty, convey the vision that underlies the use of reframing techniques. Watzlawick *et al.* (1974), for example, argue that we never deal with reality but only with images of reality, and that it is the nature of the particular images we employ that determines potential solutions (or failures of solution) to our problems.

Frequently, reframing is employed in helping the patient to develop a different perspective on the behavior of a key other in his life. Such a change in perspective can be crucial in enabling him to behave differently toward the other person, and thereby to break the circular pattern in which they are both enmeshed.

Mrs. R, for example, was an overintrusive mother who continually provoked rebellious behavior in her teenage son. Recently, this behavior had become more extreme and dangerous. In typical circular fashion, this behavior confirmed for Mrs. R that her son was "still a child" and required still further questioning, supervision, and limit setting way beyond the norm for his age; predictably, this response on her part provoked further extreme behavior on the part of her son. Mrs. R was extremely distraught by this state of affairs, but had little understanding of her role in her son's behavior. Her response to beginning exploration of the pattern made it clear that she had enormous resistance to seeing her son's behavior in interactional terms. It was also clear that some fairly immediate change was necessary, because the son's behavior was becoming increasingly reckless, presenting risks of brushes with the law or of a serious accident.

Direct recognition of her role in provoking her son's behavior and of her overintrusiveness in the affairs of both of her children was too threatening for Mrs. R to tolerate. The pattern was therefore addressed via reframing. The therapist said to Mrs. R something like the following: "I can appreciate the conflict you are feeling. You want to treat your son like a maturing person who is almost an adult, yet you feel it would not be responsible to give him too much autonomy, given the way he acts. But I think much of the reason that he acts that way is that somehow he seems to think that you need him to remain a child. For some reason, he seems to need more evidence than other teenagers do that you will not be upset by the loss of your little boy and can truly tolerate his growing autonomy. What could you do to make this really vivid to him, to make him understand that you don't need him to remain a child and that you really are ready to see him grow up?"

There then ensued a detailed discussion of ways in which Mrs. R could demonstrate this to her son. As much as possible, the therapist encouraged Mrs. R to generate her own ideas about how to behave uncharacteristically, so that her son would really get the message that she was ready to let him grow up. The reframing of the situation provided a rubric for promoting not only the cessation of the repetitively destructive intrusive behavior, but also an experimentation with behavior that would be a dramatic reversal of what the boy had come to expect.[14] Together, patient and therapist considered various ideas on how to convince the son by actions that it was permissible for him to grow up. Mrs. R's going out without leaving a phone number where she could be reached in case of emergency, "forgetting" to plan and discuss what was available for dinner, and going to sleep before the boy came home were all behaviors that made sense in this new framework and were conspicuous departures from her previous behavior.

The sources of Mrs. R's behavior toward her son, the fantasies and unfulfilled expectations that led her to initiate this pattern in the first place, remained to be explored and needed to be. But in a rapidly and dangerously escalating situation, it was necessary to find a way to break the cycle of interaction; an approach that attempted to achieve this through direct insight into Mrs. R's role in the pattern and what lay behind it would very likely have permitted the situation to get much worse before (possibly) she gained sufficient insight. Indeed, the increasing seriousness of the impasse was itself becoming a factor working against her feeling any way of accepting a full picture of the pattern in which she was participating and the needs that lay behind it without a grave threat to her self-esteem.

In considering the intervention just described, a few features are worth noting. To begin with, we may highlight the fact that in presenting the reframing, the therapist did not simply direct the patient. In *asking* what could be done to persuade the son that she was really able to tolerate his growing up, the therapist encouraged Mrs. R's active participation. She was stimulated to learn to generate new progressive behaviors, and the ideas and actions promoted were ones that felt comfortable to the patient and conformed to her personal style. Putting even the explicit suggestions in the form of questions ("How do you think your son would react if you . . . ?") further placed the patient in the role of an active collaborator, who had the ultimate decision

14. Fisch *et al.* (1982) make the point that it is difficult to suggest that someone stop doing something without giving that peson some *new* behavior that will actively replace the old. Moreover, the *absence* of behavior is less likely to be noticed by significant others than the occurrence of new behavior.

about whether to adopt a particular behavior, and who was encouraged to view the therapist's suggestions as a coparticipation in a kind of brainstorming session rather than as an authoritative directive.

It is also worth noting that the intervention was framed in a way that resonated with the patient's perception of the situation and communicated an empathic appreciation of her experience. Though there was certainly more to the pattern than the therapist indicated in his communication, the statement about feeling a conflict between wanting to let her son grow up and feeling his behavior didn't permit her to do so did accurately express her conscious experience, and even helped articulate that experience a bit more clearly. To be sure, Mrs. R was in fact (at least as the therapist viewed it) considerably more *ambivalent* about letting her son grow up than the simple statement "You want to treat your son as a maturing person . . ." expressed. But she was not ready to accept that ambivalence consciously, and the therapist's statement accurately addressed her phenomenological experience at the same time that it prepared the ground for a strategic intervention.

Moreover, it is important to recognize that the more conscious side of the ambivalence was not just a defensive facade. To be sure, it represented the side of Mrs. R's feelings that she was more comfortable with, and there was a definite (indeed strong) element of defense in her conscious disavowal of the other side. But it is in the very nature of conflict that *both* sides represent real strivings and inclinations. Speaking to one side of the ambivalence in Mrs. R's case gave the patient the benefit of the doubt, as it were, addressing the aspect of herself that she wished to affirm and that was more progressive.

Within the overall context of any therapy, it is important to communicate that the other side is seen and accepted as well; the patient needs to be helped to explore and understand the sources of his or her less socially acceptable and less conscious inclinations, and this cannot be achieved if the patient feels that the therapist's interest and support are contingent on only showing one's "nice" side. But in helping the patient to construe his or her behavior more positively, the therapist is helping to affirm shaky self-esteem and lay the groundwork for a more thoroughgoing reworking, organized around the patient's more progressive inclinations.

A related reframing was utilized in the case of Mrs. W, who had difficulty permitting her teenage daughter to express any complaints, and who also ended up thereby sowing the seeds of the very rebelliousness and unpleasantness she wanted so desperately to avoid. In her case, the therapist pointed out (accurately) that Mrs. W experienced her daughter's complaints as reflecting poorly on her parenting (a good parent would be above reproach, and her children would "respect" her and not criticize her). The complaints could be viewed very differently, however. They could be seen as indicating that Mrs. W had done a good job as a parent; she had raised a child who was independent and feisty and who respected her mother enough that she felt she didn't have to pussyfoot with her.[15] By borrowing this interpretation of the situation from the therapist, as it were, Mrs. W was enabled to interact differently with her daughter for a while, with the predictable paradoxical effect that now the daughter found less to complain about and more to say that was directly complimentary and respectful.

In the case of Dan, the focus of reframing centered on his feelings about his wife. His wife's anxiety with strangers, which led her to be somewhat socially avoidant and to "cling" to him at parties and other gatherings, was a source of considerable distress to Dan and led to much conflict in the marriage. The simple statement that "Your wife seems to feel most relaxed when she's alone with you"—the obvious complement of Dan's description of her as anxious with strangers— seemed to make a considerable difference. This different way of looking at the situation helped to diminish a pattern of bickering between them that was a source of unhappiness for both of them, and it enabled a different balance to be achieved on the foundation of this temporary reprieve.

Elliot, 2 years after having separated from his wife after many years of an unhappy marriage, continued to berate himself for having delayed so long in taking this step. The therapist noted Elliot's mentioning in passing that he had been concerned about the effects of a divorce on his children, and called attention to this factor. Helping Elliot to recast his understanding of having stayed in the marriage as due largely to his healthy concern for his children, rather than simply

15. In a somewhat similar case, the therapist noted that a son's complaints could be seen as coming out of a strong need to differentiate himself from his mother, and that when a child feels particularly close to and admiring of a parent, it is often necessary for him to work especially hard to criticize and diminish the parent so as not to be unduly influenced in his quest for his own identity. Here again, behavior that the mother viewed negatively and with alarm (and consequently responded to in a way that actually exacerbated it) was given a different and more positive meaning, which opened up the possibility of new interactional behavior.

due to his having been a fool and a weakling, proved liberating for him. He was able to affirm the sacrifice he had made for his children and to appreciate more clearly what they meant to him. Significantly, once he had gotten past the repetitive self-recriminations about staying with his wife, he was able to explore in a more productive fashion just what anxieties and needs had kept him in the marriage so long (without losing sight of the role that concern for the children had also played).

In another case—in a sense, a mirror image of the cases of Mrs. R and Mrs. W, described above—Janine, a late adolescent, was becoming increasingly bizarre in her behavior. At the same time, she was showing signs of an increasing sense of merger with the therapist. Earlier in the work, it had become apparent that the dynamic between Janine and her mother was one in which the mother subtly communicated her need for her daughter to remain merged with her, while overtly giving the message that she wished she would grow up. The therapist responded to Janine's regression with comments such as "I think you feel that you have to be desperate for my sake—that unless you show how much you need me, I'll fall apart. Maybe you could try out the idea that I can handle it if you do well."

The therapist recognized that Janine's behavior reflected a definite regression and decline in reality testing. He responded, however, in a way that attributed more control to Janine than she herself felt at that point or than most clinical theories would imply. By reinterpreting (reframing) Janine's behavior as protective toward the therapist (thereby reflecting Janine's strength as well as sense of responsibility), instead of as an expression of her helplessness, he enabled her to view recent events differently and to interrupt the cycle of decline, which had been exacerbated by Janine's sense of helplessness before what was "happening to" her. Not unimportantly, the reframed perspective was not simply a benign fiction; though not the whole story, Janine's sense that significant people in her life could not tolerate it if she did too well was a real contributing factor in her vulnerability to more severe levels of disturbance.

Michael, an extremely self-critical man, had great difficulty in disengaging from repetitious monologues detailing the same set of complaints session after session. His narratives were always seamless and left no room for a fresh perspective on any of the matters he discussed. Efforts to encourage him to explore marginal thoughts and follow unexpected associations invariably ran up against a brick wall. He would say that what he had just said *was* what came to mind and that nothing else had occurred to him.

On one occasion, when he was describing how his boss always wanted things done just his way (and vaguely implying that he subtly sabotaged the boss's directives by being overly literal in following them) the therapist commented that perhaps Michael experienced something similar in therapy—that perhaps he felt the therapist also had his way of doing things and wanted Michael to conform to it in all particulars. To this interpretation, Michael was very responsive and began to open up more than he had before. He began to recognize that he had experienced the request for marginal thoughts as a demand that he give up his own logical style and do things the therapist's way, thereby giving up control over his own thoughts.

Shortly thereafter, he mentioned that something had just occurred to him but that he didn't want to tell the therapist what it was. Rather than addressing the element of resistance in this statement of Michael's, the therapist responded with a comment that gave a positive connotation to what Michael had said. He stated that Michael had just done something important: He had made room for himself in the therapy; he had asserted that he could have some control over what transpired and did not have to conform totally to what the other person wanted. The therapist further commented that in saying that he didn't want to tell the therapist what he had thought, rather than saying that nothing had occurred to him, Michael was proving that he did not have to pay the price of appearing helpless (even to himself) in order to resist what he experienced as oppressive demands.

The quality of Michael's therapeutic participation improved after this, but, as in all therapeutic work, the change was not a once-and-for-all "they lived happily ever after" fairly tale. He continued to take two steps forward and one step back, and at times both patient and therapist were reimmersed in the old quagmire. There continued to be some periods when Michael droned on in a way that the therapist found impossible to do anything useful with, and on some occasions the question was again raised as to whether Michael was aware of any marginal thoughts on the periphery of his consciousness. He continued to respond to such inquiries primarily with the report that there was nothing there, but now he was somewhat more responsive to the notion that perhaps some thoughts had occurred to him that he simply didn't want to state.

On one occasion, he said that the only thought that had popped into his head while telling his story was that he had no marginal thoughts for the therapist; he hadn't felt that it was worthwhile interrupting his narrative to report this. The therapist responded that the thought about not having any marginal thoughts was itself a marginal thought, as valuable and useful as any other. He wondered aloud if perhaps there had been other such thoughts as well in the past that Michael had felt didn't "qualify." This gave rise to a very fruitful exploration of Michael's fears that his efforts would be regarded as not good enough or would not be appreciated, and of how he had taken to hiding rather than risk the ridicule he thought would follow if he really opened up to people.

In a wide variety of contexts, attention to the strengths and positive connotations that can be found in patients' behavior can facilitate both increments in self-esteem and the ability to hear what the therapist is saying. Indeed, it is frequently just such a focus on the positive that enables the "negative" to be addressed in a therapeutically useful way. The therapist's skill consists very largely in helping the patient to bear looking at what had seemed unbearable, and in seeing the possibilities hidden behind the curtain of despair.

7.   *Meeting the Cast of Characters: I. Rationale and Clinical Relevance*

In THIS CHAPTER and the next, we describe the use of interviews with parents, siblings, and partners as a means of enhancing individual psychotherapy. It is our belief that meeting the "cast of characters" can be extremely enlightening and of great therapeutic importance. These meetings are limited to one or two sessions at most and always take place in the presence of the individual with whom we are working. Our intent in these meetings is not to do family or couples therapy, but rather to enrich our work with the individual who is our primary patient. In this respect, our work differs considerably from the work of Bowenians, who do family therapy with one person (Carter & Orfanidis, 1976), or from the interesting work of family and couple therapists such as Framo (1981), Williamson (1981, 1982a, 1982b), and Headley (1977), who, to varying degrees, feel that confronting old issues with the family of origin directly is a crucial step in the resolution of current interpersonal difficulties.

In this chapter, we discuss the various kinds of information that can be gained from our "cast-of-characters" meetings and how this information can be used therapeutically. Having presented the rationale, we then move on in Chapter 8 to discuss when and how to present the idea to the patient. We have found that just how one prepares the individual for the meeting significantly influences the likelihood of success of this intervention. Often, the preparation is as useful as the meeting itself, and we describe in detail the premeeting planning that takes place.

We also describe in Chapter 8 a variety of formats we have developed for doing these interviews. Interviewing one or both parents, for example, involves different questions than does interviewing siblings or partners. We hope to prepare the therapist for difficulties that he or she may encounter, and with this in mind present a number of "dos" and "don'ts" based on our experience. How one uses these observations in the later work—especially in the sessions that immediately follow these meetings—is of critical importance, and we conclude Chapter 8 by discussing this in detail.

Throughout these two chapters, we address where appropriate a number of objections and/or anxieties we have heard expressed by participants in seminars and training workshops we have given on this topic. These concerns are principally those of the individual therapist, the primary expected audience for this book. For many individual therapists, what we are describing represents a venture into alien territory, as well as a departure from what they have come to feel is required by the theoretical orientation to which they try to remain faithful.

Many of these theoretical concerns, as well as the apprehensions about intervening in new and unfamiliar ways, have already been addressed in earlier chapters. Here, however, we must deal with new and different doubts and hesitations. Up till now, we have been discussing variations introduced into the basic format of individual therapy—the one-to-one encounter. Now we are introducing the idea of altering (albeit only temporarily and very occasionally) even this defining feature of the structure of the therapeutic relationship. The therapist who is used to working with people only one at a time may feel quite uneasy about the prospect of inviting others into the sanctuary—indeed, may even feel outnumbered and under siege.

We address these additional concerns of the individual therapist throughout the next two chapters, providing concrete descriptions of how to proceed and of the rationale for the particular clinical choices we describe. Here, however, we wish to address first a question that was raised by a number of *family* therapists when we first began describing these procedures. From their perspective, the question was not one of why one should see the family members at all, but rather why one should continue to do individual therapy with the patient instead of "going all the way," as one of them put it.

This question can be addressed on a number of levels. To begin with, it must be noted that there are a good many cases that we do believe are best treated in the context of conjoint family therapy; one of us (EFW), indeed, devotes a good portion of her practice to working with couples and families and to teaching such work. But it must also be said that a good deal more research is necessary before one can state with any authority a set of criteria that would point unambiguously to either family or individual therapy as the appropriate modality. We suspect that a substantial proportion of cases that present themselves clinically can be fruitfully conceptualized and treated as *either* individual or family problems.

To be sure, one would expect that different aspects of the overall problem would be addressed in one modality or the other—that is, that "improvement" or "cure" would not mean exactly the same thing in the two instances. But because changing the system of interactions in the family alters the experience and functioning of each individual in the system, and because changing any individual alters the system in which he or she participates, there should also be a substantial overlap in what is achieved.

From our perspective, what is most important at this stage of our knowledge is to refrain from viewing individual therapy and family therapy as two competing and/or alien points of view. Although we too—like, for example, Sander (1979)—regard some cases as more appropriate for individual work and some for family work, we do not believe that drawing a sharp distinction between the two is likely to be heuristically useful. As we have noted earlier, our objection to some of the integrative efforts offered thus far is that they retain a notion of psychodynamics that is essentially intrapsychic; the inevitable consequence of this is to make of individual and family treatment sharply drawn alternatives. In contrast, our cyclical psychodynamic model is an effort to provide a framework within which treatments whose main focus is on the dynamics of the individual and treatments that focus primarily on the system of interaction can find common ground. Within our framework, individual dynamics are important in any system, and the system is important in the understanding of any individual. Although such a commitment does not mean that the gap is fully bridged, it does mean that we need not abandon our understanding of systemic influences when we decide, for whatever reason, to work alone with a troubled individual. Although an understanding of the role of systemic interactional patterns can point one toward methods of working simultaneously with groups of individuals who participate in the same system, it can as readily guide individual work—and not merely as a kind of dipping one's toe in the water, but as a canny treatment of choice.

What, then, are the criteria we use in deciding whether to see someone individually or whether family treatment is called for? As noted above, these criteria cannot yet be spelled out on the basis of hard evidence or unambiguous clinical experience. Certain considerations, however, seem reasonable ones to utilize on a provisional basis and to explore further. In general, for example, it seems to us that when the presenting complaint involves a child, family therapy is likely to be called for in a larger percentage of cases than if the person perceived as having the problem (the "identified patient") is an adult. Children are particularly likely to be strongly influenced by a single system (the family) that is central to their lives; many adults are participants in significant ways in a variety of systems, and need to be addressed as individuals who are the nodal point of a number of systems rather than more exclusively as members of one predominant one.[1]

Moreover, a reasonably large number of adults can make use of the understanding they gain of the interactional patterns in which they are integrated, and can work on their own to alter these patterns and thereby change the system. It is far more difficult for a child to do so. Most children do not have the psychic resources to accomplish such a task; for them, the therapist's direct work on changing the system in which the child is developing is likely to be of considerable importance.

The chronological age of the identified patient is not, of course, the only criterion for determining whether to see the family or to work individually. Even with regard to the considerations noted thus far, it is clearly the case that a significant number of adults, too, are so enmeshed in a particular problematic relationship or system that working with them individually is likely to be frustrating. Moreover, there are some children who do seem able to thrive in individual therapy, using the new system with the therapist to initiate actions that alter the original system of the family. (This is especially likely to be able to be achieved when the therapist or someone else works with one or both

1. It must be recognized, however, that for children too the family is not necessarily the only significant system that must be considered. For many children, the school or the neighborhood peer group constitute important systems in which the children participate in ways that can have a significant impact on their personality development. Indeed, we suspect that the significance of peer influences is much underestimated by both individual *and* family therapists.

parents, even if not working conjointly with the family as a whole.) Moreover, there are some children, especially as they enter adolescence, who need to extricate themselves somewhat from the family system and can use individual therapy to help them to accomplish this.[2]

Needless to say, one of the crucial considerations in deciding whether to work individually or with the whole family is the wish of the patient. Some people don't *want* to be seen conjointly with their families. In such instances, to insist on family treatment is questionable both on ethical grounds and on grounds of clinical effectiveness; one pays a price for pushing someone in a direction he or she does not want to go. It is true that family therapists often do have to persuade people that family treatment is what is called for, and that sometimes the initial opposition to this idea is rather vigorous. In such instances, moreover, sometimes the family therapist takes a rather tough and uncompromising stand in this regard and/or uses somewhat devious means to induce the family to come in together. In such instances, ethical considerations regarding respect for individual autonomy versus paternalism are weighed against ethical precepts regarding the relief of suffering (in different configurations for different therapists). But in most instances, if after a while it remains clear that family treatment is not what is wanted by the person who first called for a consultation, there comes a point where it is both unethical and counterproductive to continue to insist.

Finally, it must be recognized that whether individual therapy or family therapy is offered frequently depends on the training and predilections of the particular therapist. This would represent an impermissible indulgence on the part of the therapist if there were unassailable evidence about which modality was best for which patient or problem; the internist who refuses to recommend surgery for a patient because he is not a surgeon (or the surgeon who regards every case as operative because that's the kind of therapy he does) is clearly to be condemned. But given the present ambiguity in most cases as to which approach is called for, as well as the shortage of mental health practitioners and the likelihood that a therapist will do best what he is best trained for and feels more confident in, it seems reasonable to include the therapist factor as a legitimate one. A good many problems are likely to be benefited by either individual *or* family therapy.

2. It should be noted that there are family therapists who claim that the family treatment modality is the appropriate medium for accomplishing this separation. In this regard, see in particular Haley (1979).

The important point is that inviting guests into a session of an individual therapy need not be thought of as a halfway measure on a path that, if followed logically and courageously, would inevitably lead to family therapy. In many instances, there are good reasons why individual therapy has been the treatment of choice. As we have argued, this is no way implies a lack of concern for issues of system and context; the special "cast-of-characters" interviews we describe here are designed specifically to incorporate such considerations into the individual therapy modality.

To be sure, inviting "guests" to sessions complicates individual therapy, in that it alters the transference and introduces many new variables. We have found, however, that our work has benefited by these meetings and that the difficulties and risks involved seem to be worthwhile. In what follows, we describe some of the clinical advantages of such interviews.

Reconstruction of the Patient's History

Although the emphasis in our approach is on present interactions, we do, like many other therapists, find that some perspective on the developmental origins of the problem is useful. But, unlike many therapists, we do not feel that the patient's recollections of his childhood perceptions alone, or even his perceptions supplemented by the experience of patient and therapist in the transference, provide a sufficient picture in many cases. If one believes that systems considerations are relevant, then one must seriously question whether access only to what has been registered by the patient himself (through recollection *or* through repetition in the transference) will provide adequate data. The patient can only experience in the transference what he at one time "noticed," at least unconsciously. Some things are simply beyond the ken or beyond the recognition of a child (or, in fact, simply of the individual involved or immersed in the experience, regardless of age). Although parents or siblings may at times recall significant events or facts that the patient has not registered, what they most often provide is rather an additional perspective out of which a *Rashomon*-like construction of reality is possible.

Margaret, a 35-year-old career woman who had recently moved to New York from California, was intensely conflicted about getting attached to a man. She vacillated between, on the one hand, almost desperate feelings of need, in which separations of even a day or two from her boyfriend were hard to bear; and, on the other hand, feelings of extreme detachment, in which she felt no affection or caring for this same man—with whom she was living and whom she planned to marry. This detachment appeared to be a defense against fears of abandonment, which could be evoked by minimal cues signaling withdrawal. For example, when her boyfriend, a successful journalist, was temporarily preoccupied with work, Margaret would begin to feel that he was losing interest and didn't love her anymore. Then, feeling detached and uninterested in response to the perceived withdrawal, Margaret would worry about making a lifelong commitment to her fiancé.

Margaret had often talked about the fact that when she was 8 years old her father had abruptly left home. According to Margaret, she had been completely surprised by this separation, because she had never seen her parents arguing. The oldest of four children and the only daughter, she had thought herself to be her father's favorite. Father was described as extremely attentive to Margaret and involved with her right up until the day he left. Margaret understood that her fear of involvement with men must be related to the loss of her father and the mistrust of "devotion" thus engendered. Nonetheless, she was bewildered as to why her reaction was as intense as it was and why she had not come to terms with something that had happened so long ago. A session with Margaret's mother unexpectedly helped answer this question.

In the presession planning, Margaret had made clear that she thought mother would be very uncomfortable talking about the separation from Margaret's father. The therapist agreed that he would not raise this issue, but would instead focus on other things. Almost immediately, much to Margaret's surprise, mother spontaneously brought up the period in their lives when father had left. Just the fact of mother's having been so willing to talk about this was an important piece of information for both Margaret and the therapist. It began a valuable process of Margaret's reexamining whether her mother was still as fragile as she perceived her.

Mother's description of father's departure contained some striking details of which Margaret had no memory. According to mother, Margaret's father had gone off to a new job in Chicago and hadn't written, called, or visited the children for a full 6 months after he left. Mother also provided useful additional information about the family structure that had existed at that time. Confirming Margaret's perception that she and her husband had never fought, the mother stated that she also had been at a loss to understand her husband's desire to leave. Mother described herself as having felt overwhelmed with feelings of humiliation and shame, especially in relation to her family and neighbors. Apparently, it was many years before mother experienced anger at her husband. Her dominant feeling had been one of pathos mixed with determination to prove to the world her self-worth by single-handedly raising four fine and successful children. Both the inaccessibility of her own anger, and her wish to preserve for the sake of her children their positive feelings about their father, had led to her never saying anything critical of him to Margaret. The mother had tried to prevent her children from feeling or expressing what she herself could not at that time acknowledge.

From this discussion it became clear that Margaret's loss had been far greater than she had realized. For one thing, she had had no recollection of the 6-month period in which she had not seen or heard from her father. Furthermore, her feelings of abandonment had been enhanced by a strong identification with her mother's pathos and an inhibition and prohibition about expressing anger. Margaret's never having expressed anger at her father had resulted in a superficial but cordial relationship between them, in which she kept him at a great emotional distance while continuing to behave as a devoted and dutiful daughter.

Margaret, like many patients who have heard some new version of events from a parent or sibling, experienced this new knowledge as highly meaningful. There is relief in being able to make sense of one's reactions. Often, as in the case of Margaret, there is also a freeing up that occurs. For instance, although she and the therapist never talked about it, Margaret spontaneously became more demanding of her father (e.g., asking him to contribute some money toward the down payment on a house), and she stopped trying so hard to be a "devoted daughter." She also became less conflicted about making a commitment to her boyfriend, though she couldn't explain exactly why and how this change in feeling occurred. As she stopped vacillating between withdrawal and devotion, her boyfriend became more consistently available, which of course further aided in her mastery of abandonment fears.

Harold, a 28-year-old civil servant, who was discontented with his career, had been born with a congenital heart defect that presented real restrictions. However, his self-imposed restrictions were considerably more severe than necessary. He had always been very close to his overly protective mother and thought of himself as much more like his mother than his father, whom he saw as punitive, demanding, and withdrawn. He knew that his mother had in effect laid claim to him when he was a child and that he had strongly identified with her, both in her anxieties and in her criticism of his father. What he did not know was how much his mother identified herself with his handicap.

In a meeting in which both parents were present, the mother, asked to tell about herself, immediately started out by saying that she, like Harold, had been a sickly child. Apparently she had had severe asthma and had been hovered over by her family. Harold could not remember ever having heard about his mother's sickly childhood, and saw for perhaps the first time just how invested his mother was in a shared image of sickliness. Although Harold had already begun to separate from his mother and was no longer the confidante he had once been, seeing his mother's need to see both herself and him as sickly angered him and led to some greater identification with his father.

Arthur C, a highly successful man in his mid-30s, was extremely critical of himself on a variety of counts. For one, he felt that he had failed to live up to his own expectation in finding a career that felt truly meaningful. He was almost self-flagellating in his contempt for the wish he sometimes experienced to live an easier, less pressured life. He was also conflicted between his desire for success and an unheeded but nagging impulse to live a less conventional life. He had been an ideal child, and as an adult had a great need to be pleasing. Tolerating the disapproval or disappointment of an authority figure was very difficult for him.

Arthur had described himself as a mature, responsible, problem-free child, in comparison to his younger brother, who had been extremely disgruntled and cranky as the result of severe digestive problems. The therapist had speculated that because his brother had been so difficult, Arthur, as the "good" child, had been generously rewarded by the pleasure and joy he brought to his parents. Interviewing Arthur's parents shed some light on just how much the mother, in particular, needed her elder son to be mature, responsible, and perfect.

The interview revealed that the mother's level of stress during the time following the second child's birth had been far greater than

Arthur had realized. The baby's digestive problems had required constant attention to what, when, and how much he was eating and had necessitated numerous visits to doctors and several stays in the hospital. Mrs. C had had to handle both children on her own, since Arthur's father was at that time at a crucial stage in building his business and had to work day and night. Mother described this period as the worst of her life.

Arthur, who had almost never heard his mother say an unkind word, was shocked to hear that mother had often felt enraged at the baby even though she knew he was blameless. Mother, a deeply religious woman, was herself shaken by these feelings. She described Arthur as her main—indeed, almost her only—source of joy and happiness at that time. Though none of the facts were actually new, mother's description of both her distress and her pleasure in the older, "easy" child was qualitatively different from what Arthur remembered. He had no memories of his mother as overwhelmed. It was not until this meeting that Arthur and his therapist got a full picture of the pressure on him to "grow up" and be problem-free. Mother herself said, "Maybe I put too much pressure on Arthur to be perfect."

Evaluating the Reality Component

Interviewing family members provides an opportunity for the therapist to measure what he sees against what has been reported. It enables him to see whether the mother is really as distant, or hostile, or all-giving as the patient says; whether the father is really as tolerant, or passive, or rigid; and so on. The point is not simply to challenge or play "Monday morning quarterback" to the patient's perceptions. It can be valuable as well to *affirm* the patient's perceptions, especially when the patient can see that the therapist affirms *some* of his or her assumptions and challenges others.

Now, of course, the therapist is not in a privileged position to perceive "reality" in a direct and unmediated fashion. He also perceives the mother's "passivity" or the father's "hostility" through the filter of his own history, cognitive structures, motives, and transferences, as well as in terms of the set created in him by the patient's earlier reports. But it is not simply a matter of the blind leading the blind. The therapist's perspective is of value to the patient for a number of reasons.

First of all, the therapist's perception is of value simply for being that of an "other." We all benefit in every aspect of our lives from such alternative perspectives. Indeed, such converging perspectives almost define what civilization—or sanity—is. Where the therapist's contribution is particularly useful in this regard is that the therapist can at times provide the perspective of another in areas of the person's life where almost any alternative perspective has been lacking—that is, in those areas that are so personal and private that others are rarely privy to them.

But the therapist's perspective is more than that of simply *any* "other." The therapist, to begin with, is in a relationship to the patient characterized by a unique mixture of involvement and uninvolvement. The therapist cares about the patient and is knowledgeable about intimate details of the patient's life, yet at the same time maintains a reflective distance not common in other close human relationships. Being freer from the immediate emotional press of the experience, the therapist does seem to us—the caveats above notwithstanding— to be somewhat less hampered by his own emotional biases in his perception of the people and events in the patient's life.[3] Moreover— and this is especially relevant to the procedures we are discussing here—the particular kind of interview we are describing in this chapter provides an unusually rich opportunity to "know" family members and to take a look at interactions between them.

Marilyn, a 34-year-old career woman with two children, often expressed contempt for her father. Described as extremely weak, he was said to rely on the patient's mother for all decisions large or small. Inept, insensitive, and almost totally "out of it" was the way Marilyn perceived her father. Marilyn had a profound sense of both loss and rage at what she experienced as her father's lack of interest in his daughter.

Prior to the family meeting, Marilyn and the therapist had examined the interactional aspects of her parents' personalities—for example, how father was "stupid" and "insensitive" in response to mother's domination, and how she in turn felt that his ineptness indicated that she

---

3. We hope it is clear that this is not because therapists *as people* are more perceptive or less biased, but because of the unique structure of the therapeutic relationship that is established.

needed to take charge. Much of the work involved sorting out the ramifications for Marilyn of having grown up in this particular family system. Attitudes toward herself, her children, and her husband were examined in terms of this family dynamic.

Part of the family system in which Marilyn had grown up, and which still seemed to be in effect, was that the children would join with their mother in her demeaning attitude toward father. The therapist speculated that he in turn was angered by their joining their mother in disparagement of him and that he characteristically expressed his anger by being "out of it" and "inept," furthering the children's belief that their mother was right. It was difficult, however, to assess from Marilyn's description alone just how entrenched this personality trait had become. Was he *really* unobservant, or did he simply not reveal his opinions? Would he be more responsive if the situation or system was altered, or had this by now rigidified into a personality trait that would be almost impossible to change? Would the therapist see father in the same way as did the family, or had they all exaggerated and distorted how "unconscious" father actually was? Would he respond to the therapist differently than he did to his wife and children? As we discuss in detail below, the answers to such questions as these are important, in that they help determine reasonable therapeutic goals.

As predicted by Marilyn, her mother and her older sister dominated the family session. They were both very articulate and volunteered answers to the questions posed. Father sat quietly and tuned out by making eye contact and faces at his 1-year-old grandson. He seemed content to let mother speak for the two of them. His wife did not speak of him disparagingly, but rather simply ignored his presence. The therapist's attempts to engage father were met with only slight success. Repeated indications of interest and support did result in some opening up, but it took a good deal of effort both to encourage father and to keep mother from taking over. Thus it did seem that though not *totally* unalterable, this was a fairly rigid system and an entrenched personality style.

However, though father was far from forthcoming in this interview, he did say *some* things that were highly meaningful to Marilyn and that helped to alter significantly her feeling that he never noticed or cared about her. When asked to comment on her mother's description of the difficulties Marilyn had given the family in her college "hippie days," father said he had secretly been glad that Marilyn had finally decided to be her own person and not to be as concerned about pleasing her mother as she had previously been. Apparently he had been silently rooting for her in her struggle for independence. Feeling himself to be overly submissive, father had great respect for his daughter's autonomous and self-respecting behavior. Though father then quickly retreated into silence, the glimpse he allowed into his feelings for his daughter made it difficult for her to see him or treat him in quite the old way.

The two clinical examples that follow demonstrate the use of these interviews as an aid in determining the extent of patients' emotional reactivity to their parents.

Kristine, a single woman of 30, found it almost impossible to be with her mother without feeling surges of intense rage. She described her mother as an extraordinarily destructive woman whose greatest pleasure seemed to be in seeing her daughter fail. Not a kind word was said to be uttered by mother to her daughter. Rather, she would vigilantly look for flaws with which to humiliate her. Kristine said her mother would be delighted to come to a session, since she would love having this forum in which to criticize her further. Even knowing that Kristine was seeing a therapist would be used as further ammunition.

With all this in mind, the therapist approached this interview with considerable apprehension. He had determined to get a look at this mother, but was prepared to exercise considerable control over the course of the interview so that the meeting would not simply deteriorate into a repetition of their standard fights. Kristine had described herself as being extremely confronting of her mother, never letting her get away with nasty innuendos.

The interview turned out to be so polite that the therapist was concerned that his patient would be disappointed that her mother hid her true colors so well. To be sure, mother was far from warm and loving. Surprisingly, however, she described her daughter in what seemed to the therapist to be rather neutral, nonjudgmental terms. All in all, the interview seemed rather flat, and the therapist feared that his attempt to protect both mother and daughter and prevent them from abusing each other had resulted in a controlled but lifeless meeting. It was not until the follow-up session with Kristine that the meaningfulness of this session emerged.

It seems that Kristine and the therapist had experienced her mother's statements quite differently. What the therapist had regarded as "neutral" statements had seemed to Kristine to typify her mother's hostile innuendos. Outraged by these perceived attacks, Kristine felt that her anger in response had been clearly visible. Not only had the therapist not experienced the mother's behavior as hostile, but he had significantly misread Kristine, who had seemed to the therapist to be feeling nothing more than slightly defensive. Kristine's outrage at her mother's statements, an outrage that she had apparently been feeling at the time, had simply gone unnoticed by the therapist. How one deals with such discrepant perceptions as these in the sessions that follow is discussed in Chapter 8. The point here is that the therapist gained a useful perspective from this interview on just how extreme Kristine's sensitivity and emotional reactivity to her mother were, as well as on how she did (or did not) express it.

To be sure, not being in possession of the epistemologist's stone, we cannot say with certainty whether the therapist's perspective or the patient's perspective was "right." But what was striking in this instance, and therapeutically important, was how different the interaction looked to the therapist and the patient. It may be true that, from the point of view of "psychic reality," what matters is whether the patient *felt* criticized. But it is our firm belief that to focus exclusively or one-sidedly on psychic reality is to miss a crucial component of a patient's difficulties. There is a difference, we contend, between the patient who must deal with a mother whom almost anyone would judge as hostile, and one who perceives a hostility so subtle or so privately construed that for almost anyone else the remarks would appear innocent. We discuss in more detail in the next chapter how one might take a different therapeutic strategy in the two instances.

Marcy had often talked about her feeling that she had failed to live up to her expectations for herself. She believed that her sense of failure was solely self-imposed and that her parents, friends, and husband held her in high regard. She and the therapist had spent a good deal of time discussing her ultrasensitivity to criticism and the readiness with which she would heap blame upon herself. When Marcy brought in her father, the therapist was alert to see whether the father was perhaps subtly critical of his daughter.

Just as Marcy had expected, father seemed proudly delighted in Marcy's accomplishments. He spoke appreciatively of his daughter's qualities both as an adult and as a child. As with many patients, Marcy was surprised to realize that her father was well aware of and empathic about some of the difficult times Marcy had experienced in growing up. She also was struck by how much more open her father was about his own feelings and difficulties than she had expected. In general, the interview seemed to have gone quite well, and father and daughter left looking as though they felt close and warm toward each other.

Again, it was not until the next session that the therapist was able to assess the actual impact of this meeting on the patient. He was surprised to hear that, following the interview with her father, Marcy had felt very depressed. Anecdotes about what a wonderful little girl she had been had been processed by Marcy as "Oh, what a disappointment I am now." Pained by thoughts of how she had not lived up to her potential, Marcy had found herself intermittently sobbing for several days following this meeting. The praise heaped upon her resulted in considerable pain, giving the therapist some perspective on Marcy's need to keep her father at a distance.

It is important to note that Marcy *knew* her father had in no way implied that she was a disappointment. Although Marcy had said this before, it was useful for the therapist to see for himself that this was in fact the case. As far as the therapist could discern, father was genuinely proud of his daughter, and there were no subtle messages to the contrary. In light of this benign interview, the severity of Marcy's reaction helped both the therapist and the patient to realize more fully just how desperately Marcy needed to be special. This insight was certainly not a new one, but the depth and extent of Marcy's need were revealed in a way that extended both patient's and therapist's understanding of what they were dealing with.

This deepened understanding of the intensity of Marcy's feelings led to new avenues of exploration. In the sessions that followed, Marcy described herself as being the "star" of the extended family as well as of her own immediate family. She had been considered the smartest of all her cousins. Apparently, Marcy's mother herself had had higher aspirations than her own siblings, and Marcy's success in school was a great source of pride to her. It became clear that it would be almost impossible for Marcy to experience as an adult the kind of adoration that she had received as a child. Although we had "placed" the father in relation to her family at the beginning of treatment by doing a genogram (see Chapter 4), it is often necessary to get at the same information from a variety of angles in order to fully understand the system and its impact on the individual.

Indeed, one important matter that is frequently overlooked in discussions of therapy is that working through of insights is necessary not only for the patient, but for the therapist as well. It is one thing to "know" something about a patient, and it is another to understand and appreciate it so fully and experientially that it becomes part of the very ground of being with the patient, so that the therapist is able to interact with the patient in a fully therapeutic way. Meeting Marcy's father and knowing how extremely Marcy had reacted to his praise brought home to the therapist, as nothing had before, just what the patient's experience was. Though one could argue that it is possible to see this same dynamic by attending to the transference, it is our belief that transference is rarely as powerful as the reactions to the *actual* family members. Moreover, one has an opportunity to gain a different perspective when one can observe both the patient's reaction and the behavior that elicits it from the outside, rather than having to process it while also being its object.[4]

Some therapists are concerned that an emphasis on assessing how realistic the patient's experience is can be judgmental and inconsistent with the spirit of exploratory psychotherapy. In our view, this concern is misplaced for a number of reasons. To begin with, as we have indicated elsewhere, the image of nonjudgmental neutrality by which many therapists believe they operate seems to us a distortion. Judgments are inevitably made in human relationships, and if therapists had to depend on a genuinely nonjudgmental attitude in order to succeed, therapy would really be "the impossible profession." What is required in essence is a *selectively* judgmental orientation, in which as far as possible the therapist's judgments are limited to matters bearing some casual role in the difficulties the patient says he wants to modify (P. L. Wachtel, 1979a). Evaluations of whether the patient's reactions are "realistic," or of when and where he misperceives the possibilities in a situation, are precisely the sorts of things the patient is paying the therapist for.

Choosing Therapeutic Directions

Assessing the reality component helps the therapist make decisions about therapeutic directions. Should the therapist, for example, work with the patient toward changing a relationship or toward accepting it with greater equanimity? If change does seem possible, what is the best way of going about it? And so forth. From our cast-of-characters

4. And, of course, it is even more valuable to be able to have *both* perspectives.

meetings, we are better able to make judgments as to how responsive a parent or partner might be to changed behavior on the part of the patient, and what kind of approach on the part of the patient the other person might respond to most favorably. We can notice further details of how the patient behaves with that person and can get a firmer hold on the reciprocal interactions that further the difficulties.[5]

Curt claimed that his father never said a complimentary word. Father was portrayed as relentlessly critical of all his children. The therapist had surmised during the course of the work that Curt's mother was extremely angry at her husband and had taught the children to "respect" but not to like their harsh and judgmental father. As an adult, Curt still tried to avoid his father's displeasure, to a degree that the therapist saw as excessive. The therapist wondered whether Curt's eagerness to please was rooted in part in a sense that father really did value him. Perhaps, the therapist thought, father was simply inhibited about expressing this overtly.

A meeting was held with Curt and his parents. Both parents seemed more self-centered than the therapist had been led to expect. Mother needed to be firmly stopped from using the whole session to talk about herself. Father, when asked to speak about his son, lapsed readily into a critical stance. Even with much encouragement and urging, father could not seem to say anything positive about Curt, either as an adult or as a child. For example, although he acknowledged that it was probably a good thing that Curt had recently become more assertive, he thought Curt was going too far with it and that he should be a more cooperative and compliant son. Expressions of wholehearted admiration or praise were just not forthcoming.

It is possible, of course, that father simply could not say anything positive in the presence of mother, since their system was that mother was the "softie" in the family and father was the "heavy." The therapist's attempt to change that system, however, by violating the implicit family rule that father should be assumed to be harsh and approached as such, was met with great resistance. This meeting led to a greater emphasis on helping Curt deal with his father's disapproval (instead of—as the therapist had earlier thought might be useful—working with Curt on understanding and registering father's conflicted efforts

5. We hope it is clear from all that has been said thus far that we do not decide on therapeutic directions unilaterally, but rather in collaboration with the patient. What we are describing here are observations that help base our own input into this decision-making process on a more expert and realistic picture of probable consequences.

to express a real but disguised regard). The patient's experience of his father was confirmed, and he was cautioned by the therapist that attempts to elicit praise would probably be futile.

Mark, age 31, felt great pity for his sister. He saw her as a "loser" who would probably never marry. Though she earned considerably more money than he did and was highly successful in her career, Mark felt acutely her aloneness in the world and regarded himself as responsible for looking after her. Despite the fact that he was only 2 years her senior, he regarded her as a child rather than a peer. In particular, he felt extremely uncomfortable with the notion that she was a sexually mature woman.

The sources of these attitudes were complex and too numerous for us to discuss here. The interview with Mark's sister was useful in enabling the therapist to sort out some of the relevant considerations, and it helped in determining where to go therapeutically. First of all, it was important to note that although this sister did seem pleased that Mark had always been protective of her, she was also bothered by their lack of closeness and the strangeness of their current relationship. She seemed more than willing, if not eager, to relate to Mark as a "friend." It became clear in this session, though, that whenever Mark's sister started to talk about her social life, Mark would rapidly change the topic.

From this session with Mark's sister, the therapist was able to see how inaccuracies in Mark's view of his sister were related to specific things he did to avoid knowing facts that conflicted with his assumptions. Furthermore, it became much clearer that by relating to her in a parental manner, he brought out the side of *her* ambivalence that enjoyed viewing her brother as protector. The response that this elicited further confirmed his feeling that she was a "responsibility" rather than a friend. In contrast to the case of Curt, just described, the meeting with Mark's sister confirmed the therapist's feeling that this relationship *would* be amenable to change.

Rita T, a 35-year-old married woman with two teenage children, felt that her mother was dissatisfied with her in a chronic, nonspecific way. She could not say exactly what it was that her mother seemed to want, but felt that her mother did not think she was a dedicated enough daughter. It was her feeling that mother still considered her a child who should take direction from her. Overt conflict seldom arose between them, since Rita usually followed her mother's suggestions or else ignored them in an "inadvertent," nonovert way.

An interview with Rita's mother helped the therapist assess just how invested mother was in being in charge and how upset she would become if Rita directly challenged her authority. Mother, when asked for a description of herself, described her work as very gratifying, since she was the assistant to the chief administrator of a large agency and had absolute control over who had access to him. She was quite direct about how good she felt about the power she had in that institution.

Further indications that mother would not relinquish power graciously came from her discussion of the family structure when Rita was growing up. The therapist had known that the patient's grandmother had lived with the family. What he had not known was that mother had felt herself to be in complete control of her daughter's upbringing, even though she was away from home all day. Mother boasted that her own mother, who looked after Rita while mother was at work, had followed her instructions to the letter and would never have done anything she had not authorized. Unlike many mothers who entrust part of their child-rearing responsibilities to a grandmother, Rita's mother felt that she had not relinquished even an iota of her power and authority.

This interview made it clear that Rita's mother was greatly invested in being the one in control. Once again, however, it was not until the following session that the therapist really understood how the patient had experienced the meeting. After the session, Rita and her mother went out to dinner together. At dinner Rita found herself talking more openly and honestly to her mother than she had done before. Apparently the session had shifted her perception somewhat, so that she saw her mother as *needing* to feel important rather than as actually being so dauntingly powerful. This shift in perspective distressed her. Though her mother's controlling behavior had been annoying, Rita had derived a certain security from perceiving her as always in control.

The interview helped the therapist and the patient anticipate both Rita's and her mother's reactions to changing the way she interacted with her. It seemed likely that mother would become sad rather than angry if Rita behaved autonomously, and that Rita would find it distressing to see her mother as vulnerable. The information gained in this instance, as in many others, included understanding of the patient's subsequent reactions, as well as what was heard and observed in the meeting itself.

A Broader Perspective on Current Difficulties

In the preceding section, we have focused on the usefulness of these interviews in assessing the current reality the patient faces in dealing with a particular family member. In this section, we are concerned with how this information helps the therapist to understand the patient's interactions with others besides the person who is interviewed.

This is not simply a matter of generalizing from observations about interactions with family members to interactions with people outside the family. There are a variety of ways in which patients' difficulties with other people in their lives can be better understood after meeting family members.

Colleen seemed to desire a great deal of emotional intensity in her relationship with her husband. She had married a strong-minded, outspoken man whom she described as being passionate and tyrannical. Often he would denounce his wife for not living up to his moral and philosophical ideals. Colleen both complained about and reveled in his judgmental nature. With the help of the therapist, she began to understand more clearly her part in the system, which allowed him to be a demanding and aggressively principled "authority."

As Colleen changed, both in terms of new ways of responding to her husband's outbursts and in eliminating her subtle invitations to him to be both judge and jury of her behavior, their marriage settled into a relatively calm partnership. When this occurred, Colleen began to feel that something important was missing in the relationship. They had no children, and she counted on him for all her important emotional gratifications. Though she felt strongly that they loved each other, she missed very much the intensity and passion that was part and parcel of their pattern of his criticism, her self-blame, and their eventual reconciliation.

A meeting with Colleen's parents shed considerable light on this dilemma. When the therapist suggested this meeting, Colleen expressed concern that her parents would have nothing to say. The therapist assumed that Colleen's perception of her parents as people who blandly saw everything as "nice" and who could not acknowledge any intense feeling at all was probably somewhat exaggerated. As it turned out, the interview more than confirmed Colleen's description. Both parents had an extraordinary degree of difficulty in describing their own personalities, even in the most superficial way. Though clearly of average or above-average intelligence, they seemed to lack the most rudimentary vocabulary of self-description. There was a flatness and dullness to their answers that was quite extraordinary.

When the patient, seen alone, received feedback regarding the therapist's perceptions, she expressed great relief and gratitude. She had never been able to fully make clear how "flat" the environment was that she grew up in. She felt that this flatness and unwillingness to acknowledge feelings led to her difficulty in knowing what she felt, and her consequent susceptibility to and even desire for her husband's pronouncements regarding her motives and behavior. The wishy-washiness of her parents was intolerable to her, and her need in her marriage to provoke "fights" when all was calm was much more understandable.

Phil often felt badly about himself because he was not the "man" he felt he ought to be. He avoided situations in which he was uncertain of how to act, and he always needed to get the lay of the land in advance so that he would not look unsure of himself. He often fantasized about women being attracted to him, but felt he could not perform as well sexually as he imagined other men could.

An interview with Phil's mother shed some light on his preoccupation with "masculinity." The mother described with pride how "wild and mischievous" Phil had been as a child and said he was a "real little man, a tough guy." Phil was also the only grandson on either side of the family, in a large family that produced many girls. He was surrounded by adoring grandparents and unmarried aunts and uncles to whom he was special. As an adult, he seemed to be longing to be the prince he once had been. Feeling that he could only win the adoration he felt he needed by acting like a man, Phil kept private (even from his wife) any feelings of need and vulnerability. As a consequence, he experienced himself as only "acting" confident and adult, though all the while feeling like a fearful little boy. He could not distinguish his true competence as an adult from the fraudulent "little man" of his youth.

Anne, an aspiring 32-year-old single career woman, was held back by conflict over feelings of competence and expertise. Whenever her own knowledge or strongly felt opinions conflicted with those of someone whom she respected or felt close to, she became "confused" and self-doubting about her own ideas. She all too readily assumed the role of the novice or "student" who was eager for advice. With her therapist, whenever she expressed herself assertively, she took pains to assure her that she did not mean to be critical or rejecting. She worried that she was being offensive in sticking to her own ideas and not accepting the viewpoint of the therapist.

Anne described herself as getting along quite well with her mother. Mother was presented as a quiet, noncontrolling sort of woman who went overboard in being unobtrusive during her stays with Anne, whom she visited rather often from her home in Wisconsin. Anne felt very close to her mother but described a feeling of "strain" at being with her for any length of time.

Just as Anne had said, her mother was a warm and pleasant woman. When asked to describe herself, she volunteered that she liked to keep things peaceful and consequently avoided arguments if at all possible. Interestingly, the example she gave was one in which she and a friend had disagreed on the occurrence of some event; rather than keep the argument going, Anne's mother had kept to herself some "proof" she had that she was right. Anne observed that this sounded strikingly like her own behavior.

What Anne did not observe and had never reported was how "hurt" her mother felt when there were disagreements. For example, mother described an instance when Anne lost her temper at mother's efforts to help by rearranging papers on Anne's desk; mother felt hurt at having been yelled at and withdrew to nurse her wounds. Not until this interview was it clear to the therapist and to Anne how she had been assuming that the rest of the world was as sensitive and intolerant of conflict as her mother.

It was interesting to note that Anne was so good at *avoiding* conflict with her mother, and her mother so good at communicating her being hurt unobtrusively (if nonetheless powerfully), that Anne had hardly ever had an opportunity to notice how her mother responded to disagreements; they just did not occur. She could not report to the therapist instances of facing her mother's hurt reactions. It was not until this interview that Anne realized at a conscious level how much she avoided threatening and "hurting" her mother. In future work, the therapist was able to use this insight about Anne's pattern of interaction with her mother to help Anne overcome her anxiety about disagreeing with others in her life.

Learning from Siblings

Meetings with siblings can be particularly useful, both in clarifying how the patient interacts with the parents and in getting some ideas as to alternative approaches. Siblings are often astute (albeit biased) observers of one another. Frequently they can describe well a pattern of interaction that the patient, being an emotionally involved participant, cannot observe very clearly. Furthermore, siblings have their own perspectives on the parents, which may differ considerably from that of the patient. Even when their perception is basically the same as what the therapist has heard, they may describe what went on in a way that the therapist registers somewhat differently. As we have stated before, it is useful for the therapist too to work through his understanding of the family dynamics. Often a sibling's perceptions and anecdotes deepen and renew more powerfully what the therapist already "knows."

Stuart had described his father as very uninvolved with his sons. He always seemed to Stuart to be disappointed in their accomplishments and to compare them unfavorably to the children of his friends. A meeting with Andy, Stuart's brother, confirmed this perception. He too described father's aloofness and lack of attention to his sons. Though this was, of course, no surprise to the therapist, Andy's attitude toward father was angrier and less resigned than his brother's.

Andy described in considerable detail an incident in which he had eagerly awaited his father's return from a business trip in order to show him a trophy he had won, only to be met with some extremely disparaging comment. Though Stuart had conveyed to the therapist his feeling that father was highly critical of *all* his sons, his brother's story deepened the therapist's understanding of just how rejecting father had been. Furthermore, the brother, unlike the patient, saw mother as acquiescing in and perhaps even encouraging father's detached and rejecting attitude.

Carole would become very upset when her mother was angry at her. She submitted to what she regarded as unreasonable demands in order to avoid the unpleasantness of a bitter scene. Assuming that mother, once angered, would stay angry led Carole to avoid confrontations. She very much wanted to become more assertive with mother, but often found herself almost immobilized with anxiety about incurring mother's wrath. This anxiety seemed to the therapist so out of proportion to the kind of anger that one could reasonably expect that it had the quality of a phobia.

For instance, if mother asked Carole to come to dinner so that some new friends would get a chance to meet her daughter, Carole could not say no even if she had already made other plans. Firmly believing that her mother would go into a tirade at such a refusal, and that her anger would be of indefinite duration, Carole resignedly submitted to this pressure. Having received some indication from Carole that her older sister Judith had in recent years learned to handle their mother, the therapist decided to ask the sibling in to discuss this issue. It was felt that Carole could perhaps model her sister's behavior, since they were both responding to the same person.

Judith described mother in much the same way as did Carole. The fact that they perceived mother the same way was of course important, since only if Carole perceived her sister as up against the same attitudes would her ways of dealing with this be relevant. According to Judith, mother did regard "loyalty" from her children as requiring submission to any and every request. Negative responses to her requests were met with accusations of disloyalty and threats of abandonment. Like Carole, Judith until just a couple of years ago had "quaked with fear" at mother's screaming. With the support of her husband, however, she had begun to try to stand up to mother. What she had discovered was that mother stayed angry for no more than a week and then would gradually warm up again, acting as if nothing had happened.

This discussion proved to be quite useful to Carole. Although the two sisters had often conversed about their mother's tyrannical attitudes, the questions asked by the therapist changed the focus of the discussion from shared groaning to strategic problem solving. With the help of the therapist, Judith was able to articulate clearly just how she had managed to change her behavior and what the results had been. Though this was by no means entirely new to Carole, it was spelled out in a way she seemed to be better able to use. She had always in some sense known mother's anger wouldn't last, but she now felt she could attempt to test this out, aided by a decision to borrow still another page from her sister's efforts and literally keep a chart of how long her mother's anger lasted.

Shortly after this meeting, Carole began to make some inroads into becoming more assertive with her mother. It is, of course, hard to know exactly what helped—that is, whether it was the information gained from this meeting or perhaps simply the act of holding this session, which conveyed an optimistic problem-solving attitude on the part of the therapist.

Correcting the Tendency to Blame

When we work with an individual in psychotherapy, the picture we get of family members—most often the patient's parents—may be one-dimensional in a number of respects. We learn about the parents in the context of how they influenced the course of the patient's development. We see the parents almost exclusively through the patient's eyes. Even any reports of the parents' own view of themselves or of how they are regarded by others is filtered through the consciousness of the patient. Since the patient has come to us primarily to discuss those aspects of his life about which he is dissatisfied, as therapists we tend to evaluate the parent–child interactions with a negative skew, even when the patient himself is speaking positively. Many therapists we know first became aware of their negative bias when they themselves became parents. Only then did they have a natural empathy for the difficulties of parenting, which could serve as a corrective for the hitherto unacknowledged tendency to see parents' behavior as only slightly less than villainous.

There are of course ways in which this bias is corrected for, even in the ordinary course of individual therapy. The good therapist helps his patient to see his own responsibility for the course his life took, as well as how he was influenced by his parents. He also helps the patient to see positive aspects of his own personality (and therefore of his upbringing) as well as the problematic ones. Nonetheless, we believe that upon reflection most therapists would agree that their pictures of patients' parents are considerably more negative than they would be if the parents were the patients.

Meeting a parent face to face as another human being, rather than as a phantom in the life of the patient, makes it possible to develop a much more three-dimensional and subtly nuanced picture. For a short while (to be described in detail in Chapter 8), we treat the parent somewhat as if he or she were our patient, inquiring into the parent's own personality and trying to listen with as much empathy as we can muster to the difficulties he or she describes.

Often our patient is surprised by the self-awareness demonstrated in the parent's answer to our request to "tell me about your personality." In many families, parents (even when the children are adults) do not share their internal life with their children. Just knowing that a parent is capable of introspection is often a positive experience for a child.

We as therapists may also be "softened up" by parents' expressions of emotional distress. We may, for example, sympathize to some degree with their "hurt" at being emotionally cut off from their offspring, even while we may feel confirmed in our judgment that our patient's emotional withdrawal has been necessary and warranted. Or we may feel sympathy for how anxious they seem in the session, or how grateful they feel at having been asked to attend. Even this little bit of firsthand knowledge of the parent is a useful corrective to the all-too-human tendency to build a case against those we don't really know. And it is invaluable in enabling us to apply a more comprehensive and realistic perspective in our efforts to be of assistance to the patient.

Enabling the Patient to See Parents More Positively

Patients in individual therapy often express a lot of negative feelings about family members. These negative perceptions seem to be enhanced by the process of therapy. Therapists, especially early in therapy, condone or even encourage the patient's "blaming" of family members, even while knowing that the "truth" is subjective and immensely complicated (E. F. Wachtel, 1979).

There are many reasons why therapists may find it useful or necessary to "blame" family members. For one, it helps alleviate the patient's feeling of self-contempt and helps him to have more empathy for his own difficulties. Secondly, many patients doubt the validity of their feelings, and the therapist aims to help the patient feel firmer about and value his own perceptions. Very disturbed patients in particular need help in seeing their "badness" or "craziness" as a response to heretofore unarticulated parental provocation.

Often, seeing parents more realistically means being able to acknowledge their shortcomings and faults—an undertaking a thin line away from blaming. Therapists often know that the "negative" picture, though a necessary corrective to previous denial, is in fact itself a distortion. Nonetheless, it is often necessary to accept and not to challenge these distortions in order to establish a therapeutic alliance. Only when the patient feels that he is accepted and cared about by the therapist does the therapist have enough leverage for his interventions to have a significant impact.

At later stages of the work, however, it has seemed to us that patients are often quite receptive to a revised, more complex and circular account of family history. As trust in their own perceptions, as well as in the therapist's, becomes firmer, they can now afford a more generous and systemic understanding of family members' "loathsome" behavior. Many patients *wish for*, not merely tolerate, a more positive view of family members. Meeting family members gives the therapist an experience from which he can cull some positive perceptions, which in turn can be presented to the patient. Just as judicious "blaming" has its place in therapy, so too does the planned use of positive statements about parents.

Most patients have at least some wish to see their parents positively and can take a step toward doing so by identifying with the *therapist's* more positive perceptions. The therapist, because of his special role vis-à-vis the patient, is in a uniquely powerful position to help alter the patient's ideas, feelings, and perceptions regarding his parents. Positive statements the therapist makes about the parents are often given more weight than similar statements made by someone not as significant to the patient.

Most therapists believe that caring about and valuing one's patient is an important part of what is therapeutic. By incorporating the therapist's good feelings about him, the patient can begin to feel better about himself. What we wish to add here is that just as patients can feel more positively about themselves by taking in the therapist's positive perceptions of *them*, so too can they incorporate the therapist's positive attitude toward aspects of their *parents*. Since we all consciously or unconsciously identify with our parents, viewing them more positively makes us feel prouder of ourselves. When meeting parents, it is useful for the therapist to look carefully for admirable qualities and to give the patient feedback on what he sees.

One might, for example, tell a patient in the next interview that "I was impressed by how outspoken and direct your mother was in regard to her feelings"; "Your mother seemed to be quite a zestful and energetic woman"; "Your father is a handsome man"; "Your mother is observant"; "Your father seems comfortable with your mother's assertiveness"; "Your mother seems to be very intuitive and sensitive to others' feelings"; or the like.

This discussion is not meant to deny the also common experience of patients' having a stake in a negative view of the parent. There are times when the therapist's making a positive comment about the parent will be experienced by the patient as a failure of empathy or as siding with the parent against the patient. Such concerns need to be addressed, and we do so in the next chapter. For now, we are merely pointing out that having met the parent in the flesh gives us more material to reexamine and modify the skewed picture the patient has presented. Furthermore, though we might say similar things based solely on inferences from what we have heard the patient say about the parents, basing our statements on actual encounters gives what we say much more credence.

A Sample of the Patient's Interactional Style

Inviting a guest to a session, whether it be a parent, a sibling, a spouse, a child, a lover, or even a friend, gives us an opportunity to observe firsthand our patient's interactional style. Frequently, in these sessions, we have seen our patients acting in a manner that came largely as a surprise to us. Though the patients may have told us about behaving this way in certain situations, patients' descriptions often are but a vague allusion compared to what we see in these sessions. People are rarely so self-observant that they can accurately convey just how they act. It is difficult to know, for instance, just what it means when someone says he "withdraws" in the face of conflict. Even detailed questioning designed to get very specific behavioral descriptions—something it will be clear we are strongly committed to—often does not elicit information that conveys nearly as richly the flavor and nuance of what the patient does.

Many therapists would contend that one gets such a firsthand opportunity to observe from the transference. We would agree, but only in part. The transference, to be sure, gives us a vivid interactional sample; however, as we have already indicated, in our view it is far from an exhaustive sample and not a sufficient substitute for knowing how the patient interacts with others. From a systems perspective, as from a cyclical psychodynamic perspective, the person's behavior and experience depend greatly on the context. Although it is often possible to find transference behavior that resembles in some way what one might see in the person's interaction with others, such behavior is often only a subtle hint of what becomes extraordinarily vivid in these sessions.

It is certainly true that sometimes transference reactions themselves are extremely powerful and vivid, and we are certainly not claiming that transference reactions are always a pale shadow. But we do insist that the instances in which the patient's proclivities are powerfully enacted in the transference do not exhaust all his important interactional behavior. Some patterns will be enacted particularly powerfully in the transference. Others are much more likely to become evident in other relationships. Despite prevailing myths, all therapists are not equivalent. Each of us have characteristics that inevitably enter into shaping which aspects of the patient's personality and of the patient's conflicts are most powerfully engaged in relation to us.

By holding sessions with significant others, we are able to observe a wider range of interactional style than we can by relying on the transference interactions alone. We have found it very useful to examine later with the patient just how he acted with the visitor in the session and to compare it with his way of being with us. Often we have held a number of sessions with different significant people in the patient's life. Doing this enables us to compare, for instance, how an individual acts with his sibling with how he acts with his spouse. Such comparisons often open up important avenues of exploration.

Jane, after years of waffling back and forth, finally resolved to ask for a separation from her husband, Ken, to whom she had been married for 8 years. After having announced this decision at home, she asked whether she could bring in her husband for one meeting, with the hope that they could work out a way to handle the separation that would be least harmful to their two young children. Problem-focused meetings such as this are described in detail in the next chapter. Here we wish simply to illustrate how observations deriving from these sessions can differ from those obtained in the transference.

For weeks prior to this separation, Jane had discussed with the therapist the rationale for separating. The therapist felt that Jane had a good deal of clarity as to her reasons and goals in making this move. In the sessions, she described what she would say and to some extent had already said to her husband regarding what she hoped to accomplish by a trial separation. For this reason, it came as quite a surprise to witness an actual discussion of the separation between the two of them.

Confused as well as hurt, Ken kept asking for clarification, and the two became embroiled in what seemed like a hopelessly entangled argument about the "logic" of what Jane was saying. In contrast to the articulateness with which she had expressed her feelings in individual sessions, she now became extremely vague.

Jane had told her therapist that she wanted to be free to explore other relationships and to use these experiences to get a better perspective on how strong her feelings were for her husband, as well as on some of her negative feelings toward him. In the session, however, she simply said that she wanted to separate temporarily because she was worn out from their quarreling and needed a rest. Obscuring the fact that she wanted an opportunity to evaluate the relationship, she said instead that she wanted them to "date" each other rather than live together, so that she would not have to deal with the aspects of Ken that she found so irritating. Since she avoided any references to the idea that she would be using the separation to make a decision about the relationship, Ken did not think a separation made logical sense. "How," he asked, "would dating each other solve our problems?" As Ken pressed for clarity, Jane became increasingly vague and continued to omit the crucial point that she wished to go out with others in order to evaluate her commitment to staying with him.

Following this meeting, Jane explored in her regular session just how she had felt about the joint meeting. It seemed that she was pleased to have had the therapist's help in resolving the issue, even though that help had consisted largely of encouraging (and at times even pushing) Jane to be clearer. On a couple of occasions (in the course of 3 years' work), Jane had mentioned that friends got angry at her for not being clear about the boundaries of the relationship. The session with Jane's husband gave the therapist an opportunity to see exactly how Jane kept things vague. Jane had always seemed unusually vulnerable to accusations by her husband that she was immature or "screwed up." By being vague, in the hope of not incurring her husband's anger and of keeping her options open, Jane did appear irrational. One could easily see how her husband would perceive Jane as confused. In the session with Ken, the therapist gained information not only as to the exact behavioral components of Jane's obscureness, but also as to just how this strategy elicited the very criticism to which she was most vulnerable.

Making the System More Hospitable
to the Patient's Changing

Family members often regard the therapist and the therapy as somewhat threatening. Many parents worry that their grown children's therapy will consist largely of finding fault with their parenting. Stories abound about patients who have become angry and alienated from those for whom they had previously had seemingly positive feelings. A spouse may be troubled about the intimacy that the partner now has with a stranger, or may worry that the therapist will stir up trouble in the relationship. Though these attitudes are by no means always predominant (and in fact, some parents and spouses rejoice in individuals' finally getting the help they need), we have found that quite often our patients have to contend with the negative feelings of intimates regarding their treatment.

While it is true that some patients provoke these reactions by presenting the therapy as a place in which they can "tattle," or by using the therapist's statements as weapons with which they assault others, nonetheless the hostility that many patients encounter seems to be largely unprovoked. In these cases, we work with the patients on what they can do to alleviate the family members' largely unfounded anxiety. We have also found it helpful to suggest that a hostile family member be included in a session so that he or she will have an opportunity to meet the mysterious "therapist." Just as we may correct our tendency to distort and blame family members by meeting them in person, so too anxious family members can have *their* anxieties alleviated by meeting us and (one hopes) experiencing us as fair-minded and reasonable rather than incendiary. (In the next chapter, we discuss the format we use for meetings of this sort.)

We have found that giving the guest an opportunity to contribute to the therapeutic effort by telling us what he or she has been hoping we would know is often very helpful. Family members often feel relief in knowing that their concerns and points of view have been heard, and the sense of participation in the process softens their objections.

We may also learn in this meeting that our patient has subtly contributed to the anxieties that a spouse or parent may be feeling. If this is the case, we explore more fully than we did previously the motivation behind such behavior. Most guests leave this meeting feeling much more comfortable with the idea of therapy than they did when they first came in. Though we cannot assure a guest that individual therapy will not at times focus on the "negative" in relationships, our systemic orientation helps us convey a concern with untangling patterns in which all are caught, rather than with assigning blame.

Sometimes (with the prior consent of the patient), we will discuss our view of the patient's problem and our treatment plan. We find this particularly useful when it appears that the work requires new behaviors on the part of the individual that the family member will be affected by. For instance, if a woman is working on being more assertive, we might explain to her husband or parents why we think this is necessary. We may try to enlist their support for this change, even though they are ambivalent about how this will alter previously established roles. We may point out the ultimate benefit of such change to them as well as to the patient.

Just as therapists working individually with a child need the support of the parents in order to minimize negative reactions to changed behavior, so too can therapists pave the way for their adult patients. For some therapists, however, such a way of proceeding may raise a concern about doing for a patient what he should be doing for himself. Is it not the patient's responsibility to deal with his family's concerns about his therapy?

In our view, such a concern on the therapist's part is largely a reflection of the societal values critically examined in Chapter 1. To be sure, one must be judicious in the assistance one provides to patients. It is certainly true that assistance *can* be debilitating or infantilizing, and there is indeed much that we must all learn to do for ourselves. But contemporary therapeutic practice at times seems to reflect a degree of distrust of the easy path that would be worthy of John Calvin. As we have argued in a number of places throughout this book, we regard the attitude toward direct assistance adopted by many in the helping professions to be an oddly paradoxical and severely limiting one. In many instances, the best way to enable the patient eventually to reach a point where he is more self-sufficient is to provide him with assistance along the way. Moreover, the very ideals of self-sufficiency that presently have such currency in our society urgently require modulation and humane rethinking (P. L. Wachtel, 1983).

It should be noted that not all patients want to let the therapist help them out in this way. Some fear that even to ask the hostile family member to come in will make matters worse. They may also feel childish accepting this sort of help and prefer to do it themselves.

Moreover, for various reasons they may want to preserve the state of affairs in which the family member feels threatened by the patient's being in therapy. We have encountered as well many instances in which the patient feared that the guest would later mock or criticize the therapist and that the guest's negative opinion would undermine the patient's own positive judgments. All these reactions by the patient to the idea of bringing in a relative are interesting and revealing. Even when the decision is ultimately made not to hold such a session, we learn a great deal by raising this as a possibility.

Shortly after Donna and her husband had their first child, Donna began to have difficulty in dealing with her mother. Prior to the birth of the baby, she had dealt with her mother by gritting her teeth and being "agreeable," all the while keeping her mother at arm's length. Now that she was seeing more of her mother, she was finding herself increasingly bothered by what she perceived as her mother's critical attitudes. It no longer seemed workable simply to grit her teeth until she could get away. With the birth of the baby, the system had changed, and the old coping devices no longer worked as well. The stress of having more contact with her mother now that there was a grandchild motivated Donna to try to be more direct with her. She also found that keeping a distance no longer seemed desirable, because she wanted her child to have a chance to be close to his grandmother.

Donna was fearful that if she was direct with her mother she would hurt her. She wanted help in being assertive but not aggressive. With this end in mind, therapy sessions were used to locate just where and when Donna was uncomfortable with her mother. Role playing was used to help her practice new ways of interacting so that she didn't have to distance herself emotionally.

A week or two after Donna and her therapist had started to work on this, Donna asked her husband to join her in a session. It seemed that he was quite opposed to this new direction. He, like Donna, had kept a respectable distance from his own family. Convinced that Donna's new approach would ultimately lead to her becoming very upset, he came to the session with the hopes of dissuading Donna and the therapist from what he perceived to be a dangerous course of action. Though he was set to do battle, and one could easily experience him as intrusive and controlling (just the way Donna's mother had been described), the therapist preferred to focus on his anxiety and protectiveness toward his wife. The aim was to prevent a power struggle from developing between Donna and her husband, which would have interfered with focusing on the issues between mother and daughter. This was accomplished not only by being reassuring, but by incorporating some of the husband's suggestions and altering some strategies so that they would be more in conformity to what the husband could support.[6] Even though Donna's husband attended only one session, he became an active participant in the work rather than a bystander or even a potential opponent. (Further discussion of the compromise worked out with Donna and her husband appears on pp. 228–229 of Chapter 8.)

Eliciting the cooperation of key relatives may be particularly important in working with depressed patients. Sometimes with such patients it is useful to prescribe the symptom. This technique (described more fully in Chapter 6) involves asking the patient to "go with" his depression rather than to resist it. The patient might even be asked to increase his depression beyond what he already feels. Not surprisingly, such a prescription can at times be disturbing to a spouse or parent who wants the patient to be *less* depressed, not more. Clearly, here is another instance in which an opportunity for the therapist to meet with the concerned other can head off a potential sabotage of the treatment.

To be sure, one would eventually hope that the patient could himself deal with objections by a spouse or parent to something he regards as useful. But the point when the patient is in the midst of a depression is not the optimal time to take on such a task. We believe it is important for therapists to have both a clear sense of focus and a reasonable estimate of what the patient is capable of at any point. All too often, the ultimate achievement of whatever approximation to autonomy we social beings can attain is interfered with by an excessive concern with autonomy at every single moment. In our experience, the patient who has received the kind of assistance we have been describing does not become inappropriately dependent upon the therapist. Rather, having the experience of successfully utilizing therapeutic

6. This example may again raise for some readers the question of where the therapist's loyalties should lie and/or whether the therapist has a right or responsibility to take into account the needs and desires of other important people in the patient's life. These technical and ethical questions are addressed at a number of points throughout this book.

suggestions, he feels more confident about tackling the remaining and perhaps more difficult problems. Having previously seen the therapist "handle" effectively difficult family members, the patient has a model on which he may base his own interactions. He also knows that the therapist really understands just what he is up against.

8. *Meeting the Cast of Characters: II. Guidelines for Technique*

THUS FAR we have been describing what we feel are the many benefits of meeting with family members. These range from the help one may get in the reconstruction of the patient's history to opportunities for eliciting a more hospitable attitude on the part of important others toward potential changes by the patient. We have discussed how such meetings give us information regarding just how much distortion is involved in the patient's perceptions, as well as how he may be subtly contributing by his interactional style to the very difficulties about which he is distressed. We have also seen how these sessions can correct our unwitting tendency as therapists to blame family members, and may even lead to positive perceptions that we can give back to our patients. Precisely what information and what salient experience can be derived from such interviews depends on many variables, including characteristics of the patient, characteristics of the family member, stage of therapy, and many others. It depends as well on the skill with which one conducts the interview. In this chapter, we discuss in detail some technical guidelines for the conduct of such interviews.

Preparing for an Interview

Presenting the Rationale to the Patient

Before agreeing to invite a guest, most patients want to know why it will be helpful and what is likely to take place. In regard to why it will be helpful, the therapist can explain that one often gets a feeling for family members from meeting them that helps to clarify some of the issues the patient is dealing with. In addition, a parent or sibling has a perspective on the patient and the events of his life that can provide additional useful information.

Though most patients readily accept the usefulness of the idea, they have a good deal of concern about what exactly will take place. We have found it helpful to convey to the patient the attitude that in this meeting we will act as his agent, and at the same time will take charge and will prevent destructive confrontations. "Acting as his agent" means that we get prior approval regarding the limits of what he wants or does not want us to do. We prepare for the meeting by taking notes on the patient's preferences. We start by describing in detail the kinds of questions we generally ask and explore his feelings about those particular questions. If after exploration of his concerns, the patient still prefers that we not ask certain questions, we honor his request. We may later explore with him more fully the reasons (both conscious and unconscious) for these preferences, but at this point our goal is simply to plan the session and to give the patient as much of a feeling of control as we possibly can.

An inquiry into other topics the patient might like to explore that have not been covered by our general questions is often quite revealing. For instance, one man said that he would really like to know which of the children his mother loved best. The therapist, not surprisingly, did not raise this question in the session with the mother, but it was fruitfully explored as a concern of the patient's later in the therapy. As in this example, the unusualness of the situation can bring up issues and fantasies that have a "fairy-tale"-like quality; the therapist may be viewed almost as a magician who will cast a spell and reveal truth.

Dealing with the Patient's Anxieties

Many patients express a good deal of anxiety at the prospect of bringing in a family member. Exploring and eventually alleviating this anxiety to some degree constitute the first step in arranging for these meetings. Often the very suggestion of actually meeting an important person in the patient's life elicits responses that reveal new dynamics and conflicts and open up avenues for exploration. We regard this revelation of new facets of the patient's personality as an important opportunity for deepening understanding. In addition, we believe that exploration of the meaning of these interviews for the patient is crucial for their success.

When the suggestion is made that a parent join a session, the patient's first reaction is often an extremely anxious "I couldn't." We have been surprised by how often the anxiety seems to be based on a concern with upsetting the parent. Even with patients who have expressed a good deal of anger toward their parents, there seems to be a wish to protect the parents from feeling blamed or being attacked. On occasion, we have first found out at this point that the patient has avoided telling the parents that he is in therapy, for fear that the parents will be worried or feel guilty that their child rearing has been faulty. This has led to useful explorations of how the patient feels when a parent is upset and of his varied efforts to avoid disturbing the parent.

The other common anxiety about inviting parents in is that a parent may have very negative attitudes toward psychotherapy and feel that therapists are essentially "charlatans." Again, the patient may have avoided ever telling the parent that he is in treatment for fear of having to deal with this critical attitude.

Patients have also expressed concern about the feelings of dependency evoked by making such a request. One woman of 35 said, "I'd feel like a little girl parading in here with my Mommy and Daddy."

A number of patients have been concerned about the repercussions of such a meeting. Will the parents become intrusive? Will they want to know more about the patient's difficulties than the patient is comfortable with disclosing? There is often a good deal of anxiety about the intimacy involved in inviting a parent into the treatment room.

Some patients are quite convinced that their parents would unequivocally refuse to attend such a meeting. Again, even if a decision is made not to pursue the idea, we learn a great deal from raising the issue. How would the patient make the request? What are his assumptions about why the parent would or would not agree to come? How would he feel if the parent did refuse? How would this request and refusal be dealt with later? How are conflicts resolved? What "scars," if any, would be left by such a refusal? Patients often feel they would rather not ask than have to deal with their parents' reactions.

Reactions to the suggestion to bring in a sibling are generally much less intense, unless there has been a "cut-off" and the siblings are not on speaking terms. Often patients are intrigued by the idea of bringing in a sibling and welcome the opportunity for greater intimacy. Even if the meeting is not arranged, we get to "know" this particular relationship better by exploring with our patient his fantasies about how his sibling would react to such a request.

Inviting in a spouse or lover to a session poses very different questions from inviting parents or siblings. Here patients often show little anxiety, but rather a desire to preserve the therapist as their own private confidante.[1]

Some women patients have expressed concern about the possibility of their husbands' derogating the therapist. These women are generally very dependent on their husbands and have been working in therapy on knowing and trusting their own judgments. They have expressed concern that if their husbands find fault with the therapist, it will be difficult for them to maintain their own positive feelings. It may take a high degree of self-confidence and assertiveness for a patient to continue in therapy when a partner disparages its value.

In such an instance as this, one must also explore a patient's assumptions as to *why* the partner will have a negative reaction. Has the patient been using the therapist as a threat? Is the spouse disturbed or fearful about the changes that are taking place? Does the patient expect the therapist to be attacking or confronting of the visitor? Would the therapist seem weak and easily intimidated by the partner? Just as patients seem to feel a need to protect their parents from attack, so too may a patient worry about the therapist's having a hard time with the criticism and antagonistic confrontation of a family member, be it parent or partner.

After spending some time getting a more specific sense of the patient's anxieties, we then address their concerns in the following manner. In regard to a parent's feeling blamed, we reassure the patient that we understand that concern and will not let that happen. We explain that, on the contrary, we go out of our way to make sure that

---

1. In exploring patients' feelings about having their spouses meet us, we have noticed not infrequently that they prefer to keep us as "mystery figures." Threats to tell "my therapist" are more effective when the therapist is not a real person who can empathize with a spouse's feelings. Often it is only when we have suggested meeting a patient's partner that we discover we are being used this way.

the parent finds the experience relatively painless. Our purpose in these meetings is not to confront or have the patient confront the parent. Therefore, we work with the patient on an alternative way to utilize such a meeting and assure the patient that we will intervene in the session if it is becoming too confrontational.

Preparing the Patient to Communicate the Idea to the Guest

If a patient is concerned that a parent or partner will refuse to come in, we first review with him just what he had planned to say regarding the request. We may then coach the patient on saying something that in our experience may get a more favorable response. Sometimes we use the device of asking the patient what he could say to *insure* that the request would be met with objections. This "reverse" approach often helps highlight the way the patient may be subtly and unconsciously helping to bring about the rejection that he is anticipating.

In regard to inviting parents or siblings, we suggest that the patient tell the person that the therapist would like to hear from the family something about what the patient was like as a child. Particularly when talking to a parent, it is better to say, "The therapist wants to hear what I was like," rather than such things as "The therapist wants to hear about what went on in the family when I was growing up." We advise the patient to keep the focus on *himself*: The parent is needed to tell us more about the patient.

What we want to avoid is the patient's saying or implying in any way that the therapist wants to judge or evaluate the parent. Even though we learn a great deal about the parent in these sessions, we try to keep the content of the session focused largely on the patient; we feel that parents are more responsive if this orientation is conveyed to them in advance. Since most of these meetings are intentionally not focused on any current problem between family members, we suggest that the patient convey to the parent that the purpose is mainly to help the therapist find out more about the patient and is not intended as a meeting to work out family difficulties.

In inviting in a spouse, it is particularly important to make clear that the purpose is not to criticize, but rather to gain the spouse's perspective on the individual's difficulties or the difficulties that exist between them. If there is tension in the relationship, the patient might say, "I'd like the therapist to hear your side of things," or "I know I must be doing things that bother you, and I'd like the therapist to hear about it." We have found that people will generally be willing to come in if they are assured that it will be genuinely helpful to the patient and will not be used as a forum to fight.

With parents or spouses who are opposed to the whole idea of psychotherapy, the patient is advised not to get into a discussion on the merits of psychotherapy. He might anticipate the objection and say something like "I know you don't believe in this, Dad, but I *am* in therapy and it would help the process if you would come in and tell the therapist what you know about me." The request is thus for the parent to be a temporary "cotherapist," a temptation difficult for most parents to resist. If the parent is one who believes that one should help oneself and that it is weak to get advice, the patient might say that the therapist would like to hear from the parent on how to help foster independence.

The Issue of Confidentiality

We have been struck by how seldom patients express concern about confidentiality. Most patients seem to assume (and rightfully so) that we will respect their confidences in these sessions. If the question does come up, we assure them that we will volunteer no information that could in any way be construed as confidential. Usually at this point, if there is a nonobvious "secret," the patient will let us know (e.g., "I didn't tell my parents that I was worried about chest pains recently").

Patients may anticipate that the guest will have a question for the therapist—for example, "Why is my son in therapy?" "Why did my daughter become gay?" "Did my sister tell you about the time she . . . ?" Where questions can be anticipated, we plan out with the patient what he would like us to say. The overriding feeling of these planning sessions is one of collaboration and respect for the patient's wishes. If a question is asked that we have not anticipated, the patient must know that the therapist will protect his privacy with as general an answer as possible, and will leave it to the patient to decide whether or not he himself wishes to reveal more detail.

When to Suggest Such Meetings

An ongoing question which we have not yet resolved is when to suggest such a meeting. In our experience thus far, the question of what is the optimal point in therapy at which to have such an interview has been less clearly answered than that of how to conduct it or prepare for it. There are considerations that could lead to a number of different and sometimes contradictory recommendations in this regard. In fact, we ourselves have not always agreed as to what point in therapy is best. On the one hand, since a major purpose of these interviews is to enable the therapist to understand the patient's context in a way that ordinary therapy sessions alone cannot provide, it would seem useful to conduct these sessions early in the therapy. In this way, the therapist can be better informed from the very beginning, and can avoid some of the pitfalls and false starts that might result from forming one's picture of the characters in the patient's life solely on the basis of the patient's report.

On the other hand, our feeling is that many patients need a good deal of time in which to experience the therapist as on their side before being able to tolerate the therapist's seeing for himself what the guest is like. We have found this particularly true with patients who, prior to therapy, have been unable to tolerate consciously negative feelings about family members. With patients who are at a stage of treatment in which they are learning to recognize and tolerate their own hostile feelings, introducing "objectivity" does not seem wise.

Interviews held during a period in which a patient is intensely angry at a family member are generally not useful, except as a way to introduce the idea of family therapy if that seems appropriate. In general, unless the patient can tolerate some alternative perspectives on his own interpretation of reality or some positive feedback about family members, we postpone the interview until a later stage of therapy. We are uncomfortable doing such an interview when the patient wants the therapist only to see how bad the family member is or wants the therapist to tell the guest how much he or she has harmed the patient. Therapists must use their clinical judgment in these matters. Our guidelines are to assess how much trust and rapport we have with a patient and how able he is to tolerate a challenge to his own perspective at this point in treatment.

There are certain specific circumstances in which a decision to conduct such an interview at a particular point in the course of therapy seems more clearly called for. For example, if an intimate is expressing a lot of hostility toward treatment, we probably want to help with this situation as early as possible. Similarly, when a patient's symptoms and treatment directly involve another person, we find it useful to hear from that person as soon as we can. For instance, in one case, a patient consulted the therapist because of severe anxiety attacks. In order to come to the office, she had to be accompanied by her husband, who waited for her in the waiting room. The "systemic" aspects of this symptom seemed so pervasive that it seemed best to learn about the interactional aspects as soon as possible.

Sometimes circumstances alone lead us to suggest a meeting. An opportunity to meet with a family member who lives a great distance away should not be passed up, unless there is a clear indication that it would present the difficulties discussed above. If a parent is in remission from a life-threatening illness, one might want to hold a meeting while he or she is still alive. Meetings held under these circumstances present certain special difficulties. For one thing, patients usually feel even more strongly that they don't want the meeting to be upsetting to their parents. On the other hand, their hopes and fantasies about reconciliation are quite high, and they need to be told what they can realistically expect.

We have found that even in less emotionally charged situations, patients often have expectations that do not fit with the kind of "low-key" interviews we have found most useful. We have found it helpful to indicate that these interviews sometimes are dramatic in what they reveal, but that more often than not what we learn is subtle and communicated between the lines.

It is worth noting that whereas with some patients the introduction of these interviews seems dictated primarily by a general belief in their value (based on both theory and experience), in other instances the calling in of close intimates of the patients seems to flow organically from the questions and concerns that are salient in the work at a particular point. On such an occasion, suggesting this sort of interview does not feel to the patient or therapist like the introduction of a technical procedure (even an appropriate and comprehensible procedure), but simply feels like the obvious and logical thing to do. In effect, at these moments one has the experience of proceeding as one would naturally and spontaneously, were there no "rules" of therapy saying one shouldn't.

Patient and therapist, for example, may be puzzled about the origins of some defensive behavior. Together they may be speculating that this coping mechanism stems from the patient's response to a family crisis that occurred when he was a young child. But the patient and therapist would like to know more about this time in the patient's life, and inviting in family members to ask about the patient's reactions as a young child seems to flow naturally from what is being discussed. Or perhaps when a patient is saying that his spouse has a different view of his problems than he does, the therapist might suggest that the partner be invited in to give her views.

One occasion for calling in a guest that may not appear particularly obvious to the therapist who has practiced individual therapy exclusively is the simple instance of being "stuck." Family therapists frequently use the rule of thumb that when therapy is feeling "stuck," it is time to bring in one more person. Individual therapists need not take this as a replacement for their own rules of thumb (e.g., "look at what has evoked resistance," or "look at countertransference factors that have restricted the therapist from pursuing appropriate inquiry"). Rather, what we have in mind here is an additional, complementary perspective.

As we have suggested in a number of places, psychotherapy is an exceedingly difficult enterprise. It is easy for the therapist to feel blocked, thwarted, simply unable to make sense of what is happening or to know where to go next. In such circumstances, anything that helps to break the therapist's set—to provide the possibility of a new vantage point—is likely to be useful. In this sense, as elsewhere in life, promiscuity is likely to generate more offspring than fidelity.

Conducting the Interviews

After much trial and error, we have come up with a format for each type of interview, which seems to us to balance well the desire to get information with the wish to keep the meeting nonconfrontational and relatively pleasant for the guests. We first describe some general principles for conducting these interviews, and then discuss some specific questions one might want to ask and variations on the general principles that may be appropriate, depending on who is being interviewed or the particular circumstances that have prompted the meeting.

General Principles

In general, we have found it best for the therapist to be very active in conducting the interview. Both patient and guest become much less anxious when they feel that the therapist has certain questions in mind, and that the meeting will not be an open-ended discussion that could result in an emotional free-for-all. Since we are not embarking on family therapy, we do not want the session to leave family members with open wounds with which they will have no opportunity to deal. Conveying the message right from the start that we as therapists are in charge and have a certain format that we generally follow in meetings such as these not only reduces anxiety, but allows us to interrupt the interview to get back on the track if it is going in a direction that seems potentially destructive. As discussed earlier, we tell our patients that we will be somewhat "protective" of guests, and we do in fact bend over backward to convey respect and thanks for guests' participation.

Therapists accustomed to letting patients determine how they will use the therapy time may be tempted to start a family meeting by asking either the patient or the guest what that person would like to talk about. For the reasons just stated, we advise against such an approach. Though the therapist may feel in charge by remaining silent, a guest, especially if he has never been in therapy, may experience this stance as passive or as an abdication of responsibility (and perhaps even as hostile).

Our primary goal at the start of the session is to reduce everyone's anxiety, including our own, and we find that this is best achieved by telling the guest why we thought it would be useful for him to come in. We ask how he feels about being here and empathize with any anxiety he expresses. Sometimes the patient and guest will spontaneously begin to interact. Even if the discussion is a fruitful one, we keep control by returning to our format as soon as we can. We might say, for instance, "This sounds like it's worth discussing, but I wonder if you can hold that for a while, since I generally find it useful to get some other information first." Though this may seem somewhat rigid or obsessive to some people, we find that it serves a very important purpose in this sort of interview: It keeps the participants from doing what comes all too naturally—repeating the same old fights, the same old misunderstandings, the same old efforts to "help" that somehow never do.

Much of the conversation in these interviews takes place between therapist and guest, rather than between patient and guest. For a good part of the meeting, the patient may be little more than a listener. The experience of listening to oneself being talked about often stirs up child-like feelings of dependency, which can be discussed in subsequent individual sessions. In most of our meetings, we ask questions of the guest, and the answers are directed to us. The patient may be invited to comment on or react to what has been said if he does not spontaneously do so. We may then direct questions to the patient.

Once we have taken charge in this way, we find that he patient and guest do not talk directly to each other unless requested to do so. Being the hub around which conversation revolves may seem odd to a therapist used to working in a nondirective manner with only one individual. We have found, however, that doing this helps us keep the session in the proper emotional range.

At points during a session, we may ask family members to discuss something between themselves. We do this when we want to get a picture of the communication patterns that may be contributing to difficulties. Having been the hub of the wheel prior to this interaction, we can easily resume control by asking questions and having answers directed toward us.

Discussions with colleagues lead us to believe that one of the major factors in the reluctance of therapists to do these interviews is the anxiety they feel about sessions getting out of control and the uncertainty they have about how to conduct such meetings. The method we have just described goes a long way toward preventing "runaway" sessions. During these meetings, therapists must think of themselves as being like directors who, while giving their cast much room for their own creative interpretation, nonetheless keep the needs of the entire play in mind at all times.

Interviews with Parents of Adult Patients

Interviews with parents of an adult patient may be held with one or both parents, depending on the patient's preference. Generally, we prefer to have one parent only if the patient is concerned that coming to a session together will open up severe marital problems that exist between the parents. Even in such instances, if one of the purposes is to assess how the family system operates, it may be preferable to have both parents attend. In the case of divorced parents, we always hold the interviews separately and without the new spouses (if any).

Regardless of whether one or both parents are there, we begin the meeting by saying that though of course we have heard a good deal about them, we probably know less about them than they realize. Our interviews with family members have convinced us of the truth of this statement. Parents often have the idea that therapy consists of little else but talking about them. They are surprised and often relieved (but perhaps also disappointed) that we don't know as much as they expected. We say something like this: "Although we wanted you to come in so that you could give us some information regarding your daughter, I would find it helpful if you would start by giving me a 5-minute thumbnail sketch of yourself. What are you like? Tell me about yourself." If the parent seems confused by the question or doesn't seem to be responding usefully, we might further ask such questions as "What's your personality like?"

Some parents find this a disconcerting question and may need reassurance and encouragement to answer. If both parents are at the meeting, it is interesting to see who "volunteers" to go first or how it is determined who will start. We notice, too, whether the nonspeaking spouse spontaneously adds to or confirms what his mate is saying. Does this spouse correct the speaker? How does the speaker respond to the "correction"? Is it experienced as intrusive or supportive?

We notice what aspects of himself the parent regards as salient. Does he talk about himself in relation to his career? Does he define himself in terms of his parenting? Since the person is in our office because of his "parent" role, what he says may be skewed toward the parenting end. We try to make clear that we are interested in the parents as separate individuals and are not at this point asking about them in relation to their child.

If a parent has given only the "facts" of his life, we ask him to describe his personality. "What are you like?" "What is your personality like?" Some people have a good deal of trouble with such questions. Giving examples often is helpful at this point: "Are you outgoing or do you keep to yourself?" "Are you relaxed or on the tense side?" And so on. Most people will at this point feel reassured enough to answer the questions. If a parent seems extremely resistant to answering, we will, in the interest of avoiding a power struggle, go on to something else. Such resistance is extremely rare. If it does occur, it is itself highly informative.

After the parent has briefly described himself, we ask our patient whether anything he has just heard came as a surprise. We invite comments by our patient on what was said and ask for additions or modifications. In this way, we get into a discussion that is broader than mere information gathering. We might ask the guest to compare himself with the patient on certain personality traits. For example, if the guest says that he is not assertive, we might ask, "How would you compare yourself to your daughter when it comes to assertiveness?"

After we have talked about the personalities of the guest(s) and the patient, we then shift to a historical perspective. We do this both because we are genuinely interested in the history, and because to continue on the other course feels too open-ended and potentially volatile. It is important to keep in mind that our aim is to get information about the parent and the system, not to open up and resolve relationship problems. Obviously, there is plenty of place for strong emotion in therapy, and avoidance of conflict and difficult issues is most certainly not our general rule. But in these particular interviews, we find that their specific and limited (though highly important) purpose is best served by proceeding in the manner described here.

Inquiry into the childhood of our patient goes something like this: "What was your son like as a baby? What was he like as a young child? What memories do you have of him as a child? What stands out? Were there stages in his childhood that seemed particularly difficult for him?" Notice that we use the word "stages." This is an attempt to normalize and reassure the parent so that he will feel comfortable talking about difficult times.

With the hope that we might be able to give the patient something positive to counteract negative feelings about parents, we ask the parents what they remember as especially nice times they shared with their child. Reminiscences about the past often bring about a feeling of emotional closeness that has been long missing from the relationship. Not infrequently, the patient is surprised by the parent's memories. "Sentimentality" is taboo in some families. Sanctioning such reminiscences by making them part of the "facts" we need to know may help the reticent to be more emotionally expressive.

We may ask a parent to comment on how a child has changed

over the years: "How do you see Emily now? How does she seem different and how the same as when she was a child?"

Depending on our patient's prior approval, we may ask as well what the parent sees as the child's current difficulties. Not uncommonly, patients who have previously avoided discussing this sort of thing with their parents find it liberating to have a "forum" where such a discussion is sanctioned and perceived as safer than it ordinarily might be.

Generally, it is helpful to ask parents about the patient's relationship with his siblings as a child. Did they fight? Were they close? How did the patient deal with the siblings (e.g., aggressively, protectively, competitively)? Patients often are surprised by how much insight their parents have regarding their personalities. Despite inevitable distortions, parents are often astute observers of their children.

We are particularly interested in parents' observations of their children at times of great stress in the family. We might ask, for instance, "How did John react when his father died?" "How did David handle his sister's accident?" Often parents have given a lot of thought to their children's personalities. They are generally willing to share their observations if they feel confident that the therapist is in control of the situation. Not infrequently, our patient may regard the parent's observations as biased and hostile. Reactions to "hostile" comments vary, of course, from patient to patient. Docile acceptance of criticism, bitter retorts, or humorous quips on the part of our patient may come as a surprise to us. If the parent's remarks lead to a heated confrontation, we interrupt the argument with a variety of techniques, which we discuss in a later section.

Interviews with Siblings

We begin interviews with siblings in much the same way as we do our interviews with parents. Again, we find a short thumbnail personality sketch by the guest a good way to open up a variety of issues. As is the case when parents are interviewed, we have had at least one planning session with our patient, so we know what topics are to be avoided if at all possible. Generally, we ask the sibling the following sorts of questions: "How do you see your brother's relationship with your parents? How does it differ from your own relationship with your parents? What stands out in your mind about your brother when he was a child? How did he get along with your parents then? How did the two of you get along? Do you see your brother as having changed over the years? In what way? What do you see as current difficulties your brother has? How do the two of you get along now?"

This last question, of course, opens up the issue of conflict between the two of them. Depending upon the nature of the conflict and the degree of hostility between the siblings, a discussion of the issues between them may prove fruitful. Many siblings are on cordial but cautious terms. If the conflicts are relatively mild, an opportunity to open up about what is bothering them in the safety of a therapist's office may be quite productive. If, on the other hand, the discussion turns to a heated and bitter confrontation, the therapist is well advised to follow the suggestions to be given below for "cooling down" the meeting.

In one section of Chapter 7 (see "Learning from Siblings"), we describe using our meetings with siblings to gain a clearer picture of both the problems in dealing with parents and possible "solutions" to them. If our patient has difficulty in dealing with his parents, we find it useful to ask the sibling whether he experiences the same difficulty. If he does *not*, we try to assess whether the difference lies in how he perceives the parent, or in the way he acts and is in turn treated by the parent. We assume that if the parents treat one sibling differently from the other, they are responding at least in part to behavior on the part of a child that provokes or at least permits a particular way of interaction. Thus, if the sibling says he does not have the same problem with a parent, we ask why this might be the case. Siblings of patients often have useful insights into the differences in the way they and the patient interact with their parents.

Interviews with Partners

We usually begin these interviews by asking the partner what he or she feels is important for us to know that our patient might not have emphasized enough. Generally this will elicit some discussion of the personality differences between the partners. We are careful here to try to keep the discussion of differences from rapidly escalating into a "fight." Problem-focused interviews are discussed below, but for now we are describing interviews with partners where there is no obvious or pressing conflict between them.

Generally (having obtained the prior consent of our patient), we say something like this (with a light tone): "Here is your opportunity to tell us all those things that you've probably wished we knew about your wife. We want to hear your perspective on your wife's difficulties." Specific questions such as "How do you see your wife's relationship with her mother?" will vary, of course, with the particular problem being discussed in therapy.

With partners, we are particularly interested in their patterns of interaction. We might, for instance, ask the partner, "What do you do when your husband is depressed? Do you try to get him out of it? If so, how?" Though we keep the focus as much as possible on the problems of our patient rather than on disagreements between the partners, we do want to learn as much as possible about how the partners interact and how this system of interaction may contribute to the patient's difficulties. To this end, we are more apt in these sessions than in others to ask the partners to discuss something or to direct the conversation in a way so that they talk to each other rather than to the therapist. The possibility that this may open up a discussion of conflicts that are best dealt with by marital therapy is, of course, a very real one. We do not, however, suggest a referral for marital therapy unless we have already explored this with our patient prior to this meeting.

Interviews to Deal with Specific Issues

The interviews we have described thus far are not intended to deal with and resolve specific conflicts between our patient and significant people in his life. On certain occasions, however, we find it useful to hold more problem-focused meetings. Earlier in the chapter, we have discussed our position on helping a patient deal with a family member who is opposed to the therapy by inviting that person to a session. In a session of this sort we do *not* ask for a thumbnail sketch, because the "guest" generally enters the session feeling angry and resistant. Instead, we acknowledge the guest's feelings about coming to a therapist and thank him for his willingness to meet with us despite his convictions to the contrary. Again, we find that compliments go a long way toward gaining the cooperation we need for these sessions to be helpful.

Often, after this sort of beginning, the visitor is responsive to our invitation to tell us what he thinks we might need to know about his personality before proceeding to the problem at hand.

Next we tell the guest that we have the impression that he is opposed to, or at the least not enthusiastic about, the patient's being in therapy, and we invite him to talk about this. Often this leads to a discussion that presents the guest's position somewhat differently than the patient has described it. Our questioning and empathy enable the guest to talk about his feelings in a way that may make more sense to our patient than the barbs and "nasty" comments that have occurred at home.

Many partners or parents are, at the core, frightened by the possibility of unknown changes. Their opposition is seldom a simple matter of intellectual convictions. They fear and fantasize about the therapist who may turn their loved one against them. Empathizing with their anxieties, and offering assurances that the thrust of our work is self-understanding, not criticism of others, often help to allay their fears.

It is especially important in these interviews to make sure that the guest has an opportunity to air his gripes and to give his perspective. If it is agreeable to our patient (which it almost always is), we may suggest that on occasion, perhaps every 3–4 months or so, the person come in to give us an update on his view of things. Giving guests the feeling that they are participants, even if in a very occasional way, and that they have access to us (with our patients' permission) if they are feeling concerned about what is happening in treatment, usually makes them much more accepting of the patients' individual therapy.

Sometimes a partner may be concerned about a specific therapeutic technique (e.g., prescribing the symptom, or assertiveness training). Straightforward explanation about the expected benefits of the approach the therapist is taking is often enough to make the partner more tolerant of the work being done.

Sometimes therapeutic strategies need to be altered if they will cause too much upset at home. We try to "negotiate" approaches with guests that they, as well as the patients, can live with. In Chapter 7 (see pp. 209–210), we have given the example of Donna, whose husband preferred that his wife simply see her mother very infrequently rather than that she learn to be more assertive. In a joint meeting, therapist, patient, and spouse agreed to alter the treatment plan to partially accommodate it to the husband's feelings. A compromise was reached. Donna would see her mother more frequently alone or just with the baby, and on those occasions she would practice being more outspoken. They also agreed to reduce the total number of contacts that involved the husband, and when these did occur Donna would behave as she had before—that is, she would be "cordial" and nonconfrontational.

One could argue, of course, that therapist and patient should not cater to the guest's preferences. It is our feeling that the therapist must assess the relative benefits of compromise versus persistence. When compromise does not seem wise or possible, the therapist can try to engage the guest in an exploration of his anxieties about the approach being taken. Individual therapy may be recommended in some cases if the guest seems amenable to such a suggestion.

Techniques for Facilitating Interviews and Deflecting Confrontations

Emphasizing Positive Factors

In keeping with our general orientation toward keeping these interviews low-key and nonconfrontational, we try as best we can to attend to and give immediate feedback regarding the positive factors that we note. For instance, we may observe out loud that the patient and the guest seem to enjoy each other's humor. With couples, we emphasize complementarity whenever we see it. If the wife is cautious and the husband flamboyant, we might comment on how they seem to balance each other nicely. If we are interviewing our patient and a sibling, and we notice that they both become very animated when discussing some childhood events, we might comment, "When you reminisce about your childhood I can really sense the closeness that's still there, despite the differences you now have." A similar comment might be appropriate between parent and child. Comments such as "Your face looks so soft when you talk about Joanne as a baby" or "You seem very proud of Michael" set a positive, warm, and accepting tone to the interview.

The point is clearly not to effect a Pollyanna-ish denial. But it must be kept in mind that these sessions are conducted differently from our regular therapy sessions. We are not attempting here to breach either party's defenses or to confront them with material they have been working hard to ward off. Our aim, rather, is to gather information and to gain a fresh perspective on the matters we have been exploring individually with the patient. To be sure, this is most fruitfully done when we can go beyond the cliches that have obscured real understanding for them both, and in this sense we *do* want to explore ideas and experiences that have heretofore been obscured by defenses. But we keep clearly in mind two things as we attempt to achieve these goals: first, that the guest does not share our previous experience and understandings together (and may not even share the therapeutic goal), and therefore that we have a responsibility to the guest not to thank him for cooperating by upsetting him; and second, that the most effective way of enlisting the genuine cooperation of this one-time participant is to put him at his ease and make it clear that this will not be an adversarial interaction. Thus, while we do address in these sessions matters that may be uncomfortable or distressing for one or the other participant, we nevertheless try to notice and comment on behaviors by the guest or interactions between the patient and the guest about which we genuinely feel positively.

We might, for instance, say to a guest that although he clearly has a problem with his temper, the fact that he recognizes his problem is a positive factor in their relationship. We might say to a parent who is being criticized by his child that we are impressed by how he is listening without striking back. We might point out to a couple that they seem able to put arguments behind them though they remain unresolved, and to join together as parents without involving their child. These examples are meant only to give the flavor of what it means to focus on the positive. If one keeps this orientation in mind, one will in fact find many positive factors. Some individual therapists may feel a bit inhibited at first about being so explicitly supportive. But if one grasps what we are after here, it will be clear why we proceed in this fashion.

Dealing with the Eruption of Arguments

It is important to keep in mind that the meetings we have thus far been discussing do not have as their goal the resolution of conflicts or reconciliation of family members. Thus, when heated disagreements arise—and as much as we try to prevent this from happening, it is not an infrequent occurrence—we do not generally feel in a position to help the patient and the guest reach some real accord. Rather, our aim is simply to cool things down enough so that the wounds are not worse than before the meeting, and to bring the session back to a tone in which the goals of the session can be pursued. There are several techniques for doing this that are derived from the practice of family therapy.

REFRAMING

We have already discussed the general uses of reframing in Chapter 6. Here, we concentrate on the specific use of reframing for cooling down a heated confrontation. One might say, for instance, "I am struck by how responsive the two of you are to each other. The anger I am witnessing attests to how involved you still are with each other. Rather than dismissing each other, or detaching yourself emotionally, you both seem to care deeply about what the other thinks and feels."

This of course reframes the fight into a sign of something positive between the two. It will generally lead to rapid toning down of the fight, either because the participants will reflect and comment on this "interpretation," or because of the paradoxical effect of the statement (i.e., to fight is to show that you are attached, and this demonstration of attachment is regarded by the patient and the guest as undesirable).

PRESCRIBING THE ARGUMENT

Another method discussed earlier, which has important applications in gaining control of sessions like these and not letting confrontations get too hot, is to prescribe the argument. We might say to the patient and the guest, "I'm glad you are getting into a fight. This gives me an opportunity to observe how you fight and communicate with each other when you are feeling frustrated, angry, and misunderstood. It would be helpful if you would continue the argument for a while longer so I can really see the two of you in action. Be sure not to tone it down or stop it just yet." If they then stop, the therapist might say, "I'd rather you didn't stop just yet. What could you say to provoke each other?" This, of course, like the first intervention, introduces an "observing ego," which in itself changes the nature of the conflict.

INVITING COMMENT FROM ANOTHER FAMILY MEMBER

If there is more than one guest, one could invite comment by that person on the conflict between the others. This technique is called "gossiping in the presence of the other." It goes something like this: Suppose a mother and daughter are arguing. The therapist might ask the father a number of questions, such as "Does it seem to you that this is the way they usually argue, or is it different because it is in this office?" "How does it go after such a fight?" Or "How do you find out about it?" All these questions invite speculation about the system, which again interferes with the escalation of the disagreement.

INTERRUPTING THE DISAGREEMENT

The therapist might also interrupt the argument by inviting the participants to comment on it themselves. For example, "Hold on a minute. Would you say this is the way you and your mother typically argue? How long would an argument like this go on if I hadn't interrupted you? How do you usually resolve it? Do you talk about it later or just act as if it never occurred?"

All of the techniques just described have in common the fact that they deal with the argument in a way that gives information about the system, without attempting to resolve the content of the disagreement. If none of them work, it is also possible to interrupt simply and directly by calling a halt to what is transpiring. One might say, for example, "I know that you are both upset and angry right now. I have a feeling, however, that you've had this argument many times before and that this is not something that can be resolved in one or two meetings. I'd be happy, of course, to refer you for family therapy if you would like to try to work out this disagreement. For now, though, I'd like to use this time to ask you some more questions about your daughter as a child. I understand that it may be difficult to shift gears this way, but I really do think that this is not resolvable right now and our time would be more productively spent on something else."

Responses to such a statement tell us a good deal about the system. Is there flexibility? Can people shift when asked to do so? Who in the system starts the argument up again? Who responds to provocation? All this information is invaluable in knowing what our patient is up against and how he deals with it, and it helps us determine future therapeutic strategies.

By saying that we could refer the family for family therapy, we are planting an idea without pushing something on the family, yet what we have said leaves the impression that there is a way in which conflicts can be resolved if the family members so desire.

When Family Therapy Is Recommended

Generally, as just noted above, our goal in the meetings we have been describing is to meet the cast of characters, not to resolve conflicts between them. Conflict resolution of this sort usually requires the skills of a trained family therapist, and attempting this task is something many individual therapists are not comfortable with. In general, this is a task we do not undertake with our individual patients.

There are some occasions, however, in which a request for help of this sort will be honored. Sometimes the problem is so circumscribed that it seems likely that one or two meetings with a third party could really help resolve the conflict. When we do this, we advise the patient that if these meetings don't help, it might be wise to see a family therapist.

Potentially circumscribed problems include, for example, issues such as a husband's opposition to his wife's return to school, a relative who is "temporarily" staying too long and not looking for his own apartment, or a conflict over living in the city or the suburbs. Though all of these could reflect long-standing and much more extensive conflict, the therapist can use his knowledge of his individual patient to make a reasonable assessment of how likely it is that these issues are much more involved than they seem.

One might perhaps ask: If the problems are so "simple," why does the patient need help with them? Wouldn't it be better for him to master these difficulties on his own? In our view, being able to ask for or accept help when offered rather than being stoically self-sufficient is in itself often an appropriate goal of treatment. We make our decision in these cases on the basis of the dynamics of the particular individual. If a patient is generally far too dependent on others and does not trust his own judgment and abilities, we would be more reluctant to offer assistance. In such an instance, we would work with the patient on the issue of his inaccurate perception of his own powerlessness or neediness. Coaching or assertiveness training might be indicated (cf. P. L. Wachtel, 1977a).

For many patients, however, the experience of our being willing to help them or even to indulge their "unnecessary" wish for assistance may be very important and may contribute to a sense of being valued, which can then be internalized. Though we do not endorse all aspects of Alexander's idea of the "corrective emotional experience" (Alexander *et al.*, 1946), we do find that this is a useful way to conceptualize much of what is valuable in these interviews.

Interviews in cases of chronic and far-reaching (rather than circumscribed) conflict, though generally ill-advised, may be useful when there is reluctance by one or more family members to consult a family therapist. Exploring the issues in one or two meetings with the individual therapist may be more acceptable to all concerned. Though in some ways the contact may make it a bit more difficult to shift to another therapist, having a productive experience in these sessions may make for greater willingness to embark on a course of family therapy. In effect, a difficult transition is achieved in place of no family therapy at all.

Colleagues and patients alike have inquired about the advisability of the individual therapist's working with both one individual in the family and the family as a whole in ongoing treatment. It has been our experience that this does not work out well. Being the therapist to the whole family interferes greatly with the work of individual therapy. Issues of confidentiality, the specialness of the support and rapport between therapist and patient, and the unique "acceptance" of the patient's perspective would all be significantly compromised by an extended combination of individual and family therapy with the same therapist.

Similarly, family therapy will be untenable if one family member has a "special" relationship with the therapist. Not only may the others feel that there is bias in the therapist's judgments, but one individual's talking to the therapist between family sessions may undermine the powerful pressures to change the family system that family therapy attempts to generate. For these reasons, we advise even those individual therapists who are comfortable with and experienced in family therapy to refer the family to a colleague if ongoing family work seems an appropriate treatment modality.

In such instances of referral, it is not unusual for one individual in the couple or family to be reluctant. If such is the case, we often find it useful to present the rationale in a way that emphasizes the positive personality traits of this individual that have become evident in the meeting we have just had. We might say, for example, something like this to a husband who has been expressing a good deal of anger in the session: "I can see that you have some very strong feelings about what has been going on between you and your wife. I'm impressed with your openness and willingness to share these feelings with me. Your candor and forthrightness make me think that consulting a family therapist could prove beneficial. I think you would use it well." Traits such as lack of defensiveness, a desire to understand what is happening, and a willingness to look at one's share in the difficulties should all be emphasized in recommending family treatment to a "resistant" or hesitant individual.

Signs of deep caring and concern for one another are also emphasized if present. One might say that such caring is the foundation stone of successful family therapy, and thus that these family members have the prerequisite for benefiting from such treatment. If one senses a great deal of resistance, it is best to offer the suggestion but then back off from pushing it too strongly, since this is likely to rigidify resistance.

If a marital separation seems to be in the offing, it is useful to stress that consulting a family therapist in no way means making a commitment to stay in the relationship. This is a common misconception that should be corrected. We explain that couples treatment will help them resolve whether or not they want to stay together, and may help prevent an acrimonious separation.

The Session After

The session following a meeting with a family member is frequently full of surprises. As described in Chapter 7, often we are not aware of the impact of certain statements on our patient. We learn in the session after just how the patient perceived what was said by both the therapist and the family members. We generally start out by asking the patient what he got out of the session. Often the patient will focus on an aspect of the meeting that we hardly noticed.

Inquiring into how representative of the guest's behavior this sample seemed is quite important. Does the patient feel the therapist got an accurate picture of the guest, and if not, why? We ask how the conversation between them differed (if it did) from talks they have had on their own. If it differed, how does the patient account for the difference? We are usually eager to know how the family interacted after the meeting. How did the guest feel about the session? We wonder what the patient may have learned that was new.

We find it particularly useful to discuss with the patient anything we have noticed about the system of interaction we have witnessed. How do arguments escalate? Why does the guest persist in behavior that is aversive to the patient? How are they trapped in vicious circles? What is the patient's contribution to the circular interaction?

Colleagues have often expressed concern about the patient's requesting their opinion about family members after such a meeting. In our view, feedback from the therapist is a reasonable expectation on the patient's part. Having said that it would be useful for us to meet with the family, it would not be appropriate for us then to take a noncommital, analytic stance. What kind of feedback to offer, however, depends on the particular dynamics of the patient and what we feel he needs at this point in treatment.

In some instances, we might wish to confirm the patient's perceptions and say something like "I could see the defensiveness you've described." If the interview came out of a desire to understand the patient's history better, we will share with the patient any new perspectives we have gained. Similarly, if the guest, particularly if it is a parent, has revealed to us some aspect of his personality or values that illuminates the particular difficulties and dilemmas of our patient, we share that insight too.

In one instance, the mother of a 35-year-old woman described her feelings about her daughter very much the way the mother of a newborn might describe them. She stated that she thought about her daughter constantly; even when she was working or busy with other activities, a part of her mind was on her daughter. Since our patient had never described her mother as clinging or possessive or symbiotically merged with her, this statement came as quite a surprise. It threw a good deal of light on the difficulty the patient had had with separations.

Recognitions such as these are frequent outcomes of these meetings and are explored in depth in subsequent sessions. Frequently it is helpful to share positive impressions of the guest with our patient. The question arises, however, as to what to say when the patient has strong negative feelings about the guest that for him have been confirmed in the meeting, but that are not echoed in the therapist's experience of the same person. We have stated earlier that we generally do not do these interviews at a point in therapy when the patient still has a strong need to blame. Because of this prescreening, it is rare for the situation just described to occur in a way that cannot be tactfully handled.

Exploring what the guest said or did that was experienced negatively, and trying to see that behavior in the context of the history of the relationship, usually give the therapist an empathic understanding of the patient's perspective that satisfies the patient's need for affirmation. The therapist might say something like this: "I can see how you could experience your mother that way, given all that has transpired between you, but, not being the target of her criticism or personally invested in the relationship, I saw another aspect of her that I'd like to share with you."

Sometimes, of course, the problem is the reverse: The therapist's impression of someone important to the patient is a negative one that is not shared by the patient. Obviously, it is unlikely to be therapeutic simply to say to the patient, "Your wife was homelier than I had expected" or "I didn't think your father was very bright."

The first step in dealing with such reactions is the same as it would be in the ordinary course of individual work with a patient—to examine oneself for possible countertransference sources for such reactions. It is useful here to note that even when one proceeds in traditional fashion, without calling in family members, one will have strong reactions to patients' parents, spouses, and other intimates. (Indeed, one of the lines of objection to our procedure by more traditionally inclined therapists is that they get vivid pictures of the patient's close associates without it; certainly such impressions are a varying mix of counter-transference distortions and empathically accurate perceptions.)[2]

The special problem that arises in the present context is that the patient now wants to *know* the therapist's impressions of the other. He recognizes that the therapist is now forming his impression on the basis of actually seeing what the family member in question is like,

2. We hope that our overall presentation in this book makes it clear why we believe that in fact, notwithstanding the many useful impressions that may be received without such interviews, a significant increment in knowledge and understanding of the patient's interpersonal world is achieved by the method described here.

and not just on what the patient describes the person as being like. Dealing with this situation when the therapist's impressions are largely negative can be difficult. Three general guidelines can aid in handling the task effectively.

First, the therapist relies on the same kind of tact that he employs in every other aspect of therapy. Much of what the therapist has to tell patients in the course of therapy is unpleasant by conventional standards. Part of the therapist's skill consists of being able to present difficult issues in a way that will be constructive and will further the growth of the patient. This skill does not leave the therapist when he introduces interviews with relatives into the work; it can be relied on in the framing of comments to the patient in response to questions about the therapist's impressions of the guest.

Second, the general strategy of positive reframing discussed previously comes in handy in the situation being addressed here. As the reader who has mastered the discussions of positive reframing and connotation will be aware, there are ways of communicating a particular trait or observation that can place it in a different context or give it a different meaning than one of mere criticism. This perspective takes us a step further than considerations of tact alone, in that what is presented is a kind of new construction or creation that has a kernel of truth but recasts that kernel into something rather different from what the patient might ordinarily make of it.

It should be noted, incidentally, that the positive connotation may be given not so much to the guest as to the patient himself. For example, the therapist might say, "I think you've underestimated what a difficult time you've had in dealing with your mother and how remarkable a job you've done in coming through it intact. I can see why you experience her as sweet and supportive, but there's a subtle undertone of criticism that's hard to deal with because it's hidden. I think you've been taking too much of the blame onto yourself for the distance in your relationship."[3]

---

3. The foregoing might be a therapeutic reworking of an initial reaction to the mother of "What a bitch!"—a reaction that, if shared in unmodified form, would indeed be likely to be unhelpful. The skill of the therapist lies very largely in transforming raw impressions—whether negative or positive, of the patient or others—into therapeutically effective communications. Much of this book is devoted to enlarging the therapist's repertoire of forms and contexts in order to increase the likelihood of fashioning such effective comments.

Finally, the therapist is aided in communicating negative impressions by the recognition that often therapeutic growth requires the patient to confront unpleasant realities that he has heretofore avoided. Being in a position to share with the patient a "negative" impression of someone close to him can be an opportunity for the therapist, as well as a ticklish challenge. When this opportunity for honest examination of an inconvenient truth is undertaken in combination with considerations of tact and of the possibilities of varied connotations for the "same" perception, the therapeutic work can be considerably enhanced.

Coda: Psychotherapeutic Practice and American Individualism

OUR FOCUS in this book has, of course, been on the process of psychotherapy. But it is important to note in closing that broader issues underlie the rethinking of psychotherapy we have been discussing. Behind the conceptions that have dominated individual psychotherapy in the past century is a vision of man that is a product of our social system and that guides our lives in more ways than we generally recognize. Individualistic thinking, particularly of a sort that stresses the separate responsibility of each person for himself and minimizes our interdependency, is a central feature of our society and shapes our assumptions about political and moral issues as it does our assumptions about psychotherapy.

The many, sometimes surprising ramifications of this attitude— for our sense of self, for our health, for our environment, for our feelings of contentment or deprivation, and for the fragile web of society—have recently been explored in detail in a book by one of us (P. L. Wachtel, 1983). We cannot address them in detail here. But we do wish to point to one or two key themes that provide a larger context for the psychotherapeutic considerations you have just read.

To begin with, we must note that Freud's thinking, from which so much of modern psychotherapy derives, was shaped by the assumptions of the society in which it evolved, much as it also contributed powerfully to changing those assumptions in important respects. As discussed in the aforementioned book, Freud's theories show insufficiently recognized consonances with the economic theories that were beginning to dominate Western society at that time. The notions that guided the development of modern industrialized societies departed sharply from the views of economic life (and implicitly of human nature) that had guided people over the preceding millenia. Until rather recently, our understanding of the relations between people, of the rules of social intercourse, and of the experience of its participants placed a central emphasis on membership in a community and on the necessity of restraining the individual quest for personal gain in favor of more enduring shared values. But as the modern era began, there was what the social historian Karl Polanyi called a "great transformation," in which for the first time the pursuit of individual gain was regarded as a legitimate—indeed, as the overriding—aim of human behavior.

As we have noted elsewhere, this transformation led as well to a new conception of the very nature of the individual:

> Over time people came less to be perceived in terms of their context and their roles in society and more as autonomous actors who made independent decisions regarding personal gain and loss. By now this view pervades not only economic activity but personal life as well. If the gains of marriage, for example, do not exceed the drawbacks, we are far more likely than people in prior eras to go our separate ways. Marriage for us is not primarily a matter of fulfilling a social role but rather a contract between two people, to be terminated when it no longer brings its expected rewards. (P. L. Wachtel, 1983, pp. 123–124)

Where society was once conceived of as an organic unity enveloping those within it, now, following Hobbes and Locke, we are offered guiding images of separate individuals—implicitly living outside of society at that point—deciding on the basis of perceived gain to *create* a society and live within its constraints. This was essentially the vision accepted by Freud as well, as his "primal horde" theory in "Totem and Taboo" (1913/1955) makes clear. And it is this atomistic vision of an essential separateness that is the dominant vector among us today. It affects not only our ideas about psychotherapy, but our attitudes toward taxes, welfare, the possibilities of controlling pollution, and the inevitability of traffic jams.

We conceive of ourselves very largely as autonomous individuals who just happen to be members of a family and of a society. In many respects, we conceive of psychotherapy as the means of increasing that autonomy still further, of helping us to differentiate from our families and free ourselves from the pressures of society to conform. These goals have remained central for psychotherapists because they are in important respects salutary ones; many individuals have bettered their lives by achieving precisely such a differentiation. But we have tended not to balance this attention to autonomy with a sufficient appreciation of the fact and the necessity of interdependence. The conceptual framework that most psychotherapy shares with the society at large makes it easy to conceive of our ethical responsibility to the patient as requiring that we ignore almost totally the needs of those around him. Parents are often seen as intruders if they inquire into their children's therapy, and spouses all too often take on the role of villain (while the spouse's therapist has the same perception in reverse).

Philip Rieff, an acute social critic and lifelong student of Freud's thought, notes that

> Freud speaks for the modern individual, elaborating his sense of sep-arateness from the world and even from the most beloved objects in it. . . . the successful patient has learned to withdraw from the painful tension of assent and dissent in his relation to society by relating himself more affirmatively to his depths. His newly acquired health entails a self-concern that takes precedence over social concern and encourages an attitude of ironic insight on the part of the self toward all that is not self. (Rieff, 1959, pp. 329–330)

Rieff, it is important to note, is not a polemical anti-Freudian. Quite the contrary: He is extraordinarily appreciative of Freud, and shows unconcealed disdain for those theorists—among them the neo-Freudians whose thinking provides a foundation for many of the points we make in this book—who would temper Freud's stark message. But he is shrewd enough to recognize that Freud both responded to and gave unprecedented power to a vision of mankind deriving centrally from our severing of the ties that had given meaning to our lives through most of human existence. Ours, says Rieff, is a culture "constantly probing its own unwitting part," a culture so concerned with liberating the individual from cultural forms and restrictions that it is essentially an anticultural culture. The "Psychological Man" that Rieff views as our chief character type is obsessed with autonomy. Yet, as Rieff notes, culture must also be understood as a "design of motives directing the self outward, toward those communal purposes *in which alone the self can be realized and satisfied*" (1966, pp. 3–4, italics added).

For Rieff, this is a melancholy message; yet so great is his respect for Freud and for his articulation of the modern psyche that he sees no alternative. In *The Poverty of Affluence* (P. L. Wachtel, 1983), we find the roots of an alternative in a recognition of the ways in which Freud unwittingly replicated the atomistic vision of the economists—a recognition that enables us to see how our lives continue to be dominated by economic definitions of well-being and how economic guiding vectors continue to predominate in American lives, despite this supposedly being the era of "Psychological Man." We note there that the seeming dead end to which Rieff thinks Freud's theories have tragically but brilliantly brought us has an opening: one in which new values can reintegrate our newly liberated psychological selves into a web of firm but flexible relations, and in which the pursuit of happiness is no longer conceived of as a zero sum game.

In the present volume, our focus is more narrowly on the process of psychotherapy. Contribution to technique, rather than social criticism and examination of values, is our aim. But many of the same considerations can be seen as underlying our arguments. Most of all, we wish to underscore the necessity of understanding the interdependence that inevitably links our fate to that of others. Autonomy is a dangerous and illusory aim. Psychotherapy should be liberating; that much is true. But of all the illusions from which we need to be liberated, few are as pervasive or as likely to lead us astray as the illusion of the autonomous individual. The fullest development of the self is indeed our aim. That facet of individualism that affirms the dignity and worth of each individual and treats as bedrock the concrete experience of individual human beings is one we endorse wholeheartedly. Indeed, it is in the very pursuit of that aim that an appreciation of the critical role of those around us is crucial. As we have put it elsewhere (P. L. Wachtel, 1981b, p. 15), "only in concert with others can we achieve the conditions for harmony within."

References

Ackerman, N. *Treating the troubled family*. New York: Basic Books, 1966.

Alexander, F. *Psychoanalysis and psychotherapy*. New York: Norton, 1956.

Alexander, F., French, T., *et al. Psychoanalytic therapy*. New York: Ronald Press, 1946.

Aponte, H. Underorganization in the poor family. In P. J. Guerin (Ed.), *Family therapy: Theory and practice*. New York: Gardner Press, 1976.

Aponte, H., & Van Deusen, J. Structural family therapy. In A. Gurman & D. Kniskern (Eds.), *Handbook of family therapy*. New York: Brunner/Mazel, 1981.

Bakan, P. *The duality of human existence*. Chicago: Rand McNally, 1966.

Bateson, G. *Steps to an ecology of mind*. New York: Ballantine Books, 1972.

Beutler, L. *Eclectic psychotherapy: A systematic approach*. Elmsford, N.Y.: Pergamon Press, 1983.

Bloch, D. A. & LaPerriere, K. Techniques of family therapy: A conceptual frame. In D. Bloch (Ed.), *Techniques of family psychotherapy*. New York: Grune & Stratton, 1973.

Boszormenyi-Nagy, I., & Spark, G. *Invisible loyalties*. New York: Harper & Row, 1973.

Boszormenyi-Nagy, I., & Ulrich, D. Contextual family therapy. In A. Gurman & D. Kniskern (Eds.), *Handbook of family therapy*. New York: Brunner/Mazel, 1981.

Bowen, M. (Anonymous) On the differentiation of self. In J. Framo (Ed.), *Family interaction: A dialogue between family researchers and family therapists*. New York: Springer, 1972.

Bowen, M. *Family therapy in clinical practice*. New York: Jason Aronson, 1978.

Breuer, J., & Freud, S. Studies on hysteria. *Standard Edition* (Vol. 2). London: Hogarth Press, 1955. (Original work published 1895.)

Carter, E. A., & McGoldrick, M. (Eds.). *The family life cycle: A framework for family therapy*. New York: Gardner Press, 1980.

Carter, E. A., & Orfanidis, M. Family therapy with one person. In P. J. Guerin (Ed.), *Family therapy: Theory and practice*. New York: Gardner Press, 1976.

Chambless, D., & Goldstein, A. J. Agoraphobia. In A. J. Goldstein & E. B. Foa (Eds.), *Handbook of behavioral interventions*. New York: Wiley, 1980.

Coyne, J. Strategic therapy with depressed married persons. *Journal of Marital and Family Therapy*, 1984, *10*, 53–62.

Dell, P. Beyond homeostasis: Toward a concept of coherence. *Family Process*, 1982, *21*, 27–42.

Dollard, J., & Miller, N. *Personality and psychotherapy*. New York: McGraw-Hill, 1950.

Erikson, E. *Childhood and society* (Rev. ed.). New York: Norton, 1964.

Fairbairn, W. R. D. *An object-relations theory of the personality*. New York: Basic Books, 1952.

Fay, A. *Making things better by making them worse.* New York: Hawthorne, 1978.

Feldman, L. B. Marital conflict and marital intimacy: An integrative psychodynamic–behavioral–systemic model. *Family Process,* 1979, *18,* 69–78.

Feldman, L. B. Dysfunctional marital conflict: An integrative interpersonal–intrapsychic model. *Journal of Marital and Family Therapy,* 1982, *8,* 417–428.

Feldman, L. B., & Pinsof, W. M. Problem maintenance in family systems: An integrative model. *Journal of Marital and Family Therapy.* 1982, *8,* 295–308.

Ferreira, A. J. Family myth and homeostasis. *Archives of General Psychiatry,* 1963, *9,* 457–473.

Fisch, R., Weakland, J., & Segal, L. *The tactics of change.* San Francisco: Jossey-Bass, 1982.

Fogarty, T. F. The distancer and the pursuer. *The Family,* 1979, *7,* 11–16.

Framo, J. Rationale and technique of intensive family therapy. In I. Boszormenyi-Nagy & J. Framo (Eds.), *Intensive family therapy.* New York: Harper & Row, 1965.

Framo, J. Foreword. In J. K. Pearce & L. J. Friedman (Eds.), *Family therapy: Combining psychodynamic and family systems approaches.* New York: Grune & Stratton, 1980.

Framo, J. The integration of marital therapy with sessions with family of origin. In A. Gurman & D. Kniskern (Eds.), *Handbook of family therapy.* New York: Brunner/Mazel, 1981.

Frank, J. *Persuasion and healing.* New York: Schocken, 1973.

Frankl, V. *Man's search for meaning: An introduction to logotherapy.* Boston: Beacon Press, 1959.

Freud, A. *The ego and the mechanisms of defense.* New York: International Universities Press, 1946. (Original work published 1936.)

Freud, S. Totem and taboo. *Standard Edition* (Vol. 13). London: Hogarth Press, 1955. (Original work published 1913.)

Freud, S. Beyond the pleasure principle. *Standard Edition* (Vol. 18). London: Hogarth Press, 1955. (Original work published 1920.)

Freud, S. Inhibitions, symptoms, and anxiety. *Standard Edition* (Vol. 21). London: Hogarth Press, 1959. (Original work published 1926.)

Friedman, L. Integrating psychoanalytic object-relations understanding with family systems intervention in couples therapy. In J. K. Pearce & L. J. Friedman (Eds.), *Family therapy: Combining psychodynamic and family systems approaches.* New York: Grune & Stratton, 1980.

Gill, M. M. *The analysis of transference.* New York: International Universities Press, 1982.

Glick, I. D., & Kessler, D. R. *Marital and family therapy.* New York: Grune & Stratton, 1980.

Goldfried, M. *Converging themes in psychotherapy.* New York: Springer, 1982.

Greenson, R. *The technique and practice of psychoanalysis.* New York: International Universities Press, 1967.

Grünbaum, A. *The foundations of psychoanalysis.* Berkeley: University of California Press, 1984.

Guerin, P. J., & Pendagast, E. G. Evaluation of family system and the genogram. In P. J. Guerin (Ed.), *Family therapy: Theory and practice.* New York: Gardner Press, 1976.

Gurman, A. Contemporary marital therapies: A critique and comparative analysis of psychoanalytic, behavioral, and systems theory approaches. In T. Paolino & B. McCrady (Eds.), *Marriage and marital therapy*. New York: Brunner/Mazel, 1978.

Gurman, A. Integrative marital therapy: Toward the development of an interpersonal approach. In S. Budman (Ed.), *Forms of brief therapy*. New York: Guilford Press, 1981.

Haley, J. *Problem solving therapy*. San Francisco: Jossey-Bass, 1976.

Haley, J. *Leaving home: Therapy with disturbed young people*. New York: McGraw-Hill, 1979.

Hartmann, H. *Ego psychology and the problem of adaptation*. New York: International Universities Press, 1939.

Headley, L. *Adults and their parents in family therapy*. New York: Plenum, 1977.

Hoffman, I. The patient as interpreter of the analyst's experience. *Contemporary Psychoanalysis*, 1983, *19*, 389–422.

Hoffman, L. *Foundations of family therapy*. New York: Basic Books, 1981.

Horney, K. *New ways in psychoanalysis*. New York: Norton, 1939.

Jackson, D. D. The question of family homeostasis. *Psychiatric Quarterly Supplement*, 1957, *31*, 79–90.

Kaplan, H. S. *The new sex therapy*. New York: Brunner/Mazel, 1974.

Kerr, M. E. Family systems theory and therapy. In A. Gurman & D. Kniskern (Eds.), *Handbook of family therapy*. New York: Brunner/Mazel, 1981.

Kohut, H. *The restoration of the self*. New York: International Universities Press, 1977.

Kramer, C. *Becoming a family therapist*. New York: Human Sciences Press, 1980.

Laing, R. D. Mystification, confusion and conflict. In I. Boszormenyi-Nagy & J. Framo (Eds.) *Intensive family therapy*. New York: Harper & Row, 1965.

Malcolm, J. *In the Freud archives*. New York: Knopf, 1984.

Marks, I. Behavioral psychotherapy of adult neurosis. In S. Garfield & A. Bergin (Eds.), *Handbook of psychotherapy and behavior change* (2nd ed.). New York: Wiley, 1978.

Masson, J. *The assault on truth*. New York: Penguin, 1984.

Masters, W., & Johnson, V. *Human sexual inadequacy*. Boston: Little, Brown, 1970.

Messer, S., & Winokur, M. Some limitations to the integration of psychoanalytic and behavior therapy. *American Psychologist*, 1980, *35*, 818–827.

Minuchin, S. *Families and family therapy*. Cambridge, Mass.: Harvard University Press, 1974.

Minuchin, S., & Fishman, C. *Family therapy techniques*. Cambridge, Mass.: Harvard University Press, 1981.

Minuchin, S., Montalvo, B., Guerney, B. G., Rosman, B. L., & Schumer, F. *Families of the slums*. New York: Basic Books, 1967.

Paul, N. The role of mourning and empathy in conjoint marital therapy. In G. Zuk & I. Boszormenyi-Nagy (Eds.), *Family therapy and disturbed families*. Palo Alto, Calif.: Science & Behavior Books, 1969.

Pendagast, E. G., & Sherman, C. O. A guide to the genogram. *The Family*, 1977, *5*, 3–14.

Penn, P. Circular questioning. *Family Process*, 1982, *21*, 267–281.

Piaget, J. *The origins of intelligence in children*. New York: International Universities Press, 1952.

Piaget, J. *The construction of reality in the child*. New York: Basic Books, 1954.

Pinsof, W. Integrative problem-centered therapy: Toward the synthesis of family and individual psychotherapies. *Journal of Marital and Family Therapy*, 1983, *9*, 19–35.

Rieff, P. *Freud: The mind of the moralist*. Chicago: University of Chicago Press, 1959.

Rieff, P. *The triumph of the therapeutic*. New York: Harper & Row, 1966.

Sager, C. *Marriage contracts and couples therapy*. New York: Harper & Row, 1978.

Sager, C. Couples therapy and marriage contracts. In A. Gurman & D. Kniskern (Eds.), *Handbook of family therapy*. New York: Brunner/Mazel, 1981.

Sander, F. M. *Individual and family therapy: Toward an integration*. New York: Jason Aronson, 1979.

Schafer, R. *A new language for psychoanalysis*. New Haven, Conn.: Yale University Press, 1976.

Schafer, R. The interpretation of transference and the conditions for loving. *Journal of the American Psychoanalytic Association*. 1977, *25*, 335–362.

Schafer, R. *The analytic attitude*. New York: Basic Books, 1983.

Searles, H. Positive feelings in the relationship between the schizophrenic and his mother. *International Journal of Psycho-Analysis*, 1958, *39*, 569–586.

Searles, H. *Collected papers on schizophrenia and related subjects*. New York: International Universities Press, 1965.

Segraves, R. T. *Marital therapy: A combined psychodynamic–behavioral approach*. New York: Plenum, 1982.

Selvini Palazzoli, M. *Self-starvation*. New York: Jason Aronson, 1978.

Selvini Palazzoli, M., Boscolo, L., Cecchin, G., & Prata, G. *First session of a systemic family therapy*. Unpublished manuscript, Milan Center of Family Studies, 1978

Selvini Palazzoli, M., Cecchin, G., Prata, G., & Boscolo, L. *Paradox and counterparadox*. New York: Jason Aronson, 1978.

Skynner, R. *Systems of family and marital psychotherapy*. New York: Brunner/Mazel, 1976.

Skynner, R. An open-systems, group-analytic approach to family therapy. In A. Gurman & D. Kniskern (Eds.), *Handbook of family therapy*. New York: Brunner/Mazel, 1981.

Stampfl, T., & Levis, D. Essentials of implosive therapy: A learning-theory based psychodynamic behavioral therapy. *Journal of Abnormal Psychology*, 1967, *72*, 496–503.

Stierlin, H. *Psychoanalysis and family therapy*. New York: Jason Aronson, 1977.

Stone, L. *The psychoanalytic situation*. New York: International Universities Press, 1961.

Sullivan, H. S. *The interpersonal theory of psychiatry*. New York: Norton, 1953.

Wachtel, E. F. Learning family therapy: The dilemmas of an individual therapist. *Journal of Contemporary Psychotherapy*, 1979, *10*, 122–135.

Wachtel, E. F. The family psyche over three generations: The genogram revisited. *Journal of Marital and Family Therapy*, 1982, *8*, 335–343.

Wachtel, P. L. *Psychoanalysis and behavior therapy*. New York: Basic Books, 1977. (a)

Wachtel, P. L. Interaction cycles, unconscious processes, and the person–situation issue. In D. Magnusson & N. Endler (Eds.), *Personality at the crossroads: Issues in interactional psychology*. Hillsdale, N.J.: Erlbaum, 1977. (b)

Wachtel, P. L. On some complexities in the application of conflict theory to psychotherapy. *Journal of Nervous and Mental Disease*, 1978, *166*, 457–471.

Wachtel, P. L. Contingent and noncontingent therapist response. *Psychotherapy: Theory, Research and Practice*, 1979, *16*, 30–35. (a)

Wachtel, P. L. Karen Horney's ironic vision. *The New Republic*, January 6, 1979, pp. 25–28. (b)

Wachtel, P. L. What should we say to our patients: On the wording of therapists' comments to patients. *Psychotherapy: Theory, Research and Practice*, 1980, *17*, 183–188.

Wachtel, P. L. Transference, schema and assimilation: The relevance of Piaget to the psychoanalytic theory of transference. *The Annual of Psychoanalysis*, 1981, *8*, 69–76. (a)

Wachtel, P. L. The politics of narcissism. *The Nation*, January 3–10, 1981, *232*(1), pp. 13–15. (b)

Wachtel, P. L. Vicious circles: The self and the rhetoric of emerging and unfolding. *Contemporary Psychoanalysis*, 1982, *18*, 273–295.

Wachtel, P. L. *The poverty of affluence: A psychological portrait of the American way of life*. New York: Free Press, 1983.

Wachtel, P. L. On theory, practice, and the nature of integration. In H. Arkowitz & S. Messer (Eds.), *Psychoanalytic and behavior therapy: Is integration possible?* New York: Plenum, 1984.

Wachtel, P. L. Integrative psychodynamic therapy. In S. Lynn & J. Garske (Eds.), *Contemporary psychotherapies*. Columbus, Ohio: Charles E. Merrill, 1985.

Wachtel, P. L. You can't go far in neutral: On the limits of therapeutic neutrality. *Contemporary Psychoanalysis*, in press.

Watzlawick, P., Weakland, J., & Fisch, R. *Change: Principles of problem formation and problem resolution*. New York: Norton, 1974.

Weeks, G. R., & L'Abate, L. *Paradoxical psychotherapy: Theory and practice with individuals, couples and families*. New York: Brunner/Mazel, 1982.

Weiss, J., Sampson, H., & The Mount Zion Psychotherapy Research Group. *The psychoanalytic process: Theory, clinical observation, and empirical research*. New York: Guilford Press, in press.

Wheelis, A. *How people change*. New York: Harper & Row, 1973.

Wile, D. *Couples therapy*. New York: Wiley, 1981.

Wile, D. Kohut, Kernberg, and accusatory interpretations. *Psychotherapy: Theory, Research and Practice*, 1984, *23*, 353–365.

Williamson, D. S. Personal authority via termination of the intergenerational hierarchical boundary: A "new" stage in the family life cycle. *Journal of Marital and Family Therapy*, 1981, *7*, 441–452.

Williamson, D. S. Personal authority via termination of the intergenerational hierarchical boundary: Part II. The consultation process and the therapeutic method. *Journal of Marital and Family Therapy*, 1982, *8*, 23–37. (a)

Williamson, D. S. Personal authority in family experience via termination of the intergenerational hierarchical boundary: Part III. Personal authority defined and the power of play in the change process. *Journal of Marital and Family Therapy*, 1982, *8*, 309–333. (b)

Wynne, L. C., Ryckoff, I., Day, J., & Hirsch, S. Pseudo-mutuality in the family relations of schizophrenics. *Psychiatry*, 1958, *21*, 205–220.

Index